OUTBACK LEGENDS

Evan McHugh is a journalist who has written for newspapers, television and radio. His previous books include *The Stockmen: The Making of an Australian Legend*, *Outback Stations*, *Bushrangers*, *The Drovers*, *Birdsville*, *Outback Pioneers*, *Outback Heroes* and *Shipwrecks: Australia's Greatest Maritime Disasters*. Evan's book about true crime in the outback, *Red Centre, Dark Heart*, won the Ned Kelly Award for best non-fiction in 2008. He lives with his wife in the Hunter Valley, New South Wales.

OUTBACK LEGENDS

Evan McHugh

MICHAEL JOSEPH
an imprint of
PENGUIN BOOKS

MICHAEL JOSEPH

UK | USA | Canada | Ireland | Australia
India | New Zealand | South Africa | China

Penguin Books is part of the Penguin Random House group of companies
whose addresses can be found at global.penguinrandomhouse.com.

Penguin
Random House
Australia

First published by Penguin Random House Australia Pty Ltd, 2017

1 3 5 7 9 10 8 6 4 2

Text copyright © Evan McHugh, 2017

The moral right of the author has been asserted.

Cover design by Alex Ross © Penguin Random House Australia Pty Ltd
Cover photograph © Darren Clark Photography
Typeset in Sabon by Samantha Jayaweera, Penguin Random House Australia Pty Ltd
Colour separation by Splitting Image Colour Studio, Clayton, Victoria
Printed and bound in China by RR Donnelley Asia

National Library of Australia Cataloguing-in-Publication data is available.

9780143797296

penguin.com.au

MIX
Paper from
responsible sources
FSC
www.fsc.org FSC® C144853

CONTENTS

Leg One

The LandCruiser was packed with camping gear and fully serviced. It had all-terrain tyres freshly fitted. I was outward bound again.

It was rainy for the first part of the trip, passing the Hunter Valley's coal mines, vineyards and horse studs on the Golden Highway to Denman, climbing the eastern flanks of the Great Dividing Range through Merriwa, then crossing the range and settling into top gear on the undulating western slopes to Dunedoo.

Morning coffee and a first-rate chunky beef pie at the White Rose Cafe. Then on to Mendooran, Gilgandra and Warren. As the afternoon wore on and the Truckasaurus (my years' old nickname for my 100 Series Landy, for which I'm just starting to develop a fondness) gobbled the kilometres, the clouds started breaking up and the road dried. At my first overnight stop, Nyngan, in the New South Wales central-west, a chilly winter sky was coloured orange, red and yellow by the setting sun.

My journey in search of outback legends had begun. Over the years I'd written about many people and events in outback history. While some of those people (such as R.M. Williams, Sidney Kidman and Tom Kruse) were revered by previous generations, it struck me that, in modern times, there is a lack of similarly impressive figures. This may be a consequence of a 'media cycle' that moves so quickly it can no longer afford people even as much as Andy Warhol's 'fifteen minutes of fame'. Or perhaps the outback no longer resonates with the wider population. Yet my experience has been that there are still plenty of people out there who deserve our respect and admiration. To prove it, the rubber had to hit the road.

The next day was another easy drive. A couple of hours on the road got me to North Bourke for morning coffee and a micro-waved packet pie. From there, heading north-west, the plains grew wider and the skies got bigger. After two-and-a-half hours on the road, I got a burger for lunch in Cunnamulla. Beyond Eulo, when the unfenced roads grew narrower, the scrub grew sparser and the motorists coming the other way started waving as they passed, I was back in the outback.

I was meeting my first 'legend' at the Toompine Hotel, a rustic, iron-roofed place surrounded by blue-grey mulga and gnarled eucalypts. There's a community hall and sportsground near the pub, but no houses to give substance to the locality.

I'd arrived before my subject, so I set up camp – a swag, a table and a folding chair – in what I thought was a good place.

Terry Picone and I had made our plans by phone a week earlier.

'Terry, I'm doing a book on outback legends and I think you'd make a good subject. You've been an outback bookmaker for twenty-five years or more.'

'Oh, Ev. I don't think I'm that person,' he replied. 'There's plenty of others that would fit that description more than me. But now that you mention it, I have been thinking of going out to Bedourie for the camel races.'

'I'll go if you go.'

'Could you work for me?'

'I don't know anything about bookmaking, but if you're prepared to risk it, I'm there.'

So we went. For both of us it involved a journey of more than 2000 kilometres each way: me from Lake Macquarie on the New South Wales Central Coast, and him from Moree, in the north of the state.

An hour after I'd set up camp, the sun was dipping behind the trees and turning a bank of cirrus blood-red in the clear outback air. Corellas, pigeons and finches were flying and chattering back to their nightly roosts.

Terry pulled into Toompine and we shook hands, having not seen each other face to face since I'd last been in Birdsville for the races about five years earlier.

Terry – fiftyish, quietly spoken, with his ubiquitous magnetically linked reading glasses hanging unclasped on his short-sleeved shirt – was accompanied by another bookmaker he's known for years, Gordon Turner. Gordon was in his seventies but retained an impish manner that went with his diminutive size. He and Terry had known each other for so long that they'd got to the stage where they could say pretty much whatever they were thinking, without fear of the consequences. As they bantered, feigned offence, then sparred some more, I came up with a nickname for them: the Odds Couple. It might have stuck, except Terry already had a nickname.

1.

'Arthritis'

Terry Picone
(1959–)

Terry Picone is based in country New South Wales, but his heart is in the outback. Toompine is one of his favourite places, and the pub is owned by a mate of his, outback caterer 'Dogger' Dare. After Terry arrived, he got access to the local hall and we shifted camp indoors. We were still in swags but we had a roof over our heads instead of a bit of canvas.

Terry likes the outback so much that he wants to celebrate his sixtieth birthday at the Toompine Hotel. However, his wife Bethelle told him, 'You can have your birthday there, but you'll be on your own.'

Terry is a member of a bookmaking dynasty that spans three generations. Back in the 1920s, Terry's great-grandfather Domenica and great-grandmother Maria, originally from the island of Salina, near Sicily, were so impressed by Moree's artesian waters that they bought two cafes in the town and sent two of their sons to run them.

Terry's grandfather Jack stayed, with his wife Madge; the other son left during the Depression. One of the saviours of the business during those hard times were penny iceblocks. Up to 350 a day were sold to schoolchildren with the slogan, 'Can be licked – but not b-eaten.'

In an article on the Picone family for the Moree and District Historical Society, Jill Burling recorded:

> The Picone café was well known as welcoming Aboriginal customers and many Aboriginal women at Nana Picone's funeral remembered the fact that if she found them playing truant from school she offered them a treat of freshly baked cakes at the end of the week if they agreed to go to school.

Around 1945, Jack got involved in bookmaking. One story has it that the interest grew from Madge taking 'penny bets' in the cafe. These became so lucrative that Jack decided there was more money in making book than making coffee and took out a licence. Another story, told by Terry's uncle Bruce, was that Jack started out as a punter but worked out that it was more profitable to take on the punters than be one of them. Eventually the cafe was leased to a Greek family, then Terry's father, John, gave up teaching to join Terry's grandfather, then Uncle Bob gave up driving taxis and was lured into bookmaking along with Uncle Bruce.

In an interview with renowned racing authority Bill Weate in *The Bookmaker* (March 1992), Bruce explained how John showed him the ropes:

> There were no betting boards in those days, so I asked John what I should do.
>
> John pointed across the betting ring to fellow bookmaker Sammy Wyatt and said: 'If he calls out two-to-one, you call out three-to-one.'

Jack and his three sons soon became known as 'the Big Four'. According to Terry: 'Some wag nicknamed them "the Big Four" because it was quite an achievement, I suppose, to have one family as a bookmaking family. It was a big operation, you know, to have, say, fourteen different bookmakers – the base was at Moree – going all across the state on Saturdays, and south-east Queensland, too.

'My grandfather used to do the western circuit. He'd go to Dubbo, Warren, Gilgandra, and as far down as as Parkes and Orange. And then Uncle Bruce and Dad just did the north-west slopes, so Tamworth, Quirindi, Gunnedah – all through there. Uncle Bruce did the New England area. When Dad finished at the horses, he would rush to a greyhound or harness meeting that night. Most weekends he wouldn't get to bed before 3 a.m. on Sunday.'

Terry is talking about a time when horse racing was much bigger in the country than it is today, with regular race meetings at all of the locations he mentioned. The family also extended its operations into southern Queensland to races at St George, Toowoomba, Goondiwindi, Texas and Stanthorpe.

The Picone home was the Big Four's headquarters. Years later, when Terry's grandmother reported a telephone fault, he was present when a bemused phone technician said that, from what he could tell from the street, the house had once had sixty phone lines running to it.

According to an article by north-west racing chronicler Bill Poulos, the technician then asked:

'Exactly what type of business was here[?]'. . . Terry just smiled.

'I'm not exactly sure what it was but they tell me it was big in its day,' he winked.

Bill Poulos described the Picone family as the essence of racing in New South Wales, especially the northern regions. He
claimed that some race meetings wouldn't start until the Picones
turned up.

As the Picone business grew, it also diversified. In 1958, family members drew a large outback-Queensland cattle station in
a land ballot. The family continues to own rural properties and
real-estate investments to this day.

An indication of their prosperity, and the pride they took in
it, comes from an advertisement they placed in the *North West
Champion* on 6 December 1962 to celebrate Moree's centenary:

1925–1962

In the thirty-seven years that we have known this town, it has
been our privilege to know it as a centre vibrating with progress
and expansion.

These years have seen our family a part of varied business
ventures; and these ventures, thanks to Providence, have
developed into successful enterprises.

In this year, 1962, as we celebrate the centenary of our
town, we join with all other citizens in taking a brief look into
the future. Truly, if economic indications are a guide, and if
the progressive spirit of a people be fully weighed, we can look
forward to years which will see even greater development and
progress than we have round us today.

It is our sincerest wish that this district will continue to go
forward; it is our desire, through developmental effort, to make
some contribution to this progress.

The advertisement was endorsed by Jack, John, Bob and
Bruce Picone.

Jack Picone in particular had a great community ethic. He was chairman of the hospital board for many years, and active in the Lions, Rotary, the Police Boys Club and the Youth Club. He was conspicuously absent, however, from the Moree Race Club Committee.

'Probably back in those days there might have been a bit of a class thing,' Terry explains, 'because there was a bit of blue-blood sort of aristocracy. The committees – I've seen old photos – [were] all the landed gentry sort of people.'

Terry was the first Picone on the Race Club Committee. Nevertheless, the high esteem in which Jack was held is clear from the fact that the maternity ward of the Moree hospital was named 'The Picone Wing' in his honour.

Jack also enjoyed special treatment at his local bank. A bank teller explained to Bill Poulos that Jack never did his banking during business hours. 'He always came in the back door after we had closed in the afternoon,' she said. 'Occasionally, if we ran out of money – which was not unusual if we misjudged our cash order – we would ring Jack and borrow from him until our cash order came in.'

Jack's generosity extended throughout the community. He once helped a Moree local to buy a house with an interest-free loan for the amount needed. There was only one string attached. The person had stayed at Jack and Madge's home and dropped a cigarette on his mattress, burning a hole in it. Jack said he'd give him the loan if he bought them a new mattress.

Jack also helped out another Moree local, now a media personality, Max Hitchins. In 1962, Max and his brother inherited the Imperial Hotel from their father. The death duties on the place amounted to £20000, which the young men didn't have.

Jack went to see their accountant and reportedly said, 'I understand the Hitchins boys are in financial trouble. How can I help them?' After the accountant explained the situation, Jack wrote out a cheque for the amount (worth about $550 000 as at 2017). He charged no interest and asked for no documentation of the loan.

All he said was, 'Tell them to give it back whenever they can.'

In 1966, the Big Four became three when Bob relocated to Sydney. By then, Terry's father, John, had come to be regarded as one of the leading bookmakers in New South Wales. According to Bruce, as quoted in *The Northern Daily Leader* in 2002:

> When we used to cover the Newcastle Cup and the Cameron Handicap and bookmaker alongside all the top Sydney bookies, the punters would line up 25 deep to bet with John because he was so quick. When you bet at local races, you've got to make your own prices, you know the percentage you can bet on and John's prices were better than most, he was quick to assess the price.

John Picone's battle with punter Frank Duval, 'the Hong Kong Tiger', at the 1968 Wagga Gold Cup meeting has become legendary. Terry's brother Chris saw the bets placed with his father (aside from bets with other bookmakers) and detailed what happened to Bill Poulos:

> In the Wagga Cup, Duval backed his own horse, What Fun, in four separate bets – one bet alone was $12 000 to $8000 (6-4) and the last bet was $3000 to $2000.
>
> Duval had lost $200 000 on the first day (of the carnival) and when What Fun won the cup the next day he won it all back, plus $5000. *(Reproduced by kind permission.)*

Sadly, everything changed for the Picones in January 1977 when John, who was a chronic asthmatic, suddenly died at the age of only fifty-one. He left a wife, five sons and two daughters.

After a night of red wine and a dinner of seared steak and not much else, Terry, Gordon and I hit the road for Bedourie at dawn the next morning. From Quilpie to Windorah, the table drains beside the road were full of water: a good season in the making for pastoralists who'd endured years of drought. All the vegetation was green and incredibly vivid against the red dirt.

The local tourism industry was thriving – international terrorism had convinced a lot of people to travel domestically – and the Big Red Bash, a concert and running event held in Birdsville on the previous weekend, had attracted more than 7000 people. Now a constant stream of vehicles was passing me from the other direction. Every single vehicle was towing a camper trailer or caravan of some sort.

Unfortunately, almost none of the drivers knew the etiquette (and common sense) of passing vehicles on the outback's one-lane strips of asphalt. You have to *slow down* as you put your passenger-side tyres onto the gravel to pass, so you don't spray the other car with rocks. As it was, I was constantly being showered with stones by vehicles slewing on the edge of control at 90 kilometres an hour. It was only a matter of time before a big rock gave my windscreen an almighty crack.

'Damn!' I thought. 'Third day of travel for my new book and I'm already up for another new windscreen.' Not for the first time, I was grateful I had insurance.

At Windorah, where we stopped for tuna and salad

sandwiches, I got some sympathy from Terry and Gordo. And when we pulled into the rest area near the junction of the roads to Bedourie and Birdsville, Terry showed me the crack he'd just got. It was worse than mine.

It was the other driver's fault, but the Odds Couple were arguing about which one of them was to blame: the driver, or the passenger, who had said, 'You've slowed down enough.'

Fortunately, the cars were all coming from Birdsville. Once we passed the turn-off to the iconic town and were on the road to Bedourie, we only met one vehicle in 400-odd kilometres of sparse gibber plains and big-sky outback.

I was taken by surprise by one of the water-filled dips in the road, however, where the Diamantina was flowing about 30 centimetres deep. The road seemed flat, then there was a lip and a sheet of water that I hit going much too fast. The splash was enormous, like suddenly being in a car wash, and I was lucky I didn't drown my engine.

The little town of Bedourie was buzzing when we got there, with hundreds camped on the common around Eyre Creek, at the caravan park and out at the racecourse. A lot of people had decided to go on a bit of a tour of the outback after the Big Red Bash, and events like Bedourie's camel races, only 200 kilometres north of Birdsville, were reaping the benefits.

Out at the track, Terry (who usually fields for the Bedourie horse races) chose a camping spot near an old building that he knew had power on. He produced extension cords, and not long after we were plugging in lights for our bush camp. Luxury. We set up our kitchen, got a camp fire going with wood provided by the Diamantina Shire Council, and rolled out our swags.

People around us – in giant off-road caravans and elaborate

camper trailers equipped with all the modern conveniences – cast pitying glances at our rough and ready arrangements. But Terry seemed to like it that way.

The death of Terry's father came at a pivotal moment in the young man's life. Born in Moree in 1959, Terry went to a local Catholic school until he was seven, then to boarding school at Aberdeen, in the Hunter Valley, and St Joseph's College at Hunters Hill in Sydney.

'I didn't really know Dad very well, because I went away at seven and came back when I was seventeen basically. And he wasn't around when I was home in the holidays. I'd read a lot of stories about him, heard a lot of people talk about him.'

It was much the same for his four brothers and two sisters. And while his brothers attended the same schools, their differences in age, and the bonds with their contemporaries, meant the siblings only grew close after they completed their education.

Even during school holidays, the family might not be together. As many children at boarding school do, Terry spent a lot of holidays with schoolmates at various locations around New South Wales.

'I used to go to Merewether [a suburb of Newcastle] a fair bit. I had a good mate there. We used to go to the coast a lot with my uncle. The family has a house at Minnie Water, over near Wooli. I remember those times fondly.'

At school Terry excelled at tennis and rugby union.

'I got thrown out of the tennis team in Year 12 because the coach (a Marist brother) said I was a bad influence on the team.

I had a little transistor radio to listen to the races! I think the racing bug bit me pretty early.'

His football career included some notable highlights.

'In '76 I played at Joey's and we won the GPS Competition. I was selected in GPS Thirds, and from there I was selected for New South Wales schoolboys as a reserve, a utility player – forward and back. I realised after we had an interstate carnival – I came on as an inside-centre – that I marked Wally Lewis [one of Queensland's greatest rugby league players]. In those times I didn't know who Wally was but years later, when I saw the program, I saw "W. Lewis". They still beat us like they're beating us in State of Origin today and they beat us that day, too. So nothing's changed.'

An injury, of sorts, brought an end to his football career.

'I had a misunderstanding with a bloke from Inverell. We were playing down at the main oval. I had long hair in those days and he pulled my hair furiously, which I didn't like, so I let fly with a left. I clean missed him and my shoulder kept travelling. I dislocated my shoulder. I got a flogging to boot because, with a dislocated shoulder, I couldn't punch anymore.'

His shoulder kept popping out until he abandoned his football career.

After Terry's father died, in January 1977, he started university in March. While at school he'd been asked to list his career ambitions.

'First on his list was "bookmaker", but as there were no courses for that industry I put down "sports journalist", which led me to Armidale University.

He enrolled in an Arts degree, majoring in English.

By the end of his first semester, though, it was clear the

academic life didn't agree with him – he hadn't been to a lecture or tutorial in three months. With the exams looming, it was time to move on.

He returned to Moree and turned to his first choice: 'I thought, "Now I want to be a bookmaker."'

However, he was still only seventeen and you had to be eighteen to get a licence. He thought he'd hang around in Moree and get his licence the following year, but given his family's enthusiasm for enterprise and prosperity, he shouldn't have been surprised when he was sent to one of their properties in western Queensland.

'It was my uncle Bruce, grandfather and Mum – Mum was basically making all the decisions for me – saying, "You go up there for a while and work." You weren't asked, you were told. Uncle Bruce was gently encouraging but my grandfather was a pretty strict bloke. I remember him. He was pretty tough. He was brought up in the old school and he liked to be the boss.'

At the time, the 27 000-hectare Listowel Downs, near Blackall, on the black-soil downs, was primarily a merino-sheep operation run by Terry's cousin Steven, Uncle Bruce's eldest son. It was Terry's first real taste of outback life.

'It was great, I enjoyed it. Steven used to go away a lot. He was seeing a girl from Longreach [Wendy, a nurse, whom he later married and with whom he's had four beautiful kids] at the time so I had weekends to myself. I used to drive everywhere. On Saturdays I'd get in the car and I'd drive. It felt like I used to drive all day and night to get to a race meeting.

'I remember I drove to Injune from Listowel Downs. I left at two o'clock in the morning and got back at two o'clock the next morning.'

Given his background, his interest in horse racing was no surprise. As he puts it, his involvement was 'ingrained – stamped. It was my passion and I had an instinct for it. I just liked doing it so it's what I chased.'

Terry recalls that outback race meetings in those days were much more social events than they are today. There was more of a bush atmosphere and many more people enjoying it; whereas today, professional punters make up much more of the crowd. The racing industry was thriving and trainers were operating at, or bringing their horses to, meetings at towns like Charleville, Blackall, Roma and Tambo.

Terry returned to Moree at the end of 1977. He was still too young to get his licence, but his brother Phillip, who'd completed a law degree, had a licence and Terry worked for him and other family members for a couple of years 'getting a bit more experience'.

'During the week I'd do a little bit of toiling – they had properties in town – mainly I was a chauffeur for people. It wasn't very brainstorming sort of work but I was just marking time till I got my bookmaker's licence.'

Among the experiences was a memorable moment involving his Uncle Bruce. It was reported by Bill Poulos:

> It was August, 1981 and the great horse Kingston Town was at unbackable odds to win the 1200m Premiere Stakes . . .
>
> Big-betting bookie Bruce Picone was fielding 'the board' at Moree and betting on the Rosehill feature was lacklustre.
>
> Punters couldn't afford the short odds about Kingston Town and absolutely no-one was willing to back a horse to beat the champ.
>
> About five minutes before the jump a little old lady clutching a small, well-worn purse made her way through the betting ring ruck.

She approached Bruce's stand and waited patiently.

'Can I help you, madam,' Bruce asked.

'Mr Picone, could I please have fifty cents each-way on Kingston Town,' she politely queried.

Bruce looked down from his stand and smiled warmly.

'I'm very sorry madam, but I can't take that sort of bet.'

The little old lady nodded sympathetically.

'I understand, Mr Picone . . . how about you take half and I'll get the rest on somewhere else.' *(Reproduced by kind permission.)*

It was also that year that Terry got his bookmaker's licence. 'What happened there: Uncle Bruce – he had a few bookmakers working for him – I just did my own thing.'

Terry travelled beyond the Picone family stamping grounds to (where else) the outback. His first race meeting was in Broken Hill, western New South Wales.

'I'd heard of the St Patrick's meeting and had a strong inkling to "go bush, young man". I was very excited, of course, [it] being my first day as a bookmaker. I had staff. [Brother] Chris worked for me and I took a couple of mates from Moree. I had a win, too, which made it good.'

Fronting a betting ring takes a great deal of courage. Get the odds wrong and you can get eaten alive, despite the widely held belief that bookies never lose.

'Now that's a furphy,' Terry says. 'You can definitely lose money bookmaking. It's a judgement thing. If you're right, you win; if you're wrong, you lose. In the old days that's why it was called bookmaking. You tried to frame a book so you didn't have any liabilities on a particular race. Very hard to do.

There's an element of liability.'

Computers now help bookmakers frame their books, shape their odds and keep track of their potential losses. But back in the early 1980s, they had to do it in their head.

'It was all manual. It was good. I think it was a lot better for the brain in those days.'

Making money may be the raison d'être of bookmaking, but for Terry, there is more to it. He enjoys the whole fabric of racing – the horses, the atmosphere, the people – and, in particular, outback racing. While he concentrated his early efforts in the north-west of New South Wales, the last quarter century has seen him venturing further afield. I asked him what's driven that.

'A love for the outback,' he told me. 'There's something about the outback. It gets into your system and it's very hard to get out. An outback race meeting has got more— I don't know if it's romance or passion. It's something about western Queensland. They reckon the further west you go, the better the people. I tend to agree with that. They're great people out there. I like going out there.'

That said, with a few notable exceptions, outback races aren't awash with potential earnings and it's hard to make a profit.

'I try to. I try to cover the diesel, the wages, the food and the grog. Windscreens, yeah. You do have good days at the office. A lot of quiet days, too.'

In outback communities, horse racing is still a community event. That's particularly the case for once-a-year meetings, which may be the only social get-together reinforcing the fabric of the community. Forty years ago, when Terry started travelling to outback race meetings, the interest in horses was strengthened by the fact that a lot of people were still actually using horses in their work – going mustering and so on.

That continues to be the case with older people, whose memories reach back to the days before planes and motorcycles. Many station-owners are still actively involved in horse racing. An example is another legend of the outback, David Brook, owner of five large stations, with his headquarters in Birdsville.

'Passionate, isn't he?' Terry commented. 'Passionate horse bloke, horse owner. It's a funny mix something like that, isn't it? It's hard to explain. But once it's in there, it's in there.'

Terry has known David for twenty-six years, the period he's been attending the outback's most iconic races, in Birdsville. It's an impressive record, but one that's matched or bettered by a number of other bookmakers, including Ron Murphy, Graeme Saunders, Gary Peoples, David 'Crockett' Power, Peter Anderson, Tony Purvis and Ken Elliott.

'I went with my cousin, Glen, the first year. I think it was '89 or '90. I had two years with him and then I got a Queensland licence.

'I remember there was this bloody big dust storm. They weren't as touristy as they are today. It was more a country race meeting. There were probably half the people there are today, about three to four thousand.

'The town was deadset nothing. There was a school, a pub. The airport was just a dirt strip and people used to land and park in front of the pub. David Brook was there. I used to go and use his phone to get markets. There were no houses like there are today. It's a metropolis compared to those days.'

What drew Terry there?

'Someone said to me, "You should go to Birdsville races, it's a good outback meeting." That's all I needed. And it was great fun. It still is. Just getting a group of blokes together, a group of mates, and going out and doing that bush stuff. And try and make a bit of money along the way. Tend to come back and tell your wife how hard you worked there.'

One of the main attractions for Terry is bush camping. Wherever he goes, he rolls out a swag and camps.

'Always camp. Still camping. I got a pretty wild camp but that's the way I like it.

'The Birsdville regular staff – Geoff Poulson, Ray Tamblin, Buck Burrow and Peter Chapman – they're good blokes to have work for you and help around the camp.'

Not long after he got his bookie's licence, Terry became involved in the Picone family's contribution to the community.

At the 1989 Inverell Cup, the track was in poor condition but the race was held anyway. Tragically, the leading horse slipped and fell and nine of the fifteen horses that were following were brought down as well. Two horses were so badly injured that they had to be put down. Nine jockeys were hospitalised. Shortly after, the Picone family brought in bulldozers and excavators and rebuilt the entire track, a project that took eight months to complete. They footed the bill themselves.

Terry also made a considerable contribution to the pocket money of a group of local children. As he admitted to a reporter for ABC Rural:

> I left about $6000 in a phone box as there was a
> misunderstanding with my brother Dennis. I was on the phone
> and he put the money behind me. We drove off down the road
> and then realised that we'd left it behind.

When they went back, the money was already gone. Years later, he found out where it went. A friend in the town where the money was left told him about a time when a group of kids came into his fish and chip shop and played pinball for week after week after week.

In his 1997 book *More Fact, Fiction and Fables of the Melbourne Cup*, Max Hitchins (beneficiary of the Picone family's generosity more than thirty years earlier) related how the Moree Race Club once took out rain insurance. According to Race Club President Eric Carrigan:

> I was in Church on a Sunday morning and Terry Picone was in the pew in front of me . . . Rather than take the usual rain insurance through insurance companies, I thought we should do business locally.
>
> 'Terry,' I whispered, 'Will you bet me $6000 to $500 for rain insurance of 20 points up to midday for our Melbourne Cup meeting?'
>
> '$6000 to $600,' was Terry's reply.
>
> '$6000 to $550,' I said.
>
> 'Done!' said Terry. 'Peace be with you.'
>
> *(Reproduced by kind permission.)*

Terry was also involved in the early career of poet Murray Hartin, another outback legend, whose story is the subject of chapter five.

> Muzz and I go back a long way. We've always been mates but we didn't connect until I came back to Moree and he was working here, in the mid-1990s. He was always entertaining – great value. Murray was between jobs at one stage and I'd lost my [driver's] licence because of a misunderstanding with the police and he

drove me round for a couple of months. I think we both enjoyed it. He tells me he had to pull me into gear. I didn't realise I was that bad but he tells me he pulled me into gear a few times.

Murray wrote a poem for Terry and his wife, Bethelle, when they got married; Terry, in turn, helped Murray get his first book published. 'I can't remember how that came about. I think he just said, "Can you give me a bit of a hand and I'll pay you back when I sell a few copies?"

'The *Turbulence* poem really kicked him on and the books and CDs kept coming after that. He's going well. Very entertaining – a good laugh, a very good laugh.'

That night, we drove back into Bedourie to go to the pub for a few drinks with 'Colgate' (Trevor Stewart), the Diamantina Shire Council's infrastructure manager and Mr Fix-It. I suspect that after a day in the car with Gordo, Terry needed a break from the Odds Couple. Colgate is so-named because he has a smile so bright it can be seen from space. He flashes it often, because even when he's under pressure, he doesn't seem to stress.

Terry also introduced me to the other bookie who was in town to work for the camel races – Ken Elliot, whose nickname was 'Huff 'n' Puff'. Terry couldn't explain why, but when I suggested it was because Ken was a pretty big fella, Terry said, 'Oh no, he's lost a lot of weight.'

Terry's nickname, 'Arthritis', was earned because he's been in so many joints. I always call him 'Terry', though – it's a bit of a respect thing. It's the same with David Brook. I call him 'David' when everyone else calls him 'Brookie'. Meanwhile, Terry is the only person who calls me 'Ev'.

We could only stay for a couple of drinks because Terry wanted to ring another bookie whose speciality was camel racing. There wasn't a mobile phone service in Bedourie ('It's coming in May 2017,' Colgate told us) so we had to go to a payphone in the main street. Terry was hoping to get a bit of an idea of the form for the following day's races. The bookie was happy to help but couldn't really give him much information.

Back in camp, the Odds Couple were going to have steak sandwiches again but I put my foot down.

'We have to have some greens,' I insisted. 'I've got the makings, it'll only take a minute.' I chopped some lettuce and tomato, thinly sliced a carrot and a red onion, and mixed everything together with some Italian dressing.

'This is amazing,' they chorused as we sat down to a proper meal. 'What do you call this, Ev?' Terry asked with a wink.

'Salad,' I replied. 'You may have come across it once or twice in the past.'

'We really should try making this sometime, Gordo,' Terry said. 'I like it.'

I knew they were baiting me. The dressing had come out of Terry's tuckerbox.

We were up early the following morning to set up Terry's stand over at the betting ring. With only two bookmakers, 'ring' wasn't the right word for it, but Terry set up at right angles to Huff 'n' Puff, so it was a betting corner.

I was given rudimentary training on the computer – shown

how to enter the amount of a bet, the type of bet and the number of the camel, using different numbers on a purpose-built keyboard. As soon as you hit the last number, a betting ticket was printed out. No need to hit 'Enter' or answer 'Are you sure?' with 'Y' or 'N'.

Once we started taking bets, the reason for the hair-trigger set-up became obvious. The bets came thick and fast.

Gordo was out front holding the moneybag, taking the bets and calling them to me. 'Ten on two!' (Short for '$10 for a win on camel two'.) 'Five on three!' 'Ten each way on six!'

As fast as he was calling them, the tickets were coming out. If a queue formed, Terry would step in to help him, and I'd be keying bets twice as fast. It didn't stop from the moment Gordo started taking bets until just after the camels jumped in the first race. Then we entered the winners and printed the payout sheet. All this while trying to hear punters over the public address system, the cheering for the charity pig races, novelty events and a band.

There was no overt competition between Terry and Huff 'n' Puff. On the contrary, Ken showed Terry and I how to manually enter the camels for each race. While three of us were working Terry's stand, Ken spent most of the day on his own.

As soon as the initial odds for the next race were set, we started taking bets.

We found out later that 800 tickets had been sold for entry to the camel races. There may have been more in attendance than that, what with various people camped at the race track who were already inside before they started charging admission. Not everyone was betting but to my mind there were a lot of people for only two bookies to handle.

The format for the races was that twenty-two camels ran in four heats, then the best ran in the final. The losers ran in a gift and the young camels went in a novice event. In between races, there were wood-chopping, camp-oven throwing and damper-making competitions and running races. The $21 000 worth of prizes were mostly donated by local businesses; the economic benefit for the town must have been well over $100 000.

As for the races themselves, after the first one I was left wondering how anyone could sensibly bet on a camel. The jockeys did a mighty job, perched on the rumps of these unwieldy beasts, but the camels were quite wilful when it came to starting, stopping and loping in any particular direction.

In one race, the favourite flattened the strapper that was trying to keep it in check, then bolted before the start, resulting in its disqualification. Some camels were fast but veered from one side of the track to the other, allowing those travelling the shortest distance between two points to take the lead.

On Terry's stand, we were flat out all day. We had no breaks and no lunch, though late in the day, we managed to get a cup of chips. There were a few bigger punters about, laying some substantial bets on interstate races, which Terry followed on TV screens above the betting corner. Most people, however, were making modest bets of $5 and $10.

At the end of the day, while we were packing up, I was surprised when several people came over and said, 'Thanks for being here, we really enjoyed ourselves.'

I hadn't realised we were part of the entertainment.

Terry explained, 'Without a bookie, meetings like this would struggle. It would be a pretty lame sort of place. They definitely add to the colour of the day. A little flutter? People just like it.

It adds to the interest. Just going to watch horses go around is pretty bland. As a good friend of mine says, "It's like watching dog poo turn white."'

For bookmakers, one of the advantages of outback race meetings is that there's no outside competition for people's bets. To the best of my knowledge, none of the big international betting companies or internet betting conglomerates offered odds on the Bedourie camels. It's a different story with interstate races.

Terry told me, 'Overseas betting companies, which are a pet hate of mine, dictate betting markets and we generally follow those trends on the interstate races. For local races, I do my own form and I've got my own ideas. At races meetings in places like Moree, your biggest competitor is the TAB. So you've got to at least match that or, if you don't like a particular horse, you'll go above it.'

Unfortunately, the unreliable nature of phone and internet connections in the outback means taking bets on interstate races can be fraught with danger.

'They get some big punters in the outback who've got internet, iPhone, satphone and iPads. They've got the same information I've got and they're looking for the trends, too. They're looking to back something I miss. I've had a couple of nasty experiences at Birdsville, don't you worry. Last year was very nasty. I did $4000 on the first race in Adelaide. So that was a bad start.

'My internet broke down. It's very tricky on the internet at Birdsville. Too many people and too many users. I had the wrong price up and I paid the penalty. So that's what it's all about: be on your game, make sure you've got all the internet and information technology up to speed. If it is, I'm comfortable, but once that fails on me or breaks down, I get very jumpy, 'cos that's when I can – well, not drop my guard – but can lose a lot of money.'

When it comes to outback race meetings, he explained, book-makers can't just turn up. If there are too many, none will cover their costs. If there are too few, punters will struggle to place a bet.

'Look at Innamincka [in South Australia]. They've got only one bookmaker so they want to know that bookmaker is going to turn up.

'The outback, it's pretty hard. Once you break the ice, break the egg to get their confidence, you're right. But it takes a bit to penetrate that barrier. I had a little bit of trouble early on but it was only a matter of natural attrition.

'They said, "Nah, nah, we've got enough bookmakers at Bedourie [horse races] and Betoota."

'It was just gentle resistance. So you took the hint and you stayed away but eventually a vacancy came up and they gave me a call.'

At Bedourie's camels, Terry wasn't sure if he'd be welcome the first time he went there.

'The camels? Well, pretty tightly held. Some bookmakers can be a bit funny, they like to be a bit territorial, but generally it's all about supply and demand and everyone sort of gets along pretty well.

'It's a good thing we came, in the end, because the crowd is a lot bigger than they anticipated. It warrants another bookmaker. It would have been a bit of a disaster for the organisers if they didn't have two bookmakers. So I think it worked out well for me.'

What was it like making book on camels for the first time?

'My first experience at camel racing was very interesting. There's a lot of talent to ride a camel. There's a lot of balance to ride a camel at speed. I was a little bit apprehensive but sort of felt my way and I enjoyed the experience. I probably would do it again. I don't know whether I'd go out just for one day, but if I had a bit of a trip organised, I'd do it. I'd be into it if it might be Marree the week before. Something like that.

'As it was, we took two days each way, a day at the camp – it's five days away – about a 2000-kilometre trip. That's putting your time into what you could do closer to home. So you've got to weigh that up, but I wanted to do it. I might even do it again. All that travelling knocks you round, and doing form, and we're not as young as we used to be.

'And staffing is a problem because you're away so long. People have trouble getting away at short notice. Grab who you can when you can.

'In the early times at Birdsville I used to have a minibus – for about fifteen or sixteen years, up to eighteen or nineteen people. Probably half of those were staff and the rest were friends and acquaintances.

'You had to get a lot of gear, a lot of grog and a lot of food. The blokes that I took have got older and you're busy running round looking after them. It just got a bit too much so I wound that down a bit and just take my staff out now. They were good days, I enjoyed those. They were good fun trips – they're still good fun trips but just not as big.'

At times there was even a chef.

'I loved that part. It took the pressure off me. All the book-making part, I could handle that, but it's the camping part, looking after all those people, that's what I found difficult.'

He still has a bucket list of outback race meetings he wants to get to.

'I've got a few in the Northern Territory I want to get to. Adelaide River – I wanna work there – and the Alice Springs Cup. I want to go to Brunette Races. There's another outback one, it's like Brunette Downs. I think it might be stock horses. Harts Range, I think it's called. It's not far from Alice Springs.

'I've just got my South Australian licence and I'm looking forward to doing a few there, like Innamincka. I didn't know you can't pick and choose there [in South Australia]. The clubs tell you where to go, so I don't know what the future holds for me there. Quorn. That's in South Australia. I was going into Broken Hill one day and I called in at that little place this side of Broken Hill – Little Topar – and a bloke was there from Quorn Race Club. He said, "You should come work at Quorn one year."

'I said, "Yeah, I'll do that mate."

'So, that's part of the reason I got a South Australian licence.

'There's a lot of racecourses I haven't been to yet. I wouldn't mind doing up the top of WA but there's a bookmaker there and you've got to wait for a vacancy. I've told the bookmaker who's working at the moment, at Kununurra and Wyndham, "If there's ever a vacancy call me up."

'What's the attraction? It's somewhere different. I've never been there. And the landscape. I think it would be a great trip from Moree to Kununurra. I drove to Darwin last year from Moree.'

If he succeeds in his ambition, he may become the only bookmaker to have worked in the outback in every state and territory. At that point, he admits he'd be a bit of a legend.

Meanwhile, Terry's 'arthritis' seems incurable. For many years he was driving 150 000 kilometres. In recent times that's dropped to about 100 000 a year, but every car he's traded in has still had between 400 000 and 500 000 kilometres on it.

'It sounds a bit corny but I've always had a dream or a vision, I suppose, to have an outback property – live in the outback. I don't mind the remoteness and the quietness; yeah, pretty simple sort of chap at heart.'

It's quite a contrast to the intensity of the betting ring, where the Picone connection is as strong as ever. Terry's brothers Chris, Phillip and Dennis are bookmakers. Uncle Bob's sons Geoffrey and Michael and Uncle Bruce's sons John and Glen and son-in-law Simon Smith have been bookmakers.

At Bedourie, I noticed that people were coming up and introducing themselves to Terry. Some mentioned past experiences with him or with other members of his family. Often their memories went back decades.

As the late Bruce Picone told Bill Poulos back in 2004:

> There is something about the racing crowd; you enjoy it wherever you go. I've often been asked by people why I haven't retired but I tell them that this is as good as retirement. It's the one thing that I will always do – I love the racing and I love the people. Even if the punter beats you, you enjoy being with them and people never forget you. *(Reproduced by kind permission.)*

Leg Two

We were up before dawn on Sunday morning, packing our camp and preparing to go our separate ways: the Odds Couple 2000 kilometres east to Moree; me 700 kilometres south to Marree.

At such an early hour, the road down to Birdsville, in the wide open spaces that I'd come to love nearly a decade before, was virtually deserted. It was also quite damaged in places by floodwater. Near Lake Machattie, it was a succession of pools that were nearly 40 centimetres deep in places. The road was unsealed but well bedded with rocks so the going was firm, despite the water.

Down at Birdsville, I refuelled at the roadhouse. While I was there, I mentioned to the co-manager Bronwynne Barnes that I was interested in catching up with her mechanic husband, Peter, after that year's races.

'I want to do a chapter on his desert rescues,' I told her.

Typically, she knew where he should be but not where he was. She said she'd let him know.

Over at the bakery I caught up with Dusty Miller for a chunky beef pie and coffee. Dusty's chunky beefs are the yardstick by which I measure all others. The only trouble is that Dusty can't help tinkering with them. I reckon once you've set the bar at perfection, you should leave well enough alone. Dusty's moustache bristles at the suggestion.

South of Birdsville, the 500 unsealed kilometres of the Birdsville Track had pools of water on them all the way to Marree. The drive was a frustrating sequence of gear changes: slowing down to traverse water or rutted road, then accelerating back to a reasonable speed . . . and repeat.

The drive started in sunshine but a cloud band eventually rose and darkened in the south-west. About 100 kilometres out of Marree, it started raining lightly. In the distance, it looked quite stormy. I started worrying about road conditions. It would only take 20 to 30 millimetres of rain to turn the track to mud. I had my next interview lined up for the next morning, and I was keen to get there on time. However, it's never a good plan to work to a tight schedule when driving in the outback.

Finally, I could see Marree about 15 kilometres in the distance. The rain was still light but the storm that had passed meant conditions were quite slippery. I'd slowed down to 60 kilometres an hour, and while conditions were soft, the road surface was holding up well and I had good traction.

Then I hit a soft patch, and there was a sound of mud being thrown up under the car. The car slid a little, I corrected and all was well. I knew, in such a situation, to avoid hitting the brakes when the slide started. That can make the slide worse and lead to a rollover. When it happened a couple more times, I slowed down a little more. I still felt like I was driving to the conditions.

Then the Truckasaurus slid again. I corrected. Corrected more. Full opposite lock. No traction. Trucka was now completely sideways and all I could think was, 'Here we go.' I tried turning with the slide, to get the vehicle all the way around. No shame ending up backwards if you're still on your wheels. There was so little response from the 2.5-tonne vehicle it felt like the steering was broken.

I waited for the rolling to start.

Trucka and I slipped towards a deep drain at the side of the road then started going over the edge. Then . . . we stopped. Two wheels just off the road. Two wheels on.

I was shaken but unharmed. The engine had stalled and it took me a moment, in the total quiet, to realise Trucka was also undamaged. I started the engine and it only took two goes to reverse out of the drain onto the road.

I undid my seatbelt and got out and looked at the tyres, which have a chunky, all-terrain profile. They'd become caked in mud, so much so that there was no tread on the road. The road itself bore the evidence of the huge slide, ending at the ditch.

Less than 5 kilometres away, the town of Marree was now shining in late afternoon sunlight. I got back into Trucka and gingerly moved off. I found that, at 40 kilometres an hour, the car was quite manageable. Despite years of experience driving in outback conditions, I'd just learned something new. Fortunately, it hadn't come at a high price.

That night, while having dinner at the pub, I learned that others hadn't been so lucky. On the Oodnadatta Track, there had been three rollovers. One vehicle had been found abandoned. It was possible that the passengers had hitched a ride with someone else, but there was concern that someone might have been injured and wandered from the scene.

I counted myself very fortunate. I also noted the irony that the person I was meeting the following day was the person I'd have seen that night if I'd needed medical attention after a car crash.

2.

Finger on the Pulse

June Andrew

(1954–)

Sitting in an office in the Marree Health Service Clinic in the arid north-east of South Australia, waiting for a computer to boot up while making small talk was an odd way to start an interview with one of the most respected women in the outback. Nevertheless, nurse June Andrew and I were hoping the computer contained the email that meant the Royal Flying Doctor Service (RFDS) had given approval for her to talk to me.

We wondered whether the slow response was due to the machine or the notoriously unreliable outback internet. Still, it was as good a way as any to break the ice, and when I eventually realised I had a copy of the required email on my iPad, June was ready to chat.

I'd almost certainly encountered June once before without realising it, back in 2009. My wife Michelle and I had taken the opportunity of a break in the floods around Birdsville (where we were spending a year) to escape south for a bit of shopping. On the way back, we'd stayed overnight in Marree and saw there was social tennis on. We went down for a hit and envied the level of organisation and involvement – which we'd been striving for up the other end of the Birdsville Track. Little did we know the organisational skill was June's.

It wasn't until late 2015 that June came onto my radar. Recently retired Birdsville policeman and cowriter of *Outback Cop*, Neale McShane, suggested she would be a good subject for this book.

'The nurse down there has been there forever,' he said.

June Andrew was born in a little village in Devon in 1953 and emigrated to Australia with her parents in 1957, aged three. At first they lived with other immigrants at Smithfield Hostel, north of Adelaide, then they moved to Elizabeth and Gawler, where she and her three brothers grew up. She went straight from secondary school at Elizabeth Girls Technical High School into nursing.

'The tutor at the hospital in Gawler was going on long service leave, so we actually started training at the hospital on 15 December, before school had actually finished. School finished a week later.'

Back in those days, the 1960s, most of the learning was done on the wards. June still believes that's the best way to do it. She did two years at Gawler, then transferred to Royal Adelaide for another two years. She did midwifery and worked in Mount Gambier for a couple of years, then moved to Tasmania and did her Childhood, Mothers and Babies training for six months in Hobart. She did relieving at mothers and babies clinics around Tasmania for about eighteen months.

'I decided that wasn't what I wanted to do all the time, so I took my mum and dad back to England and met lots of relatives, and saw where I was born and where Mum was born, and where Dad was during the War, and where they met. They got married during the War. Then we came back and I wasn't sure what I should do. So I did two years in a nursing agency working in country hospitals.'

It was while she was doing that, in the town of Keith, in 1982, that she saw a job advertised for a nurse in Marree.

'I had no idea where Marree was. I'd never been any further north than Peterborough. I had to get the map out before I applied and I thought, "Oh, okay. That sounds interesting. I'll apply."'

The position had been advertised for five months. She went for an interview and was offered the job a week later.

'Can you start Monday such-and-such?'

'Yep, okay.'

At that point, she still hadn't been to Marree. Nevertheless, she gave her nursing agency a week's notice, worked until the following Saturday and drove to her parents' home in Gawler on Sunday. Then she tackled the 600-kilometre drive to her new job.

'It was dirt roads from Port Augusta, pretty well. You used to go through Beltana, the old Beltana – lots of winding roads – and then I kept driving and driving. I had a little Laser. I kept driving and I thought, "I wonder how much further?"

'I got here just before five o'clock on the Monday.'

She arrived just in time to see the last official flight from Marree's old airstrip. The dentist from Adelaide was flying out after his regular visit. He used to drive to Port Augusta and fly up on the RFDS plane. It was 6 December 1982.

June can't recall her first impression of Marree.

'Apart from "How far is it?" I don't know what I expected.

By the time I got here I was so tired I didn't take any notice. I found the Health Service okay and I thought, "Well, this'll be interesting."

'I was on six months' probation – district nurses do six months' probation – so I only had to stay for six months at least. That was the idea, but I did sort of come intending to stay for three to five years. I wanted to stay somewhere for longer. I'd sort of got sick of opening and shutting my suitcase all the time.'

When June arrived there was a nurse, Jane Walker, still working at the clinic, but she was about to leave to get married. Her betrothed was a local pastoralist, David Morton, from Pandie Pandie near Birdsville. Jane was able to give June a week to get orientated, then she was on her own. By then, she was beginning to get a feel for the weather around Marree at that time of the year.

'We had dust storms every day and the dust used to blow in. We used to have to get the shovel to get the dust out. I was thinking, "Oh, this weather's a bit different." It was pretty warm, too, because December's pretty hot.'

She met most of the community during the first week, but there was a problem. With the school year ending and people going off on holidays, or permanently, there were farewell barbecues every night. That meant June was introduced to most of the people in the dark around camp fires.

'I couldn't recognise anybody in the daylight, but they all knew who I was. It's really hard when you meet lots of Aboriginal people in the dark because it's even harder to see them in the camp fire light.'

'"Oh yeah, I met you there."

'"Yes, but . . . who are you again?"'

Back then, the railway still ran to Marree, and with railway workers the population was about 150.

She was working alone in the two-bed clinic which, despite its small size, has never been full. June was accustomed to working on her own: many of the country places where she'd worked previously didn't have doctors.

'Most of the places you only have two staff, but it was only me most of the time. One of the other ladies from one of the pastoral properties in the district – Lyn Litchfield – still did a bit of casual. She'd worked here for a while, met a fella and married up here. She only did a little bit of work then because she was busy with her kids and the pastoral property.

'I liked working by myself. I had to get used to using the radio because the telephone had only just come in. Up here they used to use the radio to talk to the flying doctor and they used to still do a lot of radio sessions. So you'd be listening to the pastoral properties.

'They had a social session when they'd just do the talking, then they had set session times for the RFDS if you wanted to do consults, which was on a different frequency. So you'd tend to keep it on the local frequency just to find out what people were doing.'

It was reminiscent of the classic scene from the 1950s film *The Back of Beyond* (which made an outback legend of Marree local, Tom Kruse) where the stations were calling each other to pass on news of Tom's progress up the Birdsville Track. Except this was as recent as 1982.

There were plenty of other aspects of life that were different to the city. There wasn't, and still isn't, a major supermarket in town and the shop had a limited range.

'I didn't order things in, but you'd have to make sure that they'd have things when ordering – that you'd actually get something that would last you for a week or two weeks. Mail used to come on the bus one day and then there'd be the mail plane on the weekend.'

Since then, the bus service has stopped, as has the train. Mail now comes to Marree by road, still only twice a week. The demise of public transport services has made the logistics of getting people to appointments harder, particularly in a town where not everyone has a car.

June's accommodation within the medical facility was functional rather than luxurious.

'It's just a room. I moved from the inside room to the side room once Jane went, because there was a bit more light. It's got the lounge room and the kitchen, which are sort of communal, but I was used to living with other people, sharing, so that made it a bit easier.

'There wasn't much TV so there really wasn't a lot to do once you finished work. I'm not a pub person because I don't drink. I'd go to the hotel maybe and have some tea occasionally.

'I liked going to the movies. They used to have movies that came on the train and they'd have them once a month or once every two months. They had the big projector with the wheels, then we had a projector with DVDs or videos and we used to do them at the hall.'

June's area of responsibility is vast.

'I've been to Clifton Hills [300 kilometres north] once because the planes were all busy. There was an accident between Clifton Hills and Mungerannie. William Creek (204 kilometres northwest), but usually the plane will beat me, and halfway across the

Borefield Road towards Roxby (130 kilometres south-west). Mostly it's just around the pastoral properties locally and the town.'

The town's population dropped from 150 to as low as 50 after the railway line closed in 1987, but it's now up to 90. However, numbers fluctuate, particularly during the cooler months of the year when tourists are passing through, backpackers are working in various businesses and pilots are doing scenic flights.

'You can vary from having many people in town one day to none the next day. The pastoral properties, when I first came, they were all younger families with kids. The kids all grew up and went away working and to school. Now they've all come back and they're all having babies. The older people are going away more, so the whole district's population has changed on and off over the years.'

Outback nursing has never been easy, but for more than a century, women like June have been at the forefront. From 1894 onwards, the Smith of Dunesk Mission, funded by Scottish woman Henrietta Smith, was based in Beltana, 150 kilometres south of Marree, with clergymen providing limited medical services in South Australia's far north. In 1907, nursing services were established at Oodnadatta by Sister E.A. Main.

Marree got its first nurse in 1912, although it took until 1916 for a clinic building to be constructed. It's now celebrating its centenary. While the first flying doctor services began in the 1920s, nurses have continued to provide the backbone of remote health services across the outback.

Remote health work isn't for everybody, but when June's six-month probation ended, she stayed. After two years, she was still there. By then, she knew everybody, having seen most of them in the clinic at least once.

She'd also found that in such places anything can come through the door. In the case of car accidents, of course, she might have to go out the door to them.

'You've got the Flying Doctor [Service], which you get onto to say that you're going out to see something or they'll ring and say that they've been notified, or the police will ring or the CFS [Country Fire Service] will ring. You go out and see what's there and then you'll contact them – sometimes from out there by satellite phone or radio, depending what's there or what you can use at the time. If a patient comes in the door, you assess them, do your initial safety things, then get onto the doctor. They'll come up or they'll say, "Can you just watch them for a while?"

'And then they'll reassess if they need to be flown out.

'Car accidents aren't nice, if it's a local, especially if we have a fatality where you can't do anything. Not very nice, but the thing is, if there's other people in the vehicle, you've got to do things to them and just try and cope with the family around. A lot of people in Marree are related. So it makes it a bit hard. I don't really like car accidents at all because you don't know what you're gonna get till you get there.'

If the planes are all busy, June may be asked to transport the patient to Leigh Creek, 100 kilometres south, where there's a doctor. In that case, they may be taken in the town's ambulance, driven by a volunteer or (now there is one) another nurse. However, while that's happening, the town may be left without any medical support until they return.

At times June has needed help and called on a couple of women in the district who have medical training. Sometimes, though, she just needs someone reliable to watch one patient while she's doing things with another patient or has to go out to another call.

'You haven't got lots and lots of staff. In the city there's usually more people around and the doctors would be a lot closer. In one way, if you get flown out from Marree to see the doctor, you'd probably get through the queue a lot quicker because they're actually expecting you and you're on the emergency queue. Usually if you're getting flown out, you're not very well anyway.'

June has also had to deal with heart attacks.

'I've had some people from the highway departments – the workers who've had heart attacks – they can be a bit stubborn. Even though they've got chest pains, they don't want to go anywhere. When they eventually do, they mightn't want to go on the plane. They'll get someone to drive them, when they have actually had a heart attack.'

Then there are asthma attacks, which can be frightening for everyone involved, especially if it's a young person's first bout.

'It's scarier for the parents, so trying to calm down the parents is sometimes harder than trying to treat the child who's actually having the attack. It's scary watching people, especially. I hadn't had a lot to do with asthmatics before I came up here.'

The triggers for asthma attacks are many. Some people only get asthma in winter. Some get it from animal fur. One of June's patients really likes horses but they trigger his asthma. Tourists and visitors have attacks because of the dust. Others who usually have asthma don't get it when they get to Marree, perhaps because the air is drier than where they've come from. Conversely, locals who have few asthma attacks can have more when they go south.

Drugs and alcohol are another part of the job that June, a non-drinker, has to deal with.

'We do have some problems with marijuana but most of them are pretty good with that. They have it at home, it's not like they go out. I did hear there was some ice around the district but I haven't had anybody come in.

'It's more when you've got the tourists through that you don't know what's gonna come in the door. The locals you sort of know what they're like so if they're different to normal, you can tell pretty much.'

It turns out that alcohol is much more of a problem.

'I have an issue with people drinking a lot. We have people who do drink a lot, so I had to get used to lots of people drinking. There were lots of fights when I first came.

'The railway workers who got paid in the middle of the week – not all of them but it'd usually be the same people – they'd have a big booze-up in the middle of the week after they got paid. Then they'd fight. I'd be seeing people in the evening during the week.

'If I heard Slim Dusty playing, there wouldn't be any fights. If they had that heavy bang-bang-bang music, there'd always be a fight and I'd have to work. I didn't really like Slim Dusty until I came up here, but if you heard Slim Dusty music, it was a good night. It's still the same now. If they have that really heavy beat music, there's always a fight somewhere.'

It's perhaps fitting that Slim Dusty's final live performance, in 2000, was in Marree. June got to see him.

'He performed at the end of the cattle drive that came down the Birdsville Track. We had about 7000 people in Marree. He wasn't up for very long – I think he did two songs – but I did actually see him and that was an experience.'

She didn't get to see much of the other events associated with the cattle drive – such as the cattle walking into the town and down to the stockyards – due to the medical needs of the sudden influx of 7000 visitors. This was despite other medical staff being sent up to help, including a doctor and a manager to assist with the ambulance.

'They had a whole lot of people come up with souvenirs and things. The trouble was they sold all their souvenirs on the first day and all the volunteers wanted to leave. That meant I had the doctor and my helpers on the Saturday and they all went Sunday morning. So it was just me again, apart from the two ladies who were doing a bit of casual work. The number of visitors went down to about two-and-a-half thousand.'

Another challenge for a nurse on her own is women giving birth. Stories abound of bush nurses performing remarkable feats to save mother and child. An RFDS pilot once put a plane on autopilot while transporting a woman who went into labour, so the child could be delivered in flight. When air traffic control was informed that there was now an extra passenger aboard, they asked nonchalantly, 'Boy or girl?'

June is similarly matter-of-fact.

'I've had lots of people in labour. All the station ladies kind of went into premature labour and had to go south early. The last birth actually in Marree was in 1993 and that's just because she was a bit quick. Usually most of the ladies go south three weeks before they're due.

'We've had travellers come through who are pregnant. We've had a few come up that are very pregnant and go into labour and we fly them out when they get here. The roads mightn't be that bad but it's a long trip for someone. We've had a big baby boom in the district lately – on the pastoral properties and a few in town. Lots of little kids around again.'

The RFDS supports expecting and new mothers with a community health nurse who comes when the plane does clinic flights to the town and stations. June does some antenatal work with people who are around or who come between clinics if they have concerns.

'We do a bit of postnatal but we haven't really had the births here for a while. They've been in the district but not actually in town.'

Among the most difficult challenges facing bush nurses (and many small communities across Australia) is depression, mental illness and suicide. While that subject is explored further in chapter five, June is on the front line when it comes to dealing with people who are struggling.

'There's been a few hangings and suicides in town over the years, which are never very nice, especially if they're people you know. Sometimes they're ones that you can do things with and others it's too late. We had one bloke, it was probably more for attention to start with, but he did try again two other times. We managed to fix that one, but there have been others . . . too late.

'There's a few people around who are on medications for mental illness, who've come up from south and are staying here now. They've been here for a few years. Unfortunately, sometimes we have people that we can't actually treat here. We had one gentleman who got flown out so many times we kind of said, "No, he can't come back." He's down in Adelaide.'

The RFDS used to have a mental health nurse visiting Marree, but the position was vacant when I visited in July 2016. It was

in the process of being advertised. June had noticed that having
the mental health service was making a difference, as locals –
especially men – were now coming to talk to her if they felt the
need.

'There are lots of mental health needs around, especially on the
pastoral properties. It's probably not so much this year – there's
lots of rain, lots of feed, so they're much happier at the moment.

'We had one of the doctors coming here for twenty years;
they were quite happy to come and talk to him. We did have
a psychiatrist coming for a while and some went to her regularly. That was more the ladies. They all said she was really
good. There's telephone consulting which they can do, which is
confidential.

'And I've been here a long time. I have people that just come
and talk to me sometimes. We just sit and talk. Hopefully we
don't get too many interruptions. We'll sit out the back maybe
and they'll just talk for an hour or so and just get whatever they're
worried about out of their system and then they'll go home and
they'll be happier.

'There've been some that have actually gone and spoken to
the mental health nurse and the psychiatrist later. Sometimes
they'll do it under their own initiative and sometimes they'll say,
"Well, can you book me in just to have a quick talk?" Which is
good. Sometimes, once they've had a good talk, they say, "Well
I'm feeling a lot better now", but you just keep an eye on them
for a while and see them a bit more regularly.

June has also reached a point where people can maintain a
degree of confidentiality by saying they're going to see her for
non-medical reasons.

'I became the Avon lady because the town wanted me to be

the Avon lady. So they could come up and say, "I'm just going to get Avon."

'It probably helps that I'm by myself, in one way. You've got to be careful when you're out and about because people ask you things and you say, "You'll have to ask them. I can't tell you."

'Unless they've said, "Yes, you can tell people."

'Some people say "Oh, yes, just tell 'em" because they'll know anyway because they're all related.'

With some of her patients, privacy isn't an issue.

'Over the years I've seen a few different animals. Lots of cats and dogs. A few horses. I sewed up my first horse out in one of the paddocks. I got really good at jumping back every time it tried to kick me but it had a really good suture union. It had a really good flap and it healed up really well.

'I had a brolga somebody brought in once. It had a sore leg that I fixed. I got registered so I could give dog and cat vaccines because the vet didn't come very often.

'The vet said, "No, I'll put you in so that you can actually do them."

'I've had to put a few animals down – especially older ones. I've put lots of kittens and things down. We try and keep the cat and dog numbers down.'

The Pika Wiya Health Service, the Aboriginal health service headquartered in Port Augusta, also brings a free vet to town every so often. They'll do free desexings, which can be a major saving, not just for the operation but also on the cost of travelling to Port Augusta (380 kilometres) or Quorn (340 kilometres) to get it done. Treatment is usually carried out behind the building, where there's good light and an electricity supply. If it's windy, visiting vets sometimes carry out procedures on the clinic's verandah.

Still, there have been moments when June has thought, 'I can't believe I'm doing this.'

'The first time I sewed up a horse. I'd never had anything to do with horses when I was little. The first time I gave a dog an immunisation, they didn't hold it quite tight enough and it moved. They've got to be muzzled preferably.

'They say, "Oh, no, the dog will be fine."

'I say, "No, somebody else said that and the dog bit me. So you either muzzle it or you hold its head or you do something with it, I'm not touching it."'

These days, more people have vehicles, and will drive to Port Augusta with their pets if they really want something done with them. That's the only option in Marree, since there are no flying vets, as there are in other areas, and the RFDS won't do aerial evacuation of an animal.

June has also forged a good relationship with a vet in Port Augusta who has been coming up to Marree for years. She can consult with him if any animal problems arise.

The nursing service June works for has operated under a number of titles over the years – Bush Nursing Service, Royal Bush Nursing and Royal District Nursing Service – but in 2006 it was taken under the wing, so to speak, of the Royal Flying Doctor Service.

When the new arrangement began, it was the only RFDS clinic in the country. It remained so until 2016, when the RFDS took responsibility for Andamooka (600 kilometres north of Adelaide) and Marla (1100 kilometres north).

'The RFDS role is still primarily the flying doctors, but it's expanded into other things as well. They do a lot more primary health things, especially from Port Augusta. They do clinic flights that go to pastoral properties or the smaller towns. Because that flight is a GP service, the RFDS is our GP as well. They've expanded the GP service and they've got extra funding for ten years for community things.

'They expanded on the things that the town was already doing and put some new things in. They have a healthy living program and they have the dietician and the fitness person that go out doing programs in different places. They do yoga, the fellas do some fitness things at the gym and they do sessions at the school where they do fitness and good eating. They're doing a lot more community health work and things other than primary health.'

Over what is now approaching thirty-five years, June was also drawn into the community. While some people say it can take decades (or in some places being born in an area) to become accepted as a local, the way to fast-track that is to volunteer for things.

'I started going to meetings to meet people, got on lots of committees and got involved with lots of community things: the Progress Association, School Council, the Country Fire Service, the Race Club, the Sports Club, the local paper.

'We didn't really have a tennis club when I came. They used to have an old court by the hotel, but that wasn't usable. Then the Progress Association got the big cement court built and we started regular tennis in the summer, in the evenings when it's cooler.

'I'm involved with the tennis, only because I like playing it. We needed some more social things that weren't just around alcohol, because everything was around alcohol and there really wasn't anything suitable for the kids. We wanted to do more things to involve the whole community. That's why we got the tennis going. So a bit more sport, which is a bit different.

'We got so many people coming that we started doing barbecues as well. They'd be coming anyway and having lots of drinks, but it was better to have some food. So we got more people coming then just for the barbecue that would stay to watch the tennis. It became a family social thing.'

Up in Birdsville, we'd tried to organise a similar social tennis night, but only ever managed to get two other couples interested. By comparison, Marree's tennis was a roaring success. Apparently, though, it ebbs and flows.

'We haven't got as many kids playing tennis at the moment. The bigger kids are more into their computer stuff now, and they like netball or basketball better than the tennis, but if you get them revved up, they'll have a hit, then they'll keep playing for the season.

'A barbecue is probably not that healthy but we did try introducing salads and stuff with it. You kind of have to cover your costs and they weren't buying salads so we went back to meat and bread. We have special barbecues where we have lots of salads and stuff. The kids love their salads – when it's a special thing and they don't have to pay for it.

'They do a lot of salads and healthy cooking things at school and dieticians that come with the RFDS and Allied Health do a lot of stuff with the kids. They do a lot of different foods. They'll bring different things up that we definitely don't get in Marree, so they get to try different things.

'There's not a lot of takeaway in Marree and most of the families do eat a lot of fruit and vegies when they're available. The fresh fruit and veg comes pretty well every week at the moment because it's tourist time. Summertime it's not quite so easy to get it. People will drive down to Leigh Creek and buy things. As long as the road is good, people will go down and buy some extra stuff down there if there's nothing here.'

June also used to edit the community newspaper, *The Hergott Herald*. ('Hergott' is a reference to the original name for Marree, Hergott Springs, alluding to the water soaks nearby that marked the southern boundary of the Great Artesian Basin.)

'We've got somebody else doing a bit more now, but I still put things on the community board. It used to be going years and years ago, then we brought it back in and we were doing really well for a while – and then some of the other ladies that were doing it dropped off and it only seemed to be me. So it got down to a couple of issues for the year and then it got a bit too much for me so we kind of didn't do any for a couple of years.

'Now we've started again. We try and do one a month but it doesn't always work – depending what's on and how busy everybody is. The younger lady doing some of it now, she's actually putting it on the computer more. I don't have to do quite as much but I still put my bits in and I do it when she's away.'

June is not currently on the School Council, although she still does things at the school. She's currently captain of the Country Fire Service (CFS), at least until she can get someone else to take over that responsibility. She's finding that age (she was sixty-two in 2016) is catching up with her.

'I have a bit of trouble climbing up in the front [of the fire truck] now – my knees don't always wanna bend – unless the adrenaline's working. I can get as far as the top, I can climb up the huge high deck, but it's getting behind the steering wheel I'm finding trouble with.'

For a small town, there's plenty for the fire service to do.

'We've had a couple of car fires, we've had some house fires, we had a caravan fire. Kids were playing with matches in the backyard and set fire to the caravan. Fortunately, they were out of the caravan before it caught fire. We've had a couple of houses that have burnt down. They burn pretty quick. The thing is, because the buildings are so old in Marree, and it's all wood, we're not going to be able to save the house – but we can save the surrounding houses. That's what the CFS told us.'

When the fireys are called to a car accident, June can find herself wearing more than one hat.

'I usually do the ambulance bit at the same time. We go along as a crew to the CFS truck and then I'd be the ambulance person plus CFS person when I got there.'

At the scene, she focuses on tending to patients while the rest of the fire crew takes care of their responsibilities. It's not like she's administering lifesaving treatment while yelling instructions to the fire crew.

'We're usually pretty good. Our fellas know what they're doing. I just do the paperwork after. Everything has paperwork – more and more paperwork.

'When it comes to driving the ambulance, we've got two nurses now which makes it a bit easier. Or you grab a local. You know who's around that can drive a manual – who isn't drunk – and isn't gonna freak out when you get there.

'Now that we've got two nurses we're going to actually do a roster – hopefully rostered volunteers – even just driving. Most of the people in Marree I've managed to get to at least one first-aid course, so they've got some basic first aid. We have regular RFDS first-aid courses every year.'

When it comes to promoting community health, some of June's initiatives have been obvious, such as organising tennis, while others have been more subtle. Film nights, while passive entertainment, are better than people going to the pub. And it's something for the kids. In 2009 she got onto *Random Acts of Kindness*, the Channel 9 TV show, to see if she could get a better film-night set-up.

'What that got us was a cinema in the Youth Centre. So we've got cinema seats, surround sound, the drop-down screen and a nice popcorn maker and the projector is up on the roof – a proper projector.'

She's also organised community swimming time at the town's pool, which is in the grounds of the school.

'We've been doing aqua-aerobics for a few years. Most of the ladies go up. That's a nice way of doing fitness things without feeling like you're actually exercising – and you keep cool at the same time. We usually do about forty-five minutes to an hour when the kids are at school, so they don't have to worry about what the kids are doing. So I'm involved with the pool in the community time.

'We used to do Ladies' Day Out. We used to go out for the day, but it's fitting it in when they can get away from kids and things. They don't always want to take the kids with them, but

the school has got creche a lot more now so hopefully we can do
a few more things during the day.'

Taking all these things into account, June has made a contribution to the town that goes far beyond just doing her job. She's
been involved in so much and done so much that more than once
I've heard her described as the de facto mayor of Marree. It's not
a title she has any time for.

'No, we don't have a mayor. We have a Progress Association,
which is the community organisation that raises funds to do
things in town. I was the president of it once. I was the secretary
for a long time. I'm the present treasurer. I'm not the mayor. I've
never been the mayor.'

In fact, Marree is not in a local government area that has a
mayor. Much of the north of South Australia is an unincorpo-
rated area administered directly by the state government. So, no
mayor. And definitely not Mayor June.

That's not to say her contribution hasn't been recognised.
She's been awarded the Order of Australia; she just can't quite put
her finger on when. When I express surprise, she says, 'I know,
I can't remember when I got my OAM. I'm terrible. I've got it
written down somewhere. The years go so quick, I've forgotten.
It would be five or six years, at least. Time goes that quick out
here.'

It was 2009 when June was awarded the OAM for services
to nursing and the community of Marree. Her citation lists her
achievements:

> Nursing Sister in Charge, Marree Hospital, for over 20 years;
> Secretary, Health Action Steering Committee;

Clinical Nurse Consultant, Central Operations Region, Royal
Flying Doctor Service of Australia;

Brigade Captain, Marree Country Fire Service, since 2006;

Brigade Administration Officer, for all but 12 months since
1983;

Brigade Training Officer, 1983-1996;

President, Treasurer/Secretary and/or Committee Member,
Marree Progress Association, for 20 years;

Treasurer, Secretary or Committee Member, Marree Picnic
Racing Club, for 20 years;

Founder and coordinator, Marree Tennis.

In March 2016, Gayle Woodford, a remote-area nurse working in a community in the north-west of South Australia, was
murdered by a member of that community. June knew Gayle, who
worked for a time not far from Marree, at Leigh Creek. Her death
exposed one of the risks inherent in remote nursing, especially in
situations like June's, where she has often been on her own.

'At emergency places and the smaller country places, you
don't have a lot of security. It's usually not the locals that we have
problems with. It's the visitors and the tourists that you really
don't know.

'You really don't know who's at the door sometimes – so you
do have to be careful – but there's always safeguards. Let people
know what you're doing and where you're going. It's always hard
to have 100 per cent cover with anything. Unfortunately, it does
happen. Not so much in South Australia, but in Queensland and
Northern Territory and places they have a lot of problems. No,
it's not nice, and it does make you think.'

June has had some experiences that made her worry.

'Not where I've felt trapped . . . A bit anxious . . . especially after we had some new groups in town that weren't very pleasant. But you don't open the door if you don't feel safe. If you don't want to open the door, you don't open the door. You've got a choice. You can ring the police – we've got the police but he's not always there – but you can always ring somebody else around town if you're worried and you know that they'll come. The town will look after the nurse, as long as they know that there's a problem.

'So, that was very, very, very sad but you can't dwell on the nasty things, and if I dwelt on the nasty things, I'd have never been in Marree this long.'

In 2017, 'this long' meant nearly thirty-five years. The five-year plan she had in 1982 has obviously changed.

'If I didn't enjoy it, I wouldn't have stayed this long. I guess [it's] the variety – the work's not always the same and over the years you try and do more community-orientated things to get people into a healthier living style.

'They've realised you can't always make everybody drink alcohol. I don't drink and I still don't drink. I did get my drink spiked a couple of times when I first came but I did tell them off very loudly. After you tell them off, they do know that you're being serious and you don't want to do that.

'I think people realise – and there are people now that don't drink that used to – that you can actually do things without being drunk. You can enjoy yourself.'

She has also enjoyed living in a small community where people are almost universally friendly, despite the occasional disagreements that inevitably arise.

'Sometimes they don't want to talk to you for a while, or you don't want to talk to them for a while, but you always say hello.

I always say hello.'

On the other side of the ledger, the community kicked a goal when it got June. The benefits have been many.

'It takes them – especially the Aboriginal community – eighteen months to two years to actually get used to you and come and see you if they've got a problem. Like I said, I'd probably met everybody after two years. They would have come to the clinic at least once. Then they realised I [was] going to stay and they came more often. They'd come and talk about their things.

'You can encourage them to see the doctors, so they get tested more. They find that they've got diabetes earlier and all those sort of things. It does make a difference because people don't like change. None of us like change really. Some people are a lot shyer at getting to know people.'

It took them a while to realise she was a keeper. When she arrived, they asked, 'Oh, how long are you staying for?'

'Well, I'm going to stay for five or six years.'

'Oh, I don't think you're gonna stay for five or six years.'

June says now, 'I'm still here.'

Having built that trust, it carries a burden that can't always be shared.

'I'm kind of at the point where people come if they've got a question, which can be a bit frustrating for other people who might be working at the time. They'll come more if they're used to you. I think they wanted a contact point and because I'm on lots of committees I kind of know what's going on with most things. Not everything; I don't know everything, but most things.'

It was at this moment that I got the title for this section of the book. For nearly thirty-five years, June has had her finger on the town's pulse.

'I think I became a point of contact, because people knew that I was here and I'd still be here.

'I get lots of the kids that come back who had moved out of town. They come and say hello. Some people will bring back their kids for us to give their immunisations because they don't like going down to the doctor who lives where they are.'

With June's decades of experience, what advice does she have for younger nurses contemplating a similar path?

'Find out a bit about the area you're going to. I didn't know anything about Marree till I came here. That was good because they could tell me everything, but it's nice to have some idea. Go and do remote area courses that they do now where they do suturing and observations and all that sort of thing. That wasn't available when I started. I was lucky that I had a suturing lesson during my training when one of the doctors in Emergency showed us all how to suture. I'd never done any until then but at least I had some idea.'

I jokingly suggested she'd been able to practise on a horse.

'You still need to know how to do it so it won't come undone. There are courses available now. Go and do something before you come.

'Realise they're not going to talk to you and come and see you straight away. You have to be approachable. Try and get involved a little bit in the town but not too much. Enough that you actually know what's going on. Going to meetings is one way to meet people, but don't get sucked onto all the committees – unless you wanna be. It is what it is, mate. I mean, I don't have family here so it keeps me busy.'

June doesn't consider herself to be an impressive or inspiring person, but when I ask her if she's met anyone who's made an impression on her, the answer is surprising.

'I think anyone who lives in the outback is a unique person. They all inspire you really. I did meet Tom Kruse. I think Lyn Litchfield, who married the pastoralist, she was here before me. A very varied life. The pastoralists themselves, I did meet some of the older ones before they passed away. They're more self-sufficient and they talk about how things have changed out there. They've changed a lot more on the pastoral properties probably than in the small towns and they have a lot more challenges. It's very weather-related as to what they can do. It's different from what I ever thought about when I was growing up.'

Over the last thirty-five years, there doesn't seem to have been a moment when June thought, 'This is my home now.' It just happened that way. By the same token, though, she hasn't given much thought to moving on.

'The time goes so quickly, and the years go quicker and quicker – well, it feels like they are. But no, there wasn't really a set time. It just became home. And thinking, "Well, what would I want to go and do?" I wouldn't want to go back and work in a hospital; I wouldn't want to work in the city. I do like Marree – I like the people, I've got lots of friends here now. It's like a big extended family because I've got no family up here.

'My parents used to come up on the race weekends, go to the dances. They used to come up every year for a while until it got too much for them. They've both passed away now, but they left me the house down near Gawler.'

She also has three brothers: one in Adelaide, one in Victoria and one in New South Wales. None of them are particularly close.

'I feel like a local because I've been here so long now. Most of the locals will say I'm a local. If they're joking, they say, "Nah, she's not a local yet; fifty years before you're a local."

'I say, "I'm not going to be here fifty years working. I'll be too old then."

'But I'm starting to think, "I'm sixty-two/sixty-three this year [2016], I still want to do some travelling."

'I'm not going to retire in Marree. Apart from the fact there's hardly anywhere to live, they'd still want to see me. They'd still want to come and talk. I'm quite happy to come back and visit when there's things on and help and things like that but I decided, no, I can't retire in Marree.

'I can't see myself not coming back and doing things when events are on or just coming back and visiting. I can see myself not working. I'm getting used to having days off now – I've had a few holidays. After thirty-three years not having days off, it's a bit different.

'When we're here, we're still on call twenty-four hours a day, but on the days off – on my week off – I don't have to stay, I can go.'

Her current thought is to retire to the house her parents left her near Gawler.

'I like it down there. It's a bit far out of town, but lots of people. It's a residential village – affordable living for people over fifty. It has a big social club and two swimming pools and all the things you need. And it's close enough to town to go to the pictures and go shopping. They have buses that go out there, taxis.'

———

Reflecting on her life and achievements, like all of the other sub-jects in this book, June isn't comfortable with any suggestion that she's an inspiring figure or, perish the thought, a legend.

'What that means, I don't know. I've just been around a long time, that's all. I don't feel like a legend or an iconic figure, but then most legends and iconic figures don't feel like it either. We're all individual and we're all different and our lives all vary. I could have gone lots of different ways over my life with my work things. I got offered different jobs at different times and I decided it's not what I wanted to do. This is not what I ever pictured doing when I started nursing; I hadn't even heard about remote area nursing.

'It sort of grows on you. You get to do a lot more commu-nity stuff and you get to know people better, and it's not like in a hospital where you see somebody, they come in, they're sick, you never know what happens when they go home. This sort of nursing, you see a more holistic sort of nursing. You get to see how things affect the whole family – the community. The children you've seen born, you get to see their children being born. I've seen the children of the children of the children now.

'The thing is, they look a bit the same as the first one. I was doing the pool one year – I was supervising – and somebody's children were up and they looked exactly like their parents did when they were in the pool.

'You think, "Oh, who have we got again? No, that's right. That's not so-and-so. That's their daughter or their son."

'That's when you realise you've been here thirty-three years. It doesn't feel like that long. I mean, I've got older, some of the other people have got older.

'The kids definitely look older because they come back fifteen years later and say, "Do you remember me?"

'And I say, "Um, no, but because you were probably a baby when you left and I think you've grown, you've got a beard, your hair has changed. I can't really recognise you but I remember you."

'It's when the tourists come back in that have been through five years ago and say, "Oh, I'm so-and-so and I saw you in so-and-so and such-and-such."

'And you think, "Okay."

'I had a gentleman who came in last month and he'd been in a motorbike accident and we'd flown him out. He'd had a broken neck. He walked in and I didn't actually recognise him because he'd had mud on him. I recognised the kids because they weren't covered in mud and on the ground in pain.

'Remote nursing is a different sort of nursing altogether. For anybody who's thinking about it – you've got to give it a little while, because it is different, and for some people this is a long way from what they're used to. I don't think Marree is that far from some places. Oodnadatta is a lot further. Places in Western Australia would be a lot further. It's more they can't just walk out the door and it's half an hour to somewhere. They find that hard.

'We don't have mobile phone coverage at the moment and we don't have good computer coverage some days. Some people live for electronic stuff so they don't cope very well up here. If you don't mind not having phone contact and you want to get away from things, it's a nice place to be.'

Leg Three

The weather had fined up a bit by the time I left Marree, and the road, still unsealed, was drying out. It was bitterly cold, a contrast to the mild weather up in Bedourie. Nevertheless, this was part of the journey I was really looking forward to. I never get tired of the approach to the Flinders Ranges. Driving south, the afternoon light was shifting on the approaching rocky escarpments, the fast-scudding clouds shadowing then highlighting the stark, bare hills.

After lunch at Parachilna, which hosts one of the outback's few 'boutique' pubs, the Prairie Hotel, I continued south. The road wound through dramatic gorges with ramparts of red and yellow stone soaring into a vividly blue sky. The mountainous landscape was virtually devoid of trees, but the winter rains had clothed the usually arid country in many shades of green.

The Flinders Ranges have always been one of the most evocative landscapes in the outback, a lure to artists and filmmakers. The area has been a location for films since the 1950s, including *The Sundowners* (1960), *Sunday Too Far Away* (1975), *Gallipoli* (1981), *The Shiralee* (1987), *The Lighthorsemen* (1987), *Wolf Creek* (2005), *Last Ride* (2009) and *The Water Diviner* (2014). The sound recordist and Foley artist for *Happy Feet* (2006),

Australia (2008) and *Mad Max: Fury Road* (2015), John Simpson, lives there.

They are also the home of the next person I was hoping to talk to.

3.

The Real Deal

Sally Brown

(1985–)

The first time I heard of Emily's Bistro was in Port Lincoln, on the Eyre Peninsula, in mid-2015. Michelle and I had gone there to visit a friend, Jack Ritchie, and his new partner, Andrea Broadfoot. One of the attractions was the opportunity to go fishing in Spencer Gulf for King George whiting, one of the finest-tasting fish in the sea.

Andrea was a keen fisherwoman, had a boat and knew many of the best spots for whiting in the waters off Tumby Bay. At the time, Andrea was a member of the local council; in 2016 she contested the seat of Grey in the federal election for the Nick Xenophon Team but narrowly lost by 1800 votes. If she'd given up a few of her fishing spots, which proved to be pure gold for whiting, she may have tipped out the Liberal incumbent.

Grey is one of the biggest electorates in Australia: a million square kilometres covering all the sparsely settled areas of South Australia and the many townships dotted across it. That means nearly everything north and west of Adelaide.

On our way back from Port Lincoln, we planned to spend a

couple of days camping in the Flinders Ranges. Every time we'd been there before, we'd been hastening somewhere else and had to tear ourselves away all too soon. Now we wanted to give ourselves enough time to do the place justice.

When Andrea and Jack learned of our intentions, they gave us one tip: 'You have to go to Emily's Bistro in Quorn and meet the amazing young woman who runs it.'

'Yeah, whatever,' we thought. We'd often been given hot tips before, only to go 'Meh' after driving up hills and down dales to find the place recommended. However, when we happened to find ourselves in Quorn, having driven up the scenic Pichi Richi Pass, what did we have to lose?

Located 50 kilometres from Port Augusta, at the end of the famed Pichi Richi Railway, Emily's Bistro is housed in the immaculately restored heritage-listed Foster's Great Northern Emporium, which was operated by the same family from 1878 until it closed in 2004. It was bought and renovated by Emily Brown in 2011 and much of the emporium's quaint character has been retained, including a flying-fox catapult system used for sending money from one side of the shop to the other, from counter to cashier. Pressed metal ceilings, timber cabinets and counters, historic memorabilia and old-fashioned sweet selections sit beside modern artisanal produce, books and homewares. The atmosphere is nostalgic, magical and enticing.

As for the bistro, the menu emphasises local produce – quandongs, warrigal greens, Kangaroo Island honey, Golden North ice cream, yabbies, kangaroo, goat and saltbush lamb. The country-style food includes sausage rolls, pies and pasties baked on the premises. On Sundays there's a traditional spit-roasted pig or lamb for lunch.

And then . . . there's Sally. Wait, what happened to Emily? It turns out her sister now owns and runs Emily's, and therein lies quite a tale.

We arrived right on closing, but even at the end of the day Sally Brown gave us a radiant smile, reassured us that getting coffee was no hassle, told us all about the Emporium and its restoration, and demonstrated the catapult. Throughout, the then thirty-year-old exuded a genuine warmth and charm that was captivating. We were probably the last customers of the day, but she had such energy and enthusiasm we felt like we were the first. The shop or Sally on their own would have been worth the visit. Together, they left a lasting impression.

A year later, I was flitting through the Flinders Ranges once again and detoured slightly in order to head down to Quorn and catch up with Sally. I hadn't contacted her in advance: I thought I'd take my chances that she'd be at the bistro and happy to have a chat. As it turned out, once again I got there near closing, and once again I was treated to that luminous smile.

When I explained who I was and what I wanted, Sally didn't hesitate to agree. However, she had a few things to do first. To keep me occupied, she gave me a quandong tart baked by her mother, some Golden North honey and a cup of coffee. Under the circumstances, I was more than happy to wait. She eventually delegated a few jobs to her father, Robert, and came over.

We quickly fell into easy conversation about the history of the place and how she came to be running it.

Sally was a fifth generation 'Quornie', as the locals call themselves, and can remember shopping in the Emporium as a child.

'My dad's from here,' she explained. 'My mum is from Kangaroo Island. I grew up 10 kilometres out of Quorn in an old settlement called Pichi Richi Pass. We had quite a lot of land and my parents started up a restaurant there called The Old Willows Brewery Restaurant. My parents built the restaurant – it used to be an old ruin.

'It actually opened in 1990. That's where the journey started – the hospitality. I was five years old when I was exposed to the industry. They operated The Willows for twenty-two years. Very successful business. We were actually known for our "Flinders Ranges Fancies", which is the kangaroo testicles. That's what we used to sell.'

Growing up on the land, on the edge of the outback, it was perhaps inevitable that Sally and her family (including three older sisters and a brother) would gravitate towards bush foods. She and her parents were influenced by people like chef and bush-food specialist Andrew Fielke, from the Red Ochre Grill.

'He's all about the bush tucker,' she says. 'Peter Jarmer as well. They were a big influence in our lives. They were the ones that helped Mum get started.'

The children virtually grew up in the restaurant. On week-ends and holidays they helped out with functions. When Sally's sisters finished school, they went straight into jobs in hospitality – managing bars and restaurants. Her brother managed to take a different career path, however, and when Sally finished school, she also wanted to do something different. She chose teaching.

'Hospitality was my life. I didn't know anything else but that. I had no-one that went to uni in my family or anything like that, so I kind of wanted teaching as an escape. I wanted to see what the other life was like. I'm actually dyslexic, so it took me an extra year at high school to get the grades to get into teaching. I studied primary school and majored in Aboriginal studies.

'Another reason I got into teaching: growing up in the country, you're looking for inspiration left, right and centre. You need something to keep driving you. If you don't have anything inspiring you, it's quite easy just to say, "It's too hard."

'To be honest, I didn't really have any teachers that inspired me. I wanted to be that teacher. I wanted to inspire children. Like I said, I'm dyslexic; I wanted to, I guess, come back to the country and inspire children and be, like, "There's a bigger world out there. You can do anything. There's no limits in the country."

'And even with this place [Emily's], we've just done it. We've created this. And when I say "we", I mean myself and my family. We get people from all over the world that come in here and just say, "Wow, we've never seen or experienced anything like this." And that's what drives us. It's all about giving people an experience – and a story as well.

'I love inspiring people. And even the children here, like, I say to them, "Oh, there's so much to do."

'Even the mountains – I used to climb Devil's Peak [697 metres high, near Quorn] in the morning, I'm a fanatic hiker – and that's actually the other reason I got into teaching, because I love physical education and hiking and music. I was a music teacher for a while. I used to climb Devil's Peak before work in the mornings. I could do that in less than an hour, up and back.

'When I was at uni, I used to work with schools in Port Augusta and do Year 10 treks with Caritas College. I used to go as a mentor and hike with the kids up through Wilpena Pound [the famed natural amphitheatre in the heart of the Flinders Ranges], just pushing them through. I'm driven by that kind of thing.'

Of course, being a student meant Sally was available on weekends and during holidays to help her mum out with the restaurant. Her older siblings had their own careers in hospitality, but until she graduated, Sally kept being drawn back.

After getting her degree, she found work not far from home, at Willsden Primary School in Port Augusta. She was the Aboriginal language coordinator. Then she went to Darwin for a year 'just to see what the other part of the country is like'.

'After Darwin I wanted to experience something different, so I went to America to work on summer camps, and I was in charge of a conference centre there. And when I was in America, I got the phone call about Emily's Bistro.'

Her sister Emily had found running the cafe too much for her. She was having health issues, and the relentless work – seven days a week, long hours, no days off – was wearing her down. When she reached breaking point, the business was forced to close.

Sally's parents rang her and asked, 'Do you want to come back and reopen Emily's Bistro and take over, or go back to teaching?'

As Sally recalls, 'My parents said, "You've got a choice. Like, no pressure with it."

'I kinda had to come back anyway because my visa was running out, and I thought, "You know what, I gave teaching a go. I've experienced that life. But this feels more like me. This is the real me – this kind of thing."'

She also had an understanding of the potential of the business and what it could do for the town and the area. So in mid-2014 she made the choice to leave America, return to the little town on the edge of the outback and reopen the cafe. Emily's Bistro reopened under new management: Sally's.

'When I reopened it, I had a full-time chef. At that time, my mum was a chef on the Ghan and the Indian Pacific. She was doing her own thing and all of that, so I was running the show.

I worked damn hard to get people to see what it's all about –
"Sally is running the show now" – and get them to know me,
believe in me and believe in what I was doing.

'Then, in November, I was in a really bad car crash. I was
actually in a head-on collision. I nearly lost my leg. I fractured my
collarbone. So I was in hospital for a while, about three months,
and then I was in a wheelchair and on crutches. It's still a journey
with that – I'm still trying to recover from that.

'The crash happened just before my Christmas bookings.
I had a lot of Christmas shows booked up ready to go. We didn't
cancel them. I missed out on them all because I was in hospital.
Mum actually had to come back and help me out. So we were all
dragged back into the bistro again, Mum helping me out again
because I still, sort of, need that support to push me through. It's
been a blessing to have her back because no-one can create what
she creates. We actually work well together; we're a team. We go
hand-in-hand.

'That was really full on, that part of my life. Even being in a
wheelchair, I was told, "You've got a choice. You can either get
back to work or sit in the house and feel sorry for yourself."

'So I chose to come back in the bistro, in my wheelchair, and
run the business again. I was determined to come back and keep
it going because this is what I wanted to do. Being back in here
was probably the best thing that I ever did because it just pushed
me through the hard times.'

It's not difficult to imagine how tough the hard times were.
Her sister had struggled with the workload. Now Sally had to
deal with the physical and emotional challenges of recovering
from her accident while managing the relaunch of the fledgling
business.

According to the saying, 'What doesn't break you makes you stronger'. So how much strength does it take when you're already broken?

In a strange twist, her accident actually brought her closer to people, including her customers.

'People come in to hear the stories. Everyone's got a story to tell. You connect with them because they've had something, an experience or even the feeling of pain, that's happened to them. It's intense.

'The accident completely changed me. It's made me realise what I've got and what I've done is pretty special. I might get a day off every now and again but you've got to put your heart and soul into this place. This is pretty much my relationship, my baby, my husband, my wife. For the first couple of years, I actually lived in the building. My house is connected. But when you're in it, you've got to be one-hundred-and-twenty-million per cent in it. You can't take time out. I'm very focused – that's just my personality. If I've got something, I'll just do it.'

Every day was up and down for a while, but Sally never forgot why she'd reopened the bistro: she was sure it would work. She never lost sight of its potential and never doubted it would succeed. She was also driven by a belief that people needed to experience the unique country style she was striving to deliver. So while Sally was getting back on her feet, the business was doing the same. As time went on, that fact became increasingly clear.

'The city folk, the locals – they love it. It gives people, I guess, time out from their homes. We're more of an elderly town, Quorn, so we get all the seniors in for coffees. Once a month I do a film night, so the screen comes down. We show a movie and I get people that come in that don't necessarily like to go to the pub. It's bringing people together, and that's what I love doing. I feel like I'm a "hostess with the mostess". I love giving people a really good experience – throwing celebrations and parties – it's important.'

As Sally says this, I can't help but think of June Andrew, a generation older and 350 kilometres up the road, telling me almost the same thing earlier that day (see the previous chapter).

'Even though people live in such small towns, it's all about making them feel that we can still experience something wonderful. You don't need to go to the city to have a good coffee or to have a good celebration. We can do that here as well.

'It's tough, like I said, growing up in the country. It's hard because you don't have these influences coming, but in saying that, it's also good because you're creating your own flavour. What we do and what we've done, we've sort of just done it.'

In the two-and-a-half years since Sally's accident, there hasn't been a day when she woke up and said, 'This is working; Emily's Bistro is a success'. She was probably too busy to notice. However, when I ask her about it, the question of what constitutes success arises.

'The way I see success and to be successful is about people – the feedback, the comments – like the people that come every year. I'll get people like yourself. You were here a year ago. You returned. People that know me, that heard my story a year ago, they come back and they say, "Oh, Sally, you're still here . . . ra ra ra . . . That's great, we'll see you next year."

'Social media. You see all the feedback on that. The growth of the business every year, every week. The people that come in here. I'll have days and the bistro will just be full. Like, absolutely. I have to turn people away. And I look up and I'm just, like,

"Wow." Even I get shocked at the amount of people that keep coming through and through and through and through – hundreds, thousands of people – every day and week. I know that it's happening because I see it and I hear feedback and it's all positive. Everyone's happy and that's what it's all about.'

In the outback, success brings its own set of challenges. For a start, in hospitality you can never be sure that thousands will come through the door on any given day. One day can be quiet, the next can see the Pichi Richi heritage steam train pull in crammed with passengers and Quorn is buzzing. Staff can be dusting shelves and tidying store rooms one day and overwhelmed the next.

School holidays, weekends and long weekends may be predictable, but in a small town like Quorn it's not like there are many people you can call in on short notice. That's especially the case in a town where tourism is a key element of most businesses. Sally finds that her parents are invaluable in filling the breach.

'In Quorn, we currently have three cafes, including Emily's Bistro. We've got four pubs as well, for a population of a thousand people. So we mainly rely on the tourists: people heading through to the Flinders Ranges. With tourists, it's up to them to decide where they want to go: it's what they see first or good old social media. So you're always on your game.

'People have expectations as well. When they come to the country, they expect that warm country hospitality, that country-style cooking. People want the stories, they want the country people. That's what we offer. I'm not just saying it; I'm from here. This is the real deal.'

That also makes it tough when you're trying to employ people, however.

'You want to make sure you've got someone that's gonna fit that mould and be true to the business. In the country it's all about the people. They want that local girl to serve them. They want the Quornie and it's a real novelty for them to experience that.'

I'm thinking that rules out dressing like a goth or multiple body piercings. Not so. She points out that she's already got tattoos. She adds that the important thing is feedback from customers saying the bistro is authentic.

You might think that making Emily's Bistro a success would be enough for Sally, but as it happens, it's about to get much bigger. I'd noticed there was a construction site next door to the building – it turns out that Sally and her parents are in the process of building a thirty-one-room motel and conference centre that's going to be called 'The Great Northern Lodge'. As if she doesn't have enough to keep her busy.

'It's going to be four-and-a-half star,' Sally says. 'We're doing that to expand the bistro. The bistro is the heart and soul, and what's to come is exciting stuff. It's going to be the next chapter in our lives. We're doing that to sustain the business. We actually need to get more staff. We're looking at probably nine to ten full-time staff with that. And just really to put Quorn on the map. That's what it's all about. Keep this going, keep the business rolling.

'To be honest, I'm learning a lot. I've gone to uni, I've done my teacher's degree. What I'm doing now, in terms of business,

I feel like I'm in the process of learning how to do it. I'm still growing with that.'

And after that?

'I don't know what's around the corner. I don't know what the next chapter will be, but after this, things will go to the next level. Like I said, it's about inspiring the younger generations in the country.'

I can't help wondering about her ambitions to have a relationship or a family. Sally doesn't mind me asking about her personal life, and explains that she's single partly because finding someone she likes is one of the things about the outback that isn't easy.

'Like I said, this business is like a relationship. I know the other things are important, and I want to have children for them to be the next me. Like, my mum [Wendy], she's incredible. What my mum has invented and created is absolutely mind-blowing. And that's where it starts. So I want to have children so that they can be the next Wendy, Sally – the next one.'

By now we were outside, looking around the construction site and imagining what the finished building will look like. Sally's vision is impressive, but a project on such a scale is also pretty daunting. There's so much that can go wrong – and the investment involved runs into the millions. There's no doubt the young woman showing me around has plenty of self-belief and energy and a huge amount of courage, but I couldn't help wondering if that will be enough. Still, the thing about failure is that, if you never try, it's guaranteed.

While we're gazing at pallets stacked with building materials, half-built walls and bare slabs of concrete puddled with water, I ask what advice she has for a young person who wants to start a business like this in some other outback town.

'Be ready to work damn hard. Be focused. Be real about it. Make sure that you're in it for the right reasons. Make sure that you've got support behind you. Have back-up plans and set yourself goals. That's so important. Know where you're going, because you don't want to feel like you're stuck.

'In the country, like I said, it's tough because there's not other young people around here. I'm thirty-one years old. I love social life. I like parties, I love live music, I love the clubs. This, for me, has been one of the biggest sacrifices in my life – to run this business. It has been probably one of the biggest challenges for me because when I was at university and I was teaching, I'd be out every weekend socialising.

'That's my big thing. I've missed out on weddings, anniversaries, birthdays, births. I've missed out on a lot of that. In saying that, I've gained more because of what's happening; and not everyone can have this.

'My mum always tells me, "If it were easy, everyone would do it."

'I know that's true. People come in here and say, "What a beautiful place. I'd love to work in a place like this."

'And I think to myself, "I'd love to give that person an opportunity. Give them maybe one, two, three, four days to do this and see if they would enjoy it."

'I work eighty hours a week, seven days a week. It's really hard: physically, emotionally, mentally. When you're in it, you've really got to be in it.'

A number of the people in this book have lived and worked all over the country, if not the world, but have chosen to live in the outback. Sally is one of them, having experienced Port Augusta, Darwin and the United States. Yet she's returned to the place where she was born and raised. What is it about the out-back that draws her back?

'I can do either/or – city or country. If I have to live in the city, well, I've done it. I feel more content in the country. I don't know what it is about the country. I know I do work every day and I don't really get an opportunity to go out and do what I used to do. It's just the space, the Ranges. There is something really spe-cial about this place.

'The city really drains me a lot. I love it. It's probably too much for me, though. I get really excited when I'm in the city and really tired. Here I just feel like I can keep going, constantly. There's something about the country where you can just keep doing it. You're not consumed by all the traffic and the people and the noise. If I'm in the city, I can go out quite easily and live the city life. In the country, I can live here and be content. That's mainly because I grew up in the country. It's because of my upbringing.'

As we walk around, Sally is obviously proud of what she's involved in and typically upbeat about the future. While the bistro and motel are an obvious complement to each other, there's another potential market – catering for the film crews and movie stars who are drawn to this part of the outback for location shooting. There are any number of comfortable places where they can stay, but few where they can do so in real luxury.

Dusk is gathering and it's getting cold and rainy when we go back inside. There, Sally mentions the one frustration she has with achieving all that she has: getting to enjoy it. Some people in the town are resentful of her success. There's a jealousy that makes it hard for her to enjoy a win when she has one.

Unfortunately, other outback people I spoke to for this book have had similar experiences with short-poppy syndrome:

a subtle resistance to anyone who aspires to more than mediocrity. Of course, it's not a syndrome that's restricted to the outback.

So, while Sally was showing me a letter from South Australia's Minister for Regional Development, Geoff Brock, congratulating her and awarding her a grant to support her project, she was wiping away a tear because there was only scattered recognition that what she was doing wasn't just good for her, it was good for the town.

It was surprising that she might think she needed permission to be proud and happy. I mean, it wasn't just for her coffee and pies that I'd made a detour. Twice.

'Sally,' I said, 'I think it's obvious but you're one of the most impressive young women I've ever met. You've earned every bit of your success.'

The hug she gave me when we were saying goodbye suggested she appreciated the acknowledgement. She is, after all, only human. In my book, this book, she is already the inspiration to others she aspires to be. Sometimes, though, it's nice to be told that.

Six months after visiting Sally, I sent her a copy of this chapter for her to review. She wrote back:

> Hi Evan,
>
> Firstly sorry for taking a while to get back to you.
>
> One word 'wow'!, brought so many tears to my eyes after I read your draft.
>
> One change since our interview – I am no longer single, I have found romance/love – it is long distance but my partner (Emma), is extremely supportive and does the journey up from Adelaide most weekends to visit me, she is high-school teacher. (not sure if this is something you would want to mention) – I didn't mention that I was gay

in the interview, however I am not sure if that was relevant (although another massive challenge living in the country and for people to accept).

I can't express how grateful I am for you believing in me and my story.

Regards, Sally

Leg Four

The weather had closed in and it was getting dark when I refuelled at the only Quorn service station that was still open. Rain squalls buffeted the Truckasaurus and it was bitterly cold as I headed south, but it was only half-past five and I thought it was better to cover some ground instead of twiddling my thumbs in a motel somewhere. I passed Wilmington and Melrose before I started looking for somewhere to stay.

By then, it was getting close to the time many towns' restaurant kitchens close, so when I got to Gladstone I got a room in the pub. The only problem was, the cook was off sick. I must have looked hungry, because the publican asked one of his customers if she could cook me something. She disappeared into the kitchen and rustled up some fish and a salad. I washed it down with a glass of white and was happy.

That night, the pub was buffeted by increasingly wild weather. The wind moaned around the corners of the building and rattled the window of my room. The haunting sounds weren't softened by the fact that I was the only person in the place.

I was on the road early the next morning, heading for Willalooka in the south-east of South Australia. On the radio they were saying that the state was in the grip of a low-pressure system that was channelling freezing air up from Antarctica. It certainly felt like it.

As I drove through the Adelaide Hills and the Mount Lofty Ranges, there were broken branches everywhere. At Mount Pleasant, it was anything but. A major hailstorm swept down and pelted Trucka. Soon there was hail all over the road.

I ended up travelling behind a semi-trailer that was edging along at only 40 kilometres an hour. After what I'd been through on the Birdsville Track a couple of days earlier, it was fine by me.

When I took a break for coffee and a pie at a shop in Palmer, the windscreen wipers had piled hail several centimetres deep on the top of the bonnet. To add to my concerns, a small crack caused by one of the stone chips that I'd received a couple of days earlier had started to grow.

While I waited for my coffee, I thought I'd make a call to the Shear Outback museum in Hay, New South Wales, to see if I couldn't chase down a phone number for another person I was hoping to include in this book, Ian Auldist. In a couple of days I'd be heading up through Hay and it would be a good chance to catch up with him.

Ian was the chairman of Shear Outback's board and a prominent irrigator and grazier in the Hay District. I'd met him the year before at the ceremony for five new inductees to the museum's Hall of Fame. As part of the event, he'd invited writers with connections to Australian shearing to a writers' forum. It was an indication of the stature of the man that everyone who was invited, from as far away as Perth (Valerie Hobson, author of

Across the Board) and the Northern Territory (Dennis McIntosh, author of *Beaten by a Blow*) agreed to attend.

I'd sent Ian an email several weeks earlier canvassing the possibility of including him in my book project, but I hadn't received a reply. That seemed a bit out of character for Ian. He's the kind of person who's always busy but never so much so that he won't respond.

I got put through to the woman who does admin at the museum. I started to explain the situation when she interrupted me.

'Oh Evan,' she said, 'haven't you heard?'

My heart sank.

'Ian died earlier this year,' she said. 'He had a very aggressive cancer.'

The news left me reeling.

I ended up sitting alone, far from home, in an empty cafe in a little South Australian town, staring out at a bleak, stormy day. I sipped my coffee. I couldn't taste the pie.

Ian was one of those people I've been privileged to meet who I've instantly respected and admired. He was the embodiment of the qualities of outback people that I value most: reliable, resilient, resourceful. He was not so much down to earth as absolute bedrock. Now I felt like the ground had shifted beneath me.

When Ian first invited me to Hay, I had no knowledge of him. Rather than embarrass myself displaying my ignorance of his background, I did a bit of research.

Ian had been farming at Hay since 1977. He grew wool; produced prime lambs; bred, backgrounded and fattened cattle; and grew crops. He had a Bachelor of Science in agriculture and had done agricultural research for the Victorian, Queensland and

Northern Territory governments and the University of New South Wales. For thirty-five years, he ran technical assistance projects and advised on livestock and natural resource management in Asia. He also provided input on biosecurity management.

For his work with Chinese and Mongolian farmers on range-land management, he was presented with a Friendship Award by the Chinese Government, the highest honour conferred on foreign experts for 'outstanding contributions to China's economic and social progress'.

He was the chairman of the Hay Balranald Landcare Network and was involved in the Hay Football Club and the Hay Rodeo Club. In 2009 he was named Hay's Citizen of the Year. The town's mayor, Mick Beckwith, said Ian was one of the Hay community's quiet achievers.

Around 2006, Ian did an interview with the Chinese *People's Daily* about the latest of several long-term projects he'd been involved with in Asia, this time in Inner Mongolia.

> Basically we are assisting that area in the period when the grassland has been heavily degraded. The project assists farmers to stop grazing animals freely on the grassland, to try to help the grassland to recover . . . The farmers responded very well. They reduced the numbers of livestock to some extent. They planned better for the storage of grains and hays so they could learn to market animals better.

The article pointed out that Ian regarded himself as a farmer like the people he was advising.

> I have the same elements in Australia: drought, lack of rainfall, marketing issues, low prices. So I have no problem communicating with farmers.

He also spoke of the experience of living and working in China.

> Chinese food is the best in the world, of course. And I've been
> very lucky to have friends to play tennis with me. It is very
> common in Inner Mongolia to have tennis courts.

And he spoke of the study tours he'd organised for his Chinese counterparts.

> I brought my Chinese friends home and gave some return
> hospitality. It was exciting for me. I treated them with
> Australian-style hospitality: killed one of my own sheep, ate
> some Australian mutton and drank some Australian beer. It was
> enjoyable.

I suspect the translator didn't realise the difference between mutton and Ian's prime lamb.

When I met Ian in early 2015, I got the same impression of him that came across in that article: unassuming but very capable; easy to talk to. I watched as he dealt with writers, shearers and graziers at everything from a formal dinner to the sheep-dog events. One moment he had his sleeves rolled up, the next he was in a jacket and tie, giving a speech. And when I presumed to make some suggestions about the running of the writers' event, he listened to me and took my advice.

There's a photo of Ian in an obituary by the Murrumbidgee Field Naturalists (recording his championing of sustainable agriculture and natural resource management in the Riverina) with students from Western Illinois University at Shear Outback in 2015, when he was seventy-three. Ian is on the board of the museum's shearing shed during a demonstration of sheep shearing.

He's in short sleeves, inspiring the next generation, and doing what many of the others in this book do: live in the outback but connect to the wider world.

I'd been looking forward to talking to Ian, finding out about his life's work and how he's taken the knowledge he gained in the outback to some of the most exotic places on the planet. It was not to be. Of course, Ian may well have been reluctant to be the subject of the kind of profile I had in mind. Some time later, I got an email that suggested as much:

Hi Evan,

This is George Auldist, Ian's son, I have been replying to his emails.

I'm sorry to inform you that Ian died only a few months ago. He had an aggressive cancer and died at the Hay hospital.

It's great that you would think to include him in your book, he did achieve a lot. I'm sure if he was alive he would be too modest to allow it and now he doesn't qualify for your title.

Good luck, the book sounds good, if I can be of any other assistance please get back to me.

Kind Regards,

George

Still, I'd like to think Ian was the kind of person who would have given me a chance to convince him about his inclusion in the book. I'd have said that while it might be embarrassing to be pushed into the limelight, it's a chance to do something he's been doing all his life: inspire people with his ideas and outlook on life. And I suspect he was the kind of person who would have sacrificed his modesty if it meant he could help me out.

Leg Five

I finished my pie, drank my coffee and continued my journey. When I got down to Murray Bridge, the weather had improved and it was no longer raining, although the bitterly cold wind was still blowing hard. The crack in my windscreen had grown another few centimetres.

I drove over to Tailem Bend for lunch (good pies in their bakery) then on to Keith. By then I knew I was going to be early for my next destination, so I took a detour over to Kingston, on Lacepede Bay. There, the wind was howling through the Norfolk Island pines on the foreshore and the sea had been whipped into wild, choppy waves that were battering the breakwaters. Seaweed was piled high on the shore; the jetty was fenced off, as waves were breaking over it. I poked around for a bit until it was time to rendezvous with the next person on my list.

As it happened, like Ian Auldist, he had a strong connection with the Shear Outback museum. He was one of the youngest inductees to its Hall of Fame.

4

Shannon's Way

Shannon Warnest

(1974–)

The citation for Shannon Warnest in the Hall of Fame at the Shear Outback museum reads as follows:

> Shannon has established himself as the best fine-wool shearer in the current era, winning the Golden Shears world shearing championship in 2000 and in 2005.
>
> Taught the basics of shearing by his father, a good shearer himself, Shannon's ability became keenly sought after by contractors, and he spent several seasons in the heat and dust of South Australia's north, shearing up to 50 000 sheep per year. His first competition win was the intermediate event at the 1993 Royal Adelaide Show, and in 1996 he organised the first shearing competition at the Angaston show. By 2009 he had won 154 open competitions with a best sequence of 44 consecutive wins and had won the South Australian championship nine times. He has best tallies of 325 lambs in eight hours in Australia, and 405 ewes and 421 lambs in nine hours in New Zealand.
>
> Shannon has been a member of an Australian team at sixteen major competitions and has travelled extensively overseas and is

a regular visitor and competitor in New Zealand and has shorn in Germany, Austria, Switzerland, South Africa, USA, Canada, Italy, Holland, England, Scotland, Wales and Norway. He won his first world title, and the world team championship with Ross Thompson, from Inverell, New South Wales, in Bloemfontein, South Africa, and his second at Toowoomba, Queensland, where he and Daniel McIntyre, [from] Glen Innes, New South Wales, also won the world team championship.

Since the inception of Sports Shear Australia in 1995, Shannon has won the Australian National Championship on seven occasions, the last six consecutively. Prior to this, he won ten Australian title events under the old Shearing Competition Federation rules. During 2001, Shannon was invited to shear at the Commonwealth Heads of Government Meeting in Brisbane. In September 2002, he received the Order of Australia medal for services to the wool industry.

Shannon was still out at a shearing school when I arrived at his home, a small farm at Willalooka in southern South Australia. Shannon and his wife, Catherine, knew I was coming. I'd rung to confirm our arrangements and Catherine had asked where I was staying. When I said I was going to find something at the nearby Willalooka pub or up the road in Keith, she invited me to stay with them.

It was very generous, and I accepted her offer, but I still tried to delay my arrival until Shannon got home. I thought it might be uncomfortable for his wife if some strange bloke turned up and hung around. It made no difference. Catherine made me feel welcome as she juggled me, her two kids and the roast dinner she was preparing.

The big log fire in their open-plan living area was doing a great job of keeping the freezing winter's evening at bay. Outside, occasional rain squalls swept over the lush green paddocks as the wind roared through the trees in the fading light.

Shannon came in not long after I arrived. It was the first time we'd met face to face, although we'd spoken on the phone. He'd struck me as being a pretty relaxed kind of person, but in the flesh there was no getting around his physicality. Shannon stands at 190 centimetres and he gave the impression of being solid muscle. Certainly his handshake was. I couldn't escape the feeling that if he'd wanted to shear me, there'd be nothing I could do about it.

There was also a curious quality about him that struck me. I've met elite athletes before and they often have a confidence that sets them apart. Shannon had that; but there was also a stillness to him that was quite noticeable. It seemed almost unnatural, until I realised he seemed to have perfect balance. It's a quality you don't often see, but when you do, it's almost all you see. The only other time I've encountered it is in ballet dancers who, for obvious reasons, always know exactly where their body's centre of gravity is. But world-champion shearers?

We had a very satisfying dinner and stayed up quite late enjoying a conversation that ranged over what had happened to Ian Auldist and the people who inspired Shannon. We talked about how Shannon got into shearing, how he'd been mentored and the day he went 'ton up', shearing 100 sheep in a day. I mentioned that a couple of years ago, I'd been talking to international shearing competition judge Winston Flood in Tasmania and he'd said of Shannon that 'he just does the Shannon thing'. Shannon couldn't really explain what Winston meant by it, but it got him thinking.

He did mention a curious aspect of his attraction to shearing. As a kid, he'd been overweight. Looking at him, it was hard to believe, but he said he was stung by a comment that was directed at him more than once: 'That fat kid will never shear.' He was determined to prove people wrong.

He's now a two-time individual world champion and two-time teams world champion, so whoever said that has long since eaten their words. I suggested the line would make a great title for a book. When Shannon said he wasn't much of a writer, I waved the thought aside. 'A mere detail.' I could almost hear my editor saying, 'Well, you'd know.'

Next morning, we were up very early. It was still freezing cold but there was sunlight breaking through as Shannon and Catherine's sheep walked in long lines out into the fields.

While Catherine was getting the kids breakfast, she told me about the hard work of running the nearby Willalooka Hotel, which the couple owned until recently. One time she'd asked Shannon to watch the bar while she ran an errand. When she came back – no Shannon.

'He's quite good at disappearing when he wants to,' she said.

When she eventually found him, she let him have it.

'I was reaching up and trying to shake him and telling him off,' she said, 'And then he just took hold of my hands and said, "Catherine, I've never laid a finger on you and I never will. I expect the same from you."'

Down at Pinindi, a sheep and cropping property where the shearing school was being held, we were the first ones there. Shannon fired up the generator and got things ready as the young learners and two other trainers came in and started work.

Shannon was happy to talk, though our conversation was interrupted by students Stephen Brooker Jones and Jaydn Stimson, who came to Shannon to check that their handpieces were correctly set up. Later, when they started crutching, Shannon gave them pointers on the different techniques.

Mostly, though, we talked, and Shannon made me realise that, for someone who claims he isn't much of a writer, he's a great storyteller.

He was born in Angaston, in South Australia's Barossa Valley, in 1974. He weighed 5.2 kilograms, the second-heaviest baby ever born in the town. (The heaviest was 5.5.) His parents had a few hectares of land, conveniently located behind the local primary school. When he finished going there, he went on to high school in nearby Nuriootpa.

'Dad was a shearer, a slaughter-man by trade, and a bee-keeper – an apiarist. When they built the house, I remember Dad working all week. He'd be away shearing or slaughtering and then all weekend he'd bloody do the bees and that. So, he could work like nothin'. I always say that Dad probably taught me to work but John Hutchinson, who was a shearer trainer, he taught me to shear.

'Yeah, Mum said I bloody shore the cat when I was eight years old. If your dad's a shearer, there's plenty of stories out there about lads doing that, but I think at twelve or thirteen I could pick up a handpiece, like, and chisel a little bit off. I could do the back leg and stuff like that.'

By the time he turned fifteen, in 1989, he was starting to struggle at school. He'd also developed a significant weight problem.

'I was 118 kilos when I was fifteen. There were two subjects

I was good at: maths (obviously, it helps out in this game, countin' sheep) and PE (or physical education). It wasn't that I was good at PE. I think they just felt sorry for me and give me good marks. But, you know, I put in.'

Around that time, Shannon and his father went to Portee Station, not far from Angaston on the Murray River, to do some work. While he was there, the owner, Ian Clark, asked Shannon if he wanted to come back during shearing and work as a shedhand.

Shannon asked his father if he could do it.

Jim Warnest said, 'Ask your mother'.

'I said to Mum, "Well, there's a heap of work comin' up around home. Perhaps if I take half a year of school off and then come back and re-do it the following year. Like, sort of, do two halves."'

That night, Shannon rang Ian Clark and said, 'I can come.'

'I remember getting to Christmas and I was supposed to go back to school.

'Dad said to me, "If you're gonna be around close to home here, Mum's gonna make you go to school."

'So I ended up going into New South Wales and getting right away; as far away as I could.'

Shannon started working as a rouseabout and wool-handler. He went to Renmark, still in South Australia, then Wentworth, then north to outback sheds towards Broken Hill. As a youngster in the world of men, he soon discovered the mateship of the sheds. When I asked him whether mateship or competition dominated, he said:

'More mateship in my experience but, you know, the competitiveness is there. Even when you leave a shed, one bloke's quick at getting out. He's the first one gone. You look at the film *Sunday*

Too Far Away [1975], those two blokes scrubbin' at the wash trough. They're scrubbin' and the towels fall off and the arses are going like that. That's competition through and through.

'When I was wool-handling [the term now used for rouse-abouts], same thing. We were up at Morgan [in South Australia] and the shearers would leave the shed and it would be the first one into the town. You'd be skitin' about it: "I had the first cold beer."

'So, right. I was rouseaboutin' so I teed it up with all the other rouseabouts that two of us – because I was travellin' with another lad – that all the other rouseabouts would cover our backsides and they'd do the big tidy up and we'd rip through the shower and be the first ones in there. Just once.

'We made it to the last ramp, at very good velocity in the car, got airborne over this last ramp, did a big broad slide and run two tyres off the rims. And all the shearers drove past, 'cos they knew what we were up to. The contractor came along – and by that time we, bloody, had one spare and we'd got one tyre back on the bead – he helped us get goin'.

'Comin' into town, the car was squealin' on the bitumen because everything was bent up. We give it a fair go. But that's from the time we went north. It's in the sheds; it gets in your blood.'

He was also getting experience with shearers' cooks.

'Back when I was rouseaboutin' – this Neville Hahn. He's long gone now but I used to ring him now and then because he ended up ownin' seven pubs and I'd ring him up about pub stuff when we got into the hotel. Real good cook. On a Friday night he'd make pasties – it was an hour-and-a-half or two hours into town – there'd be a pastie for you. And I'm hungry as and I snuck in there and grabbed a punnet of strawberries out the fridge – 'cos as a young fella you eat lots, if you're working hard you eat, even a sheila can eat as much as bloody any man – and I grabbed this punnet of strawberries and he caught me. Tried givin' me the wooden spoon and I hadn't had the wooden spoon in years. He was a cracker of a bloke.'

He'd been wool handling for twelve months when the opportunity came to shear.

'We were heading up that Wentworth Road [the Silver City Highway] again and Pine Camp was a shed that we used to shear at. And then Springwood was the next shed up, you know, another 100 kilometres up the road, and I remember the contractor saying to me, "Well, you got two options: either you can go rouseaboutin' up at Springwood or I can drop you off and you can start crutching by yourself at Pine Camp."

'That was, sort of, the start of it there. Done a week's crutching on me own with the farmer there and I wasn't goin' back rouseaboutin' after that.'

He was still only sixteen: quite young to be making his way in the world, especially when the world comprised some pretty rough, middle-of-nowhere places. It was a potent recipe for a serious case of homesickness.

'That's where I was pretty lucky at the start. Good people. I always got put with good people. Still, getting dropped off, it was a little bit daunting but, you know.'

It helped that not long after Shannon picked up a handpiece, the incredibly hard work of shearing gave him the first of many unexpected benefits.

'I was stung by the comment "That fat kid will never shear." That was one of the biggest things, I reckon, when I started shearing. You know, you get left for dead playing with your mates and all that. Here was something that I didn't have to work at to lose weight. You know, you just had to go to work. And you're eatin' better, too.

'Me mates used to say, and I used to say myself, "I'm not fat. Just Mum fed me too much." Mum and Dad were both workin' so you helped yourself to whatever was in the pantry, sort of thing.

'When I started shearing, all of a sudden you're down a pants size and you can start touching your toes – or seeing your toes – and stuff like that. So, that was an incentive at that early age.

'And then the travel. Mates I was with had never been out of their town. You go to their place and they had a little backyard and you're inside playing computer games, which didn't interest me too much.'

By contrast, Shannon was shearing at some of the most remote sheep stations in the world.

'Gawler Ranges [north-west of Port Augusta] was a big thing: Moonaree, Kangaroo Well, up to Kingoonya. Glendambo was always a favourite spot up there. You don't have to go too much further north than Glendambo and you've run out of sheep country out there. That was always interesting up there.

'Flinders Ranges is really good, too. I'd go and do a bit of huntin'. Back then you could shoot goats. Now they're worth too much. Weekends I used to stay up there a fair bit and one old fella I teamed up with a little bit.

'On a Sunday, instead of layin' around camp – and that's when you get into trouble, when you get bored – he'd say, "Righty-ho, we're gonna go and climb this hill and we'll take a rock up and put it on the pile up on the hill."

'And you get up on the top of the hill and there's a pile of rocks. He's been doin' it for years sort of thing.

'Or we'd go up to a dump and have a look and we'd find an old dingo trap, or we'd be always looking at somethin'. It interested me, too. Like, off the beaten track you see a lot more and that's where the worldwide travel [which started a few years later] come into it.

'You can go on a bus tour – you'll see the Eiffel Tower – but you go and start shearing out in the backblocks, I reckon you meet the real people. That big structure, the man-made stuff, doesn't worry me. It's bloody seeing a fox twenty foot [six metres] up a gum tree. It's stuff like that. You can't pay to see it. You gotta be there.'

That said, some experiences you wouldn't pay to have.

'You can get wool down inside your fingers – girls get it in their nipples – it can grow through your fingers and that, and up in Bon Bon [a station in the Gawler Ranges] I had me thumb swollen like this. I had a go with the needle and I couldn't get it to burst. I was thinking, "I gotta go and get this lanced or go to the doctor" but I've never comped [made a worker's compensation claim] and never knocked off to go to the doctor. Your arm had to be broken or you had to be nearly dead.

'Then this Aboriginal cook, she seen it and she ended up getting soap and sugar and grinding the soap up and makin' a paste out of it. She mixed up this, heated it up in a spoon, put it on and put on a Band-Aid. It nearly burnt my finger it was that bloody hot. Halfway through the night, it was like an orgasm: it just went *bang*. And I was way . . . and just pus come out of it. I'll never forget her. She was a bit rough around the edges, but bush medicine. You don't have to go the doctor.'

At the same time, Shannon was developing as a shearer. Pine Camp Station established a shearing school where Shannon was mentored by legendary shearer and instructor John Hutchinson.

'He probably taught me to shear but his ethics in shearing was really instrumental and that's where we're trying to head back to now. You don't walk into the bloody smoko room with no shirt on or no shoes on. No scrub, no grub, you know.

'I was shearing up to 200 at the school and doing a really good job and John had had a few mock competition runs in the shed.

'And he said, "You'll go all right at them. We'll go to Adelaide. You're shearing well."

'That was a really big turnin' point in my life. All of a sudden it's a different kettle of fish where you're performin' in front of a crowd. It's a sport and a performance. And this is where it comes back to the saying, you know, "That fat boy isn't going to make it".

'I remember going to the Adelaide Show [in 1993] and I won the intermediate and then made the open final that same day. All of a sudden, you were recognised. You weren't just that little ruddy red-faced fella down at the end melting. You're up there doing something.

'I think Melrose I missed out, and then I went to Jamestown and won the intermediate and open. As soon as you win an open, you're in. I excelled pretty quickly but at Jamestown it wasn't a big field of shearers. Then the next big one was up in Glendambo – it was a thousand bucks first prize, a Gorilla. We called $1000 a Gorilla back then. You were tryin' to go to them shows that you'd get a Gorilla.

'There was a couple of farmers – one old fella especially I ended up doing a lot with – flew up there and wanted to see me perform. There was a lot of shearers up at Glendambo. It was a fairly big show back then. We were shearin' not far from there. I'd come into town and this farmer was a bit of a bettin' man so he went around to the publican and said, "I'll have a thousand dollars on Shannon Warnest."

'This publican was takin' $20 bets on a few people and all of a sudden there's $1000 on. Now it was, "Who's this friggen Warnest fella?"

'This was in February 1994 or something. So, I'd done four or five shows by then. I was unheard of but I ended up pullin' it off up there.'

An added bonus was beating a shearer who'd been in his sights for some time. Shannon was improving quickly but this shearer always managed to outshear him in the sheds. In the Glendambo competition, Shannon finally beat him.

'That was a real "I can get you another way" sort of thing. Once that was in the system, away I went. I've won over 200 open shearing comps in Australia.'

In 1995, Shannon's growing prowess as a shearer led to his first trip to the Northern Hemisphere. While there, he shore in the 'backblocks' of Switzerland, in high mountain valleys where he met people who hadn't travelled beyond the next village in their entire lives. He also shore a lot of sheep.

'I think I shore 12 000 in eleven weeks and we got paid two francs [each] so that was about $24 000, $25 000 cash. But I was down to 84 kilos, the hardest I've ever worked. And you were right out of your element there. Like, I wish I'd learnt German at school. I was in the class but I didn't learn. Mum was German, as in forebears.

'I bought a red Falcon ute when I got home. That was my first new car. This is the second one out here [he gestures to the one parked outside the shed] so I didn't buy many new cars. In eleven weeks – you try to go and buy a brand new car in eleven weeks. That was really good.

'And when I come home, your mates that you'd come home to – it was a bit like where I went, some of them old fellas and that over there. Like, "Gee, get out and get a life."

'But all me mates wanted to sit down and listen to what I'd done and where I'd been and that was "Oh, righty-ho, I'll bloody go somewhere else now."

He was twenty at the time, and has since shorn sheep in sixteen countries (including Australia). There are so many that he struggles to remember them all; most are listed in his citation at the start of this chapter. He's also shorn in Ireland and on the Isle of Man, and wonders if Tasmania counts as the seventeenth place he's shorn 'overseas'.

Among the highlights are shearing at the Calgary Stampede in Canada and at the Waldorf Astoria in New York as part of the commemoration of 200 years of Australian wool exports to the United States.

Shearing in the foyer of the Waldorf involved a mountain of red tape and permissions, but what few people realised is that Shannon had to carry a sheep through the hotel's kitchens to get it there. The sheep left a trail of droppings. It may have been, Shannon thought, 'so we could find our way out'.

By the mid-1990s, Shannon was doing well on the competition shearing scene, but he didn't have it all his own way. One of the premier events at the time was the Diamond Shears, held in Longreach, and Shannon was finding that it was proving elusive.

'I'd got so far with ability, but that was one show that really taught me that you're not as good as you think. Not that I thought that, but I got up there and I got bloody flogged. It was different country and different ground, and I spent probably six years up there tryin' to win it.

'One year I went up there and was the most dedicated I'd been. I got up there three or four months before. "Right, I gotta shear them sheep because they're different sheep to what we shear down here." It's like some footballers, they play good on their home ground but they go to another oval and they can't read it.

'That's why I got those 200 shows. It's because I went around the world and it didn't worry me. I went in different areas but Longreach was, what do they call it, bloody Channel Country up there? The sheep are smaller, little bit of a different shape, different wool on 'em. You can breed a sheep down here, take it up there and it turns into a Channel Country sheep within a couple of years.

'For three months I didn't have a drink. Every weekend I had off I was out on the riverbank fishin' by meself. Sit-ups. Find a branch in a tree. Do chin-ups. Going for a run. I was workin' out, getting my body really fit. I'd never been to that level before.

'I don't like losing. I remember Dad used to ride TT in Australia, the open motorbikes, and he got second in Australia over at Albany. He was so disappointed and he was good enough to win it. He was a privateer, so no sponsorship, no nothing. He put everything into this motorbike and he got over there and he was two models too old. The bloke with the faster bike beat him. And you talk to him now and he says, "It was that 5 or 6 mile an hour [8 or 10 kilometres an hour] down the straight that he was quicker."

'Dad would catch him going around the corners, work his guts out and get in front and he'd go like this – around him again – every lap. I still think of that now. I wish Dad had a better bike. That's the same as shearin'. I always thought – I respect old Dad heaps – I'd go and do it for him as well. So you'd keep drivin'.

'I remember at Longreach, a weekend a fortnight before the competition, there was a cold change comin' in and because I was from the Barossa we used to have a port. That was the in-thing in the winter time, shearing: instead of having a beer after, we used to have a glass of port. So I went and bought a little bottle of port and I thought, "Right, I've come so far and this is me night off before we get focused on it again."

'I sat out at the river by meself and I remember just sittin' there fishin' and I woke up in the morning and – you know on the Falcon utes they used to have those two rods underneath the tarp at the back – I had both of them full of fish. I couldn't remember it. I had a bloody splittin' headache and two rods of fish. I've got a photo somewhere of these bloody callop all hangin'. I just kept threadin' 'em on.'

What happened two weeks later?

'I ended up twenty-third. I didn't even make the friggen semi-finals. I was just gutted. I'd got over the night I'd had by meself because it was two weeks out, but, you know, I was dead focused to win and shore shit. Just too much pressure on meself.

'That was a big learning curve, too, and that's why that bloody "Shannon's way". I was thinking about that this morning. Shearers will train and shear right up to the day. They'll go out in the morning and practise. When I've done enough and I've got me body right, I'll go fishin' a day out or two days out from a big comp. I think I learned it from that. Instead of drilling yourself into the ground wantin' it, wantin' it, wantin' it, and then when you don't, you go "Fuck, what did I do wrong?" I think that's what I did wrong.'

While Shannon was learning that mental preparation was as much a part of competition as physical preparation, he was also realising that some competitors were masters of mind games. There's not much you can do about someone's physical preparation, short of breaking their kneecaps, but there are no rules about breaking their concentration.

'I know lads who can win battles before we get up there. One bloke I'll tell you about, Hilton Barrett, he's probably one of the hardest blokes, with his off-board antics. He'd bust so many people, just the way he was. A few instances: he rung me up one day – this was before we had the nationals over in Esperance – three months out and he says, "Look Shannon, yeah cheers mate, good on ya, good luck over in Esperance. I'm out of the state finals."

'I said, "Oh, shit, I'd enjoy the battle against you."

'But I thought, "That's good 'cos that's a big kingpin out."

'I didn't take no more notice. I was away shearing and back then I had no emails or nothing, so we rocked up at Esperance and I remember they'd booked a suite out for us. You had New South Wales, Victoria, Queensland, the Kiwis in a two-storey villa looking down to the beach. I didn't know who was in the other teams or whatever but I knew Barrett was out and he was the main man at the time. Get down there and he's doing sprints up the beach in front of us all – fully fit.

'And I go, "Fuck, what's he doin' here?"

'"Oh, he made it in."

'I'm thinking, "Shit, I haven't done the preparation", because if Barrett was in you'd try to do anything to beat him 'cos he's a bloody . . . But I ended up beatin' 'im.

'A couple of other times we were in an open final and he'd bloody be the last man to be called and I'd know he was ready and sittin' out there waitin' for the last, "If you're not here in one minute."

'And I'm gettin' in me zone, looking at the sheep, and I know he's doing it to do that, and then he'd walk up and he'd put a purple wig on and then the crowd would start laughing and he'd just try and break your concentration. I'll give him everything for those off-field antics but that's Hilton. I was never in that level and I never wanted to do anything like that. But that was a good mind tool as well.

'It doesn't matter what happens up there – if you get a kicker at sheep fourteen, get over it. I've got little things I go through if I start getting in trouble on the board: little processes so you're not stuck in 'em [negative thoughts] for three sheep. If you're stuck in 'em for three sheep, well, you're out of a blue ribbon. And if you're in against an idiot – well, I can't call him an idiot because he's a very smart man – a lunatic – how's that? A lunatic like him . . .'

I suggest 'sportsman'. Shannon gets the nuance.

'Yeah. You're dead right.'

It was while Shannon was trying to win the Diamond Shears that he managed to snare a bigger prize – his wife Catherine, who was raised in western Queensland.

'I actually seen her up at Longreach in the Diamond Shears; she got up there in the learners. I had this mental photo of her, like, "She's a nice type", sort of thing. I thought I'd never see her again and I never spoke to her.

'Then she got told to get out of where she was workin' because the shearer trainer up there, Dave Sommers was his name, told her, "You've gotta get out and get with someone good."

'That's exactly right: if you want to be the best at whatever you do, learn off the best or get with the best to learn, and take bits from everyone.

'Even with these kids, I'm teachin' them but they ask a question and you think, "Oh, that's a silly question", but you've got to find an answer for it. So teaching them is one of the best things. Teaching someone else helped me teach myself as well – that was a big thing.

'With Catherine, she come down and – you know when you first seen your love of your life – I remember her walking into the lounge room. I always took a learner on the cocky run up to a mate in the Barossa, and he rung me and I had a spare spot so she come down and travelled around. We used to shear together – she wanted to get better – so I started showin' her a lot more, and then as I started to get with her, we'd probably spend more time in the shed together rather than sending her off with another team. So, "Oh, yeah, Catherine, you come with me."

Competition among shearers may not have been limited to shearing.

'You got to keep the threats away. But when she come down, she was a great inspiration. She's shorn 200 a couple of times in the shed. That's what she wanted to do, so she got there.'

Shannon also eventually won the Diamond Shears, in 1998.

'I don't know if you noticed that ring that Catherine had on. That's the diamond out of the Diamond Shears. It was a $4500 diamond at the time. I had it mounted in a ring.'

In 2000, Shannon was twenty-six and had set his sights on shearing's ultimate prize, the world championships.

'I threw everything at it. And in competition shearing I reckon it took me to a different level. No-one had really gone out of the square – that I knew of – to really understand what you need for a twenty-sheep final.

'I remember going and talking to this bloke and he said, "I'll get ya to Adelaide and there's a Robert Crouch. He used to do a lot of rehabilitation for the cricket players and football players in Adelaide – like Gillespie. I'll have a yarn to him and see what he says, what he's gonna charge and that."'

Robert Crouch was a former boxer turned fitness trainer, particularly endurance training. The word came back, "Because I've never done a shearer before, just tell him to come down to my club tonight and I'll have a yarn to him."'

Shannon and another competition shearer, Paul Auster, made their way to Adelaide to meet Robert.

'Robert said, "Well, this world champ's comin' up. I don't know nothing about shearing. What do you actually do?"

'And I said, "Look, mate, we're doin' twenty sheep – South Africa was on merinos so it was fifteen sheep. The world champs and cross-breeds are twenty – but we're gonna have a fifteen-sheep final over there and it's gonna be twenty to twenty-two minutes. That's probably all we're gonna be looking at and you're bloody full on."

'He said, "Well, look. Grab one of these heart rate monitors. Go out to the shed and just re-enact that all week. Don't do it every run, but pick out fifteen good sheep, whatever you do, set yourself a time and then go for it. Switch the bloody monitor on and then come down next Monday night with it and we'll have a look what your body's doing. Then I can understand how we can work to train ya. Keep the bloody monitor runnin' all week. Just do your stints and then I can see what your resting [heart rate] and all that is."

'I reckon 155 beats a minute was the most I could get it up to in the shed doing those fifteen-sheep stints. Friday morning was friggen 110 and Friday afternoon 100 – when you're thinking about what you're doin' on the weekend. When we downloaded this, he said, "Righty-ho, when's your next big comp?"

'We were goin' over to the Royal Perth Show to do a match against New Zealand. I got in and I was doing 145 on the grandstand. I think I peaked at 188 at this show. I came back and showed him that.

'He said, "You're not trainin' near hard enough, if you think the world champs are gonna take that. You wanna be doing that three times a week at least and you can't do it in the shed."

'I thought, "Well, shit, there it is in black and white."

'I said, "Look, I'm not good at runnin'. It just hurts too much and it's probably no good for ya runnin' on friggen knobbly old roads up in the middle of nowhere."

'He said, "Just jump on one of these machines and we'll see how you go."

'It was one of those climbing machines, a reverse climber. I got on there and fuck, I nearly bloody died. It got the heart going. Yeah, no worries at all.

'He said, "You can't just go and do twenty-three minutes on this thing. We've got to build up to it. There's a readout here, 42 metres a minute."

'We started settin' up a program. He gave me contacts for blokes that he knew had 'em [climbing machines] around the state. There was one halfway to Mount Gambier, so if we're shearing up here, two hours to Mount Gambier to do a bloody fifteen- to twenty-minute session.

'I thought, "Nah, I'd better invest in one of these."

'In the end I bought one and that's when I reckon I took it to the next level.

'Another thing I did a fair bit – through Robert Crouch – you have a look at AFL. It's not about kicking a football. Training is about jumping through bloody tyres so you know where to put your feet, your balance and all that. When I used to play football, an hour kicking a football on the oval was your training. Now, some training sessions they might even not have a ball.

'When I was goin' for the top level of shearin', I remember juggling beer bottles. Just throwing the bottle up in the air and catching it by the neck – throwing it higher and spinning it faster because the bottle slows down. It doesn't matter where you caught it. You're just focusin' for that split second to catch that bottle by the neck, and that's when things started to slow down in real life.

'If you dropped the bottle and it smashed you'd have to pick it up. While you're pickin' it up, you'd cut yourself and you're thinking about the next one. Hand–eye coordination is a huge thing for shearing. You've got a live animal that's movin'. It would be easier if you were shearing a statue but you're not. If something moves, you've gotta be there respondin'.

'I used to have a beer box and snap all the teeth off a shearing comb and just have the two riders [the outside teeth], because you've got to know exactly where they are, and just turn away and practise hittin' the middle of the V in the VB logo on the box. Then look away and as soon as you see it, you're there. Then do it other ways – stand on one foot, stand on a wobbly board.

'When I went over to Africa, I was right in the zone. I couldn't take my body any further and I reckon it helped with my thinking as well. I had confidence that I could stand up and my eyes wouldn't fall out after twenty-two minutes. I was that far ahead of everyone else there: my mental approach and knowing that my body could bloody handle it.'

Shannon was ready for the world championships, but he wasn't prepared for South Africa.

'Life was so cheap over there. We got this taxi driver one day. We'd given him $150 or $120 – it was rand over there, a dollar to five rand – and we'd run around and he waited. This taxi was out there when we needed it, rather than try and hail one down.

'We'd just hired him for the day but we said, "Well, how about tomorrow?"

'He said, "Nah, I've got this money. I'm takin' me wife on a holiday."

'I thought, "Well, shit, you wouldn't get too many jobs like this."

'We'd probably given him three months' wages in one day. [I said to him] "If you work tomorrow, you've got six months' wages and you can go on a bigger holiday."

'[He said] nah, he might be dead tomorrow or his brothers might steal it off him or whatever.

'We went out playing golf one day and we'd hit the ball into the water and this guy comes walking out of the scrub, walking around trying to find the ball. He brought it back to us for $1. He had another ten balls and once we'd bought that one back, he said, "More, more."

'I didn't want the balls, but, "Here. Go and buy yourself a pair of rubber boots if you're gonna do this."'

At last, the day of the competition arrived.

'You're standing in front of the crowd with your back to the crowd, you just go through a couple of little breathing exercises, a little bit of a routine and then you're right in the zone.

'When you walk up onto that board and get the count-down – "shearers ready" – same thing, everything just slows down. It sounds quite funny, but you know, if a sheep blinks, you can see it. A sheep might move its head like that but you're watchin' it so you know where to grab it and then you're away.

'In Africa, I could nearly see the comb. This thing goes at 2800 revolutions. Your cutter goes across twice with one revolu-tion, so you know how fast it's goin'. I remember comin' down the last side of my last sheep in Africa and I could see the cutter movin'. You think you've slowed down because you've built right up to it and I remember goin' out that last leg, last four blows, and it was just "Hurry up". I knew I'd done it but the whole thing slowed down.

'When I ended up winnin' I got 15 000 rand [about three 'Gorillas' at the exchange rate at the time]. I remember getting this bloody wad of notes in front of 3000 people and looking out and just all these eyes. It felt like they were looking at this bloody wad of money I got, not me. So I give it to the old girl. She's quite big.

'I thought, "Well, there you go, Mum. You look after that. I'm goin' out on the town."

'That was quite an experience, comin' from there, and then you get back home and someone's whinging about a bloody prickle in their finger. And I'm thinkin', "That was a really good learning curve."

'Driving through the Eden Valley to Angaston, it's the big red gums over the road and the green flats with huge big red gums, and shit, it was like time stood still for a day. And you just looked out and thought, "Shit, this is home." You know what I mean? I mean, there's no place in the world like this.'

It may have looked the same, but for Shannon, everything had changed. He soon noticed that people treated him differently.

'One thing that shits me off, and it still does today, is someone will pull you over – even when you're talking or something like that – "Oh, this is Shannon, he's the world champion". That shits me right off. They use you because you're famous around their mates – "I know him, I know this fella" – and it's that "See ya later".

'The upside of it is just here. These lads come up to you in two years' time and they've got a big smile, a hundred metres away from you, and they're telling you they've shorn their first hundred. It's a buzz.'

And they know they've been taught by one of the best.

Shannon also got involved in organising competitions. That started back in his home town, Angaston.

'You've got to put in. I've got a bloody heap out of it so you've gotta put time back in. The other thing is, we're trying to make 'em run better and because you've been around the world and shorn a lot, you know what works and what doesn't. It's exactly the same as the shearing pattern [the sequence of blows to shear a sheep]. To become a really good shearer, you're trying to pick the best out of everyone's pattern.'

Shannon was still quite young, only twenty-eight, when he was awarded the Order of Australia for services to shearing.

There was no resting on his laurels, though. Not long after, he and Catherine bought the Willalooka pub in 2002. And Shannon's appetite for competition shearing was still keen. He missed out on the world championship in 2003, to David Fagan from New Zealand, but he was fired up for the next event in 2005.

'The world champs in Toowoomba – the second one that I won – that was the hardest out of the two worlds. The first one, you're an underdog. If you win or lose, it doesn't matter to anyone. If you've done it once, the expectation is there to do it again.

'Same thing: three or four months off the grog. If some mates came round I'd have a beer, but I could perform at 100 per cent next morning. Three [beers] and that's it. "I'm goin' to bed or goin' for a run or whatever."'

He didn't just drive up to Toowoomba for the event. He shore his way up through New South Wales, trying to get into sheds where good shearers were working so he'd be under pressure eight hours a day.

After shearing in New South Wales, Shannon moved on to Quilpie and Charleville. By then, he was ready.

'Got into Toowoomba, booked into the motel, went up and had a look at the venue for the worlds, went and seen the Australian team manager and said, "I'll see you in a couple of days."

'We headed straight into Brisbane and had a charter boat booked the next day to go out fishin'. Just out on the water, gettin' right away from it. And then come back and I was fresh, sort of thing. That's probably why bloody Winston Flood says, "He does it his way."

'Everyone else is there bloody getting prepared. I reckon that sort of cooks me a bit.'

Shannon won the double – the individual and the team world championships – for the second time.

He's still competing more than a decade later, and while he hasn't won more world titles, he's been Australian champion eleven times, most recently in 2016.

In recent years, Shannon has found another way to give something back to the industry: shearer training. Over dinner, he'd jokingly explained to me how it had changed over the years.

'In Dad's day you got a flogging, in my day you got a kick up the arse, now you can't lay a finger on 'em.'

In reality, Shannon was involved in setting up a national training program with the country's peak wool organisation, Australian Wool Innovation. He and the other shearers involved in the program travelled the country three times: first to find the best techniques; second to trial the techniques; and third to demonstrate the techniques to other trainers. The result is a nationally consistent approach to shearer training encapsulated in what are called 'the five pillars of shearing'.

'The first one is gear. You don't see Craig Lowndes going to win Bathurst with a beat-up Holden. So gear is 100 per cent. When we went around Australia with this, I reckon 70 to 80 per cent of the shearers weren't getting a true cut.

'The next thing is your position – the position of your body, the position of your downtube, the position of everything. You don't have your water bottle sitting down there [he points down the board]'. If you wanna shear numbers, you have it there.' He waves off to one side at waist height.

'Your grip. The way you grip your handpiece. We've looked into that so much more. We say it's like your mum's budgie: you've got to hold it so you don't kill it but you've got to control it so it doesn't fly away. You can hold your handpiece too tight, and to move it around the sheep you've got to move your body. If you change your grip on your handpiece [so] your hand will move around the sheep, you don't have to move your body. It comes back to that big sheep – the hand speed.

'The next thing is the free hand. When I go to New Zealand shearing sheep with no excess skin on 'em, you're just controlling the sheep. When you start shearing big numbers over there, it's all about getting that sheep skin, and your free hand doesn't do nothing. Here, where we've got bloody wrinkles, you need your free hand to straighten all that out. So that's the fourth one.

'And then your entry. Where your entry points are is huge. And that's where I was talking about hand–eye coordination, getting that comb to land on the spot every time.'

When the training group delivered the five pillars concept to the shearer trainers and wool-handler trainers in Australia, they believed they could fix nearly all the mistakes on the shearing board. It was almost always one of them that was the reason a shearer wasn't working to the best of their ability.

'That was a big learning curve for training as well. It was actually training us to train the trainer – upskilling ourselves. Look at my grades at school. I'd never passed anything before – apart from maths and PE – but all of a sudden I could go out and deliver and be a certified teacher.'

In the process, Shannon discovered that there are mind games in teaching as well.

'If you get one bad egg in the class, you've gotta target him. Don't let him rule the class. If he disagrees with anything, try and stay on him. If you let him go and then he gangs up with a few people, he can change the whole class and ruin the school. So reading people's minds is a big thing.

'That Dave Sommers, when I did shearer training, he said, "You've got six or seven shearers in the shed, and as a shearer trainer, especially if you haven't got confidence, you'll go down to the other end with the slower shearer because you know you'll be able to teach him. How do you teach the bloke up the front there that doesn't wanna learn?"

'We stood in the catchin' pen and he said, "Watch this bloke. I know he just wants to get fast. Don't worry about his job; he just wants to go faster. You teach him something faster and then you can teach him whatever you want."

'This fella, all he wanted to do was win the speed shearing. That's one sheep – "Ready, set, go" – and you've gotta shear as quick as you can. And he was getting second. So we just had to cut one second off his shearing. And he was actually stepping back before he went on to the next position. You might not understand how shearing works, but stepping back first and then forward?

'I went in there and I counted.

'I said, "You're losing a second, second-and-a-half doin' this. Just keep going forward."

'And then, "Oh, yeah. Fuck! Can you watch me again?"

'Bang!

'"Oh, yeah, well you're runnin' over this hip a bit. You're leavin' a bit of wool. I reckon if you go like this, you'll get all that wool plus you'll be a bit faster. Even if you aren't, you're cleaning your job up."

'That was a good learnin' curve because you get someone on your wavelength and they eat out of your hand. That was exciting for me as a trainer. Shit. You've gone into the fastest man in the shed thinking you know nothing, and now he's influencing the next in line all the way down because he's sitting next to you, talking to you. He's the gun, everyone looks up to him 'cos he's the fastest. Now he's your best mate, so you could probably tell them to shear left-handed and they would. Because you've got him.

'Take the kingpin. If you get someone that's upset, you don't push him aside, 'cos he's gonna slowly get his group together and upset the whole class. Get him early.'

Another technique is to get students to teach each other. Shannon recalls an instance from the days when he was a learner.

'John Hutchinson said to me, "You do a really good nick, you're one of the cleanest nicks I've seen. I can't do it as good as you. Can you go down and show that lad down there? I'll jump on your stand and shear a few. Can you go and show him how you do your nicks?"

'I said, "Oh, yeah, that's bloody good. I can have a break."

'I'd go and do four and five and then this kid says, "Geez, thanks Shannon."

'You know, you're helping someone.'

Shannon has also found that there's no right or wrong way to learn things. You can tell some kids something ten times but if you show them once, they'll get it.

'One fella read a book on shearing and it worked.'

These days, he's using video as well.

'It's just another tool we use. You can tell someone fifteen times they're wobblin' their head, keep it still. Video doesn't lie. You take a video and he goes, "Shit, I didn't realise I do it that bad."

'So then you might give him something else, like stick something in his mouth like a nut on the end of a piece of string. If it's hittin' his ears, you know.'

While we've been talking, the students around us in the Pinindi shearing shed have started crutching sheep. Shannon takes some time to give them some attention, pointing out how to move and the different ways farmers want the job done. He then grabs the handpiece and shears a sheep so I can get some pictures. As he does, more than a few of the students are glancing across to watch the former world champion in action.

There's a timelessness to shearing. The biggest change in the last 130 years is the use of machine shears instead of blade shearing. Apart from that, there's little difference between a photo of shearing taken in 1916 and one taken in 2016.

As Shannon explains when he's released his sheep: 'The techniques haven't changed since Jackie Howe [who held the machine shearing record for a while and still holds the blade shearing record of 321 sheep, set in 1892]. They still take the belly off first; they do the back leg. At the world champs there was a German shearer a couple of years ago, he put 'em on the box and the first blow was up the back of the neck. But 99.9 per cent of the skilled shearers shear the belly, back leg, that pattern.'

Nevertheless, while some things haven't changed at all, others have been transformed. Sheep have changed and shearers have had to adapt. The knowledge and experience of top shearers like Shannon Warnest has made it possible to produce more good shearers than bad.

'Sheep have got a lot bigger. You can shear little sheep and get away with being out of position, off balance – but big sheep, you've gotta have it spot on. We've had to look at that a lot more and that's helped the pattern – that's helped shearing – because everything is balancing the sheep.

'It's like boxing. You don't beat someone by standing back here with a big hay-maker. You've gotta get 'im in your area and that's where you've got the most powerful punch. If your sheep is out there [he stretches his arms right out], you're off balance, you're too far. If you have a sheep here [close to his body], you're a lot more controlled.

'I keep saying to these lads, "Each section of the sheep is like you're sitting down eatin' dinner. You don't sit down and have your dinner with your plate a foot to one side and reach over. You put your dinner right in front where you can eat it and if you spill a bit it lands back on your plate. That's exactly the same as shearing. You don't want to go into another section and be shearing around here and you're off balance and stretching the wrong way and that. You put your body into that position to shear that section of the sheep."

'That's getting looked at so much.'

It explains why my first impression of Shannon had centred on his perfect balance.

The students in the shed around us are doing a five-day raw-learner course.

'At the end of the week they can walk into a shearing shed, handle wool, load a handpiece and grab a sheep without the handpiece fallin' to bits and bloody breaking their arm and that. They know how to maintain the machines, they can shear a sheep unassisted. That's where we're aiming at and we nearly have a 100 per cent strike rate.

'It's all up to the individual. Some blokes can pick it up no worries. There's a couple of lads here that on day two were nearly on their own with no experience. Then others – lads that have had a fair bit of experience – are behind 'em.

'When we take 'em to the next school, which is an improver shed, we only can take 'em up there when they can do fifty. There's probably one lad here that could go into one of them school sheds. These other lads, you can take them up as wool-handlers and keep educating them. The improver shed is when they get paid for what they do. If they can do twelve a run or fifty a day, the farmer will pay 'em wool-handler's wages which works out to about seventeen sheep a run – that's about sixty-eight sheep a day.

'It's really an introduction to the industry. Some of these lads will get a job next week. We'll find 'em work, give 'em phone numbers, put 'em on the right direction with good people to work for as well.'

There's a lot for a young shearer to learn, but just as Shannon found in competition shearing, it can all come to nothing if they don't have the right mindset.

'It's like, if we cook ninety-nine good steaks and then cook one bad one, it's like you've only cooked one bad one. It hurts you so much in the industry. There's three blokes here that I rate as where we wanna be with the shearers in Australia, but you can go next Monday and the ABC says they're beltin' sheep and the drug thing [shearers taking drugs] and all that.

'These lads, hopefully we can instil in 'em that that's not the right way to go. There's 80 per cent of the industry that are great blokes and you wouldn't go past them as people but there's that 20 per cent that fucks it up for that 80 per cent.'

He's got some pretty good advice on how to be one of the 80 per cent.

'If you don't give a shit, if you don't present yourself right, if you don't care about the industry and about what you do and tryin' to do it the best you can, you're gonna be out there shearing for someone that doesn't give a shit. You're not gonna get the good job. If you don't put nothing in, you're gonna get nothing out of it. So learn it properly. Go in there and try to put yourself around the best people to learn off. Never stop learning. It's not about goin' to work and thinking, "Oh, shit, I can't wait till Friday's here." You've got five days to make yourself better and then worry about doing something on the weekend.

'Even the money side of it. I've had the best time of my life but bought a farm. We're getting $3 a sheep. If you shear for the right bloke, you can get $4 because you're doin' a great job. But $3 a sheep: the government gets $1, spend $1 on yourself, put $1 away. If you shear half a million sheep in your life (I'm probably three-quarters of a million; Dave – the old fella there – he's probably up closer to a million), you should end up with something like $500 000 or $750 000 – putting that $1 away.'

Add in quite a bit of prize money and you can see how much Shannon has got out of shearing, and why he's putting so much back in. As mentioned earlier, he also realised many shearers' ambition and bought a pub. He and Catherine ran the Willalooka Hotel for fourteen years, until the demands of a young family became too much. Now he shears, teaches shearing and farms. He's excelled at the first two and has plenty of plans for the third.

'We've only got 800 acres [324 hectares]. We've got 80 acres [32 hectares] of flood irrigation – about a thousand ewes. We're doin' a lot of renovating [improving the country by ploughing in clay]. I'd like to get up to about 1250 ewes on that little run there – a few cows. Then we lease a couple of places. We've got a share-lease with 1800 ewes and a hundred cows and then about 800 merino ewes on another block. So with farming, I've done the best I can to get our own improvements right.'

I asked Shannon what he thought of the shearing lifestyle. At times, his answer showed flashes of temper.

'I'd recommend that to bloody any person who wants to get out there. I reckon it's just a great lifestyle. You might have to work hard. It's not something I'd recommend for fifty years because I'm a bit disappointed in the industry. At the moment sheep are at a high, cattle are at a high. Goats are worth a lot of money. However, I can go out in the bush to places I've shorn over twenty years ago and they haven't spent a cent on the infrastructure. You know, the same mattress you slept on twenty years ago. The farmer's driving around in the latest V8 LandCruiser worth $120 000 but you can't get a mattress.

'Some of the big players in Australia – and I will stand by this – some of the biggest woolgrowers in Australia are the biggest culprits. Yeah, and I'll hammer it out with anyone. I'm over it. Even this two per cent wool tax – what we're doing here – we only get a small portion of it. We're teaching these kids to respect the industry and they circle zero on the wool poll to say how much tax they want to pay. I'm not real happy with that.'

Would he want his children to follow in his footsteps?

'If they want to. I hope they learn one thing: if you're gonna do something, do it to the best of your ability. If you've got something, don't waste it, whatever it is. If they wanna play football, if they wanna be a bloody ballerina or they just wanna be a normal person, just do it. I'm not gonna take that away from them.'

———

At the world championship in Gorey, Ireland, in 2014, Shannon once again represented Australia. He placed sixth. He's been consistently at the top level of shearing competition for sixteen years. One reason for that is that he's still able to get into the zone.

'I was speaking to [New Zealand shearer] David Fagan the other day on the phone. Once you've learned them tricks and you've stored them into you, you don't lose it, sort of thing. The fitness is the biggest thing, but you can switch on and learn to switch on. Like, I could walk in that door now and it's no worries.'

Another key is that he practises what he preaches. While he's teaching young shearers that they should never stop learning, he's still learning himself.

'You never stop learning shearing. I wish I'd known what I know now when I was twenty-six or twenty-eight. Shearing has got better since then, too. Overall, it's probably another 10 per cent better. These days you see shearers do 400 a day, and 200 is good. I could do that, too, if I was young and fit and knew what I know now.'

The mind boggles to think what Shannon might have achieved twenty years ago. Not that he's dwelling in the past. He's still competing and shearing.

'A big thing was winning ten national titles. I've lost the second to last two and it's shit me off a little bit, because it's like I got to that ten and I just lost that focus. I'm trying to find it again but things change.'

At the 2012 world championships at Masterton, New Zealand, the commentators at the final described Shannon as 'the old tiger from Australia', 'a very cunning shearer; and 'a great quality shearer'. The 'cunning' comment may have referred to his delaying tactics just before the start. He took his time getting to the board, then he went to check something in his pen. Was there a problem in the pen or had he learned a thing or two about breaking his opponent's concentration?

He may not be able to match the young guns day in and day out like he used to, but he can still switch on and show them a thing or two. These days though, his preparation for competitions has to compete with family commitments, teaching commitments, farming commitments and even spending time talking to writers.

'At that top level you're gonna need everything to go for it. That bit I'm missing is what I need to be out the front. It's not like it's gone anywhere. I just haven't got time to do it.'

Whatever that bit is, you could call it 'Shannon's way'. A couple of months after we spoke, he found it again. He won his eleventh national title.

Leg Six

The sun was shining but it was still freezing cold when I left the shed. I climbed into Trucka and turned the heating right up. I drove out of Pinindi and back towards Keith, homeward bound at last. I made it to Hay in New South Wales in good time and spent the night.

The next morning I was on my way at the crack of dawn. The temperature had dropped below freezing and Trucka was covered in ice: sure enough, the crack in the windscreen had grown even bigger. It was now about 45 centimetres long, right below my line of sight as I drove. The windscreen only had to last one day, though. Once I was home, I'd have time to get the thing fixed. Fortunately, I made it.

A couple of weeks later, I was on the road again, this time for a quick run up to Moree. As it was all highway driving, the Truckasaurus stayed at home and I took my wife's Subaru XV, which has half Trucka's fuel consumption. It's got a slightly higher clearance than a regular car, which means that if I detour down a dirt track in search of a lead, I don't leave the muffler behind as I did on a regular basis with my wife's Toyota Corolla. We loved that little Corolla, until it came to ground clearance. Then, not so much.

This time my wife Michelle (who's also my photographer) had time to come, too. Our route took us up through the heart of the

Hunter Valley, lush with winter feed, then on to the Goulburn Plains, one of the richest farming areas in the country. This last point was reinforced by huge signs on nearly every silo and machinery shed, rallying support against the activities of coal-seam gas and coal-mining interests.

We were staying with Terry Picone (see chapter one) and doing some follow-up after my trip outback with him. He also had me on a promise to help out at the Birdsville Races about a month later. Apparently I hadn't done too badly as a bookie's 'pencil'.

The other person we were here to see also lived in Moree, although he ranges far and wide in the pursuit of his profession. He has achieved something that many writers aspire to but almost none ever achieve: he's written something that became a classic as soon as the ink was dry.

5.

Poem from Nowhere

Murray Hartin

(1963–)

Back in chapter two, Sister June Andrew told me about one of the unpleasant parts of her work in Marree: having to attend suicide scenes. Significantly, in a remote region of South Australia where the population is only a few hundred, she'd been called to several.

Unfortunately, June's experience is not unique. In many rural and remote communities the suicide rate is double that in cities. In some Aboriginal communities, it's higher still. Males are particularly vulnerable. When isolation, despair, debt, drought and other factors combine, tragedy is often the result.

It's a situation for which there are no simple remedies. Obviously, if you're suicidally depressed, you should do something about it. However, that's easier said than done when you think you've run out of options. It's worse still when you don't just feel like a failure, you have actually failed.

If only you could recognise that even then, it's not the end of the road. If only you could see that you're at one of those difficult intersections in life where you may have to take a different path than planned.

If only doing that was as simple as reading or hearing, of all things, a poem.

The curious thing about Murray Hartin's 'Rain from Nowhere' (2007) is that it makes happy people cry. It makes sad people cry, too, but it also gives them hope. A young farmer, facing the loss of a property where generations before him have endured, is about to commit suicide. At the critical moment, he gets a letter from his father, who frankly admits he'd once reached the same point. In true bush style, he doesn't waste words:

> *I know the road you're on 'cause I've walked*
> *every bloody mile.*
> *The date? December 7 back in 1983,*
> *Behind the shed I had the shotgun rested in the*
> *brigalow tree.*

His father explains that he was squeezing the trigger when his son interrupted him with the words:

> *Where are you Daddy? It's time to play our game*
> *I've got Squatter all set up, we might get General*
> *Rain.*

The child's innocence and hope make him realise 'there's no answer in a gun'. Out in the real world, in the backblocks of Australia, it has probably made people who are 'at risk' realise the same thing. 'Rain from Nowhere' is arguably the greatest poem written in Australia in modern times.

My road to meeting Murray Hartin actually started back in 2009. I was living in Birdsville and writing a book about the experience when I heard a bush poet recite Murray's poem *Turbulence* (1998), a humorous piece about stockman Billy Hayes' imagined experiences in a plane.

Much later, I went looking for the poem on the internet. When I can't sleep at night, fretting over something that I usually regain perspective about in the broad light of day, I recite poetry to myself: 'The Man from Snowy River', 'A Bush Christening', 'The Diamantina Drover', 'Beach Burial', 'Five Bells', 'Invictus', et cetera. I thought 'Turbulence' would make a good addition to my 3 a.m. repertoire.

I eventually found the poem, but along the way I came across 'Rain from Nowhere'. I read it, cried, and took barely a moment to realise it was a masterpiece. Not only that, the author who wrote it was still alive.

Was it possible to meet him? I'd found out that Murray and bookmaker Terry Picone (see chapter one) were mates. So when I rang Murray, I mentioned that I was also talking to Terry. They then rang each other. Neither of them wanted to participate in the book, but they were sure the other should. In the end, I think they each talked the other into it.

In Moree, I hooked up with Terry at a country race meeting where he was working with one of his brothers. We headed to Terry's home, a beautifully restored Federation-style homestead outside town, where we met Terry's wife, Bethelle, and sat down to a great meal and a great deal of red wine. And yes, I realise there's a bit of a pattern developing here.

Murray joined us later and proceeded to entertain everyone with stories of his life, poetry recitals and humour. My first impression of Murray was that, while he's a great raconteur, he isn't easy to get to know. I was expecting a sensitive, insightful poet. I found a solidly built fifty-something farmer-type who looked like he'd be more at home talking about cultivation or football than about cutting to the heart of one of the most painful issues in rural Australia.

Despite the late night, we were up again early the next morning. Terry was keen for us to have an early-morning swim in the artesian pool, for which Moree is famous. We were going to meet Murray there.

As we drove, Terry pointed out landmarks that had particular significance for someone whose family connection to the town spanned four generations. Everywhere we went, Terry knew everyone.

At the pool, or rather, pools of different sizes and temperatures suited to everything from lap swimming to having a soak in a spa, we hooked up with Murray and went for a swim. Murray reminisced about the days when the pool wasn't so elaborate (old photos show a quaint enclosed bathing pavilion), but when local kids would spend entire days splashing around.

We went for breakfast at a nearby cafe. Once again, Terry knew practically everyone. Murray did, too. There were introductions, explanations of the significance of each person, an underlying sense of community, and an unstated pride in showing it to me.

It wasn't until lunchtime that Murray and I got to sit down and talk at his 20-hectare property just outside Moree.

When Michelle and I pulled up, I said, 'This looks like the home of a bachelor.'

Murray is, indeed, unmarried, and as he invited us inside, he apologised that he hadn't cleaned the place. It looked like he'd just moved in and was still unpacking. There were dirty dishes in the sink, dirty cups here and there. I said something about a man cave.

The other impression I got, when we sat in his workspace, was that there was memorabilia everywhere – posters, photographs, figurines, knick-knacks. There were framed speeches from the various parliaments where Murray's poems had been referenced. Stories, memories, people and events from virtually his entire life jostled for position on every shelf, wall and available piece of floor space. Even the building had significance. It belonged to his father, who'd farmed the 150 hectares around it many years before.

Murray's family connection with the land reaches back generations. His father, Kevin, the son of a wheat farmer, was originally from Werris Creek, 300 kilometres south, but had moved up to northern New South Wales to 'do a bit of share farming'. He was originally at a place 40 kilometres from town, but in the late 1960s decided to get into cattle so bought a house in town and two smaller properties just out of Moree. When the bottom fell out of the cattle market, Murray's dad got a job as a stock and station agent to supplement his income.

Murray was born in 1963, the second of three children. Coming from a farming background but living close to town meant that, at school, Murray was neither a townie nor a bushie.

'Back in those days there was a big line between the townies and the bushies. The rugby club was all people off properties, so I was a bit of a cross-over because I had the connections both ways.'

His experience of poetry goes back to Moree Primary School. For two years, he had the same teacher, Paul Lawler, who inspired him and planted the seed.

'He was into his creative sort of stuff and it was great. We used to do plays. In 1973, I was a ten-year-old in fifth class: I played Flavius Maximus in *Rinse the Blood Off My Toga*. I don't know what the curriculum was across the whole countryside at that stage, but he liked the creative side of written expression.

'I wish I could find my books that I had from fifth and sixth class, because I had some pretty good stuff.'

Murray still remembers one of his first poems.

'That was "Archie and His Automobile". I was a bit of an *Archie Comic* fan and he had a jalopy and that sort of stuff. It wasn't a brilliant poem but it had a good rhythm. I remember bits of it. It was only probably three or four line verses. It's pretty daggy really:

> *Archie just got us an automobile*
> *And it had head lights that turned with the*
>   *steering wheel,*
> *With a big back seat and a big black hood,*
> *All these accessories made it seem good.*
>
> *It moved with a broom broom and a bump,*
> *It rolled over when it hit a hump.*
> *Most of the day it hogged the road*
> *And then it ended up being towed.*

Murray reckons there was probably another verse in the middle, but even so it's a pretty impressive feat of memory to recite a poem from forty-odd years ago. Most of us would have long forgotten.

'It's nothing classical, but as a ten-year-old it probably demonstrated that, yeah, I could find rhythm in a poem or the "de dah de dah de dah" which is very hard to define.'

Murray didn't consider that early poem to be the start of his writing career: his focus leaned more towards football and cricket. Later, however, when we were talking about writing, he said:

'I don't think it ever leaves you. I was writin' poetry when I was ten and eleven. I was muckin' around with it. And I always loved words and I loved learning stuff. I could recite "The Man from Snowy River". I could do that stuff and, yeah, loved it. If you can find the rhythm in a poem, you know – and sometimes it's hard. Like I was saying, my iambic pentameter is not great in a lot of my poetry, but if you hear me recite it, you won't know.'

After primary school, in 1976 he went to boarding school at Barker College, in Sydney. While he didn't perform well academically and was missing his family (his parents separated not long after he started boarding school), he was discovering a new family that would prove invaluable for his future: the rugby family.

'I was pretty handy. Well, I had a great mate, Terry Buckland, and when I was ten, at the Gwydir Carnival, whoever it was moved me from playing prop to five-eighth [now known as fly-half] outside Terry, who had bright red hair and was just a freak. He was throwing dummy flick passes at ten, before they'd been invented, all this sort of stuff. He was so good that I worked out to just hang back and be there when he'd finished doin' his stuff. That ended up getting me to the State Carnival two years in a row. Terry sadly got killed in a car accident at sixteen; he could have been anything that bloke.'

Murray should perhaps take more credit for his own ability. Down at Barker, he got put in the fly-half position in the 13As. The next year he got moved to the centres, where he played throughout school, finishing in the first fifteen.

Around the same time, while home on holidays, he got to experience rodeo riding.

'I came third in an under-thirteen poddy-calf ride. That was my rodeo experience.'

He pointed out a prize ribbon among the other memorabilia.

'That golden sash there, that's my connection to rodeo.'

In his third year at Barker, Murray had had enough of boarding school.

'I got homesick in third form [year nine] and I come home for a week and I didn't want to go back.

'Then Dad said, "You gotta go back."

'At the end of fourth form [year ten] he says, "You can come home now."

'I said, "I wanna stay." I wanted to stay for the mates, the rugby, the girls started in fifth form [year eleven] at Barker.

'And there was no drama. I wasn't thinking about the drought. I wasn't thinking about the money. I look back at it now and it was tough times – '78, '79, '80. It wasn't good and Dad's forkin' out probably four grand a year for me.'

At the time, it may have appeared that the money wasn't being well spent. Murray failed English. The school yearbook in his final year said he was going to do a farm apprentice course and start a Border Leicester stud. The reality back in Moree was quite different. The drought that had gripped the country for years was getting worse. Interest rates were heading into the teens.

'I got home but really, we only had 3300 acres [1335 hectares], so, as Dad said, there was barely enough to keep him and my brother going, let alone me.'

Murray went back to Sydney and got a job as a mail boy for a fuel company, Amoco. He started studying communications.

'And that's when I failed communications. After failing English, I failed communications. As a journalist and a poet that's a pretty good thing behind you, isn't it?'

A couple of years later he was still in Sydney, working for Amoco, playing rugby and sharing a house with three mates from school. He was making a decent income and spending it on having a good time. The drought, meanwhile, was making national headlines and evening news bulletins. Something struck a chord.

'It came on about the plight of the Snowy Mountains cattlemen who were shooting cattle. There was plenty of food in the Kosciuszko National Park but they weren't allowed to access it. And really I couldn't get my head around how that could be. How could some boffin make the decision that it was better to keep the grasses of the National Park pristine [by not allowing grazing] while all the people there – when those Parks are in those bushfires and that – they're the ones that do the work? So, yeah, I sat down from an emotional point of view and wrote that poem [*Rural Facts*, 1983]. And it's still powerful; it still stands up. I rarely do it but it still stands up.'

I suggested to Murray that it wasn't a typical reaction from a young, knockabout lad living in a city. Surely good poetry doesn't just pop out of nowhere. Murray's answer was surprising.

'I'd knocked a couple of things up before then. If we had a party, I'd knock a silly poem up, but I could always do that. See, that's the thing, I don't think you ever lose that. I always say to people about journalism, you can't be taught to write. You can be taught how to improve your writing, but if you can't write, no-one's gonna teach you how to write. It's gotta be in there. You can't just wish to be a writer and then learn to be a writer. It's sort of just there; it's like a destiny.'

Destiny is one thing, but all the talent in the world won't help you if you don't get a few breaks. Sometimes, they may not be obvious. For Murray, that was the case when it came to establishing a connection with then Manly Rugby Club coach and future national radio host Alan Jones.

'Alan Jones goes back to '83, when I played rugby for Manly. We do have a sort of a volatile relationship. He basically tried to kick me out of the club because I didn't turn up for a game one day, which I suppose is a fairly serious offence.

'I'd been graded – second grade. He'd plucked me from fourth grade for a first-grade trial game against Randwick marking [Australian international] Lloyd Walker, and I was nineteen, so I was very young, and I actually played pretty well, and I got graded to second grade.

'Later in the season I'd been injured and I was coming back through fourth grade.

'It had been pouring rain and I rang Manly Club [the night before the game] and they said, "No, it's been called off."

'So I went out on the turps that night and I got smashed. I didn't turn up for this game and it wasn't off. It was transferred to another oval. Christ! And then he just tore strips off me, told me I'd no friends in the club and just . . . reduced me to tears.

'I remember my sister saying, "Well, go and play for someone else."

'And I thought, "Nah, stuff that. I'll tough it out."

'So in the trial game, I played first grade against Randwick. Now, in the last game of the first round, I played fifth grade on the wing. But I hung in there. And Alan had a wonderful thing called 'the team of the week'. When you've got five grades in a club, they can become a bit elitist at the top end. And he brought in the team of the week and the fifth-grade second rower could be named alongside Steve Williams, the Australian captain, in the team of the week. It was just wonderful for the club. All the first grade and everybody cheerin'.

'Well, the next week he named me in the team of the week and said, "He's had a bit of a tough time but he's hung in there."'

Murray feels that Alan had been testing his commitment. He'd passed, but it was one of the toughest things he'd ever faced.

Not long after, Amoco was bought out by BP and Murray was retrenched. He headed back to Moree, where he had an interview for a job selling machinery. Then he got a telegram from Caltex that said, 'We want you to come down to Newcastle and inter-view for the position as the sales rep at Tamworth.'

He rang up and said, 'Oh, look, it's okay. I've just got a job.'

As soon as he hung up, he realised, 'Gee, that was dumb. Then I couldn't get back on and I was shitting bricks, and got back on and says, "Yeah, okay, what'll I do?"

'I got there and they said, "Yeah, right-o, you've got the job."

The boss – the sales manager – had previously been the sales rep at Tamworth and played for the Tamworth Pirates. He was a rugby man, I played rugby; so I don't know how good I was for the job but *bang*, all of a sudden I got a two-week, fast-track, pretty-well-hopeless introduction to being a sales rep.

'The first place they took me – apart from the depot and where the brick toilet out the front of my office was – was the Tudor Hotel, the home of the Pirates rugby team.'

Murray worked for Caltex for two years before switching to TNT. While he was in Tamworth, he didn't do any writing, apart from the occasional party piece. However, Tamworth is known as the country music capital of Australia, and its annual festival, held in January, is a national event. In 1987, someone had the idea of organising a bush poetry competition, the Australian Poetry Championships, in conjunction with the music festival. Murray decided to enter.

'I won with the drought poem and then the second poem, that I wrote that day, was the one about the gunfight between the koala and the possum ['The Ballad of Kev the Koala and Ringtail Pete' (1987)].'

Shortly after, Tamworth's *Northern Daily Leader,* edited by Ann Newling, ran a double-page 'local boy done good' story about Murray's success. Then TNT sacked most of its country sales staff. Murray and a colleague got transferred to Sydney, only for him to get fired shortly after he got there.

'I went back to Tamworth to try and find work. I was twenty-four and I'd been a sales rep. The age and the jobs were a bit out of whack. So a lot of it was, "Oh, no, sorry. You wouldn't want this job."

'I said, "Well I'll take any bloody job."'

He worked as an assistant electrician (for an electrician who played rugby) at Kerry Packer's Ellerston Station in the upper Hunter. He got a few days' work as a handyman at a school in Tamworth, which gave him the opportunity to do the old joke, 'What makes you so handy? I only live round the corner.'

'Two weeks of that. Four days over a two-week period. It was fun but it wasn't gonna make me any money. So that following Saturday a couple of mates and I went riding around on our push-bikes, heckling some mates playing cricket. Shane Chillingworth was playing cricket and his wife was Ann Newling.

'She saw me when I was heckling her husband and said, "I

know you're looking for work. Come on the sports desk for five days. You can obviously write; see how you go."

'And she gave me those three lessons: twenty-five words or less in the first sentence; tell your story in the first three sentences; don't use big words. I was a sports journalist first up, then I did court and police rounds, and sub-editing. Then I was editor of the *Country Leader*, I went downstairs as editor of *The Tamworth Times*, had a bit of a fling in Sydney in the 1990s casually sub-editing for the *Tele* and the *Mirror*.

'Ann was magic. You might not remember but last night I was telling you about some of her protégés: Michael Carroll is now the editor of *The Sunday Telegraph*; Murray Kirkness is the editor of the *New Zealand Herald*.'

Always being around words – his and other people's – was invaluable in forming Murray's ability as a writer.

'You can't learn to write but you can certainly learn how to improve your writing, vocabulary and add colour to a story while having the right balance – story first, colour second.

'There's that wonderful story about the two poets – Shakespeare and the other bloke [possibly Christopher Marlowe] – about the bow-legged man walking down the road. How would you describe it? And the bloke says, "Well, I cast my eyes upon the road and I saw a man whose legs were bowed." And he said, "Right-o that's not too bad. Shakespeare, what do you reckon?" And he said, "What kind of man is this who walks with his balls in parentheses?" Same information, look at the reaction.

'It's working out a way to say things and not just using the standard clichés. You've got to be very careful; you can't be too cute. Some of the stories I wrote as a sports journo, I was tryin' too hard: "This horse was comin' home faster than a kid on the last day of school". I thought it was good at the time but it was actually a bit clumsy.

'Court reporting was a good education. All kids should be taken to court in primary school to see someone get sent away, see how someone can walk in and then not walk out a free person.'

In 1988, the second poetry competition was held in Tamworth. The venue was the Kentucky Fried Chicken car park. It was far from ideal, although Tamworth during the music festival is bursting at the seams and a lot of people end up performing wherever there's room for a crowd to gather.

'I was encouraged to boycott by my stand-in editor because he thought it was wrong to have the Australian Poetry Championships in the car park of an American fast-food company. No-one noticed I'd boycotted it.'

The following year, Murray got a call from the organisers to say they couldn't hold the competition because they couldn't get a sponsor.

'I said, "How much do you need?"

'They said, "$200."

'Serious! *The Northern Daily Leader* was across the road from the Imperial Hotel and that's where my young mate, Matty Wynn, was the publican. He was the youngest publican in Australia – nineteen, twenty, twenty-one – at this stage.

'I said, "Windog! Maaate! Listen, what are you putting on in January? Do you wanna host a poetry competition there for a few days?"

'He said, "Yeah, how much?"

'I said, "$200."

'He said, "Bring it on."

'And they were gonna let it go. For the price of 200 bucks

Terry Picone at the Bedourie Camel Races, western Queensland, in 2016.
Photo Evan McHugh.

Terry Picone (left), author Evan McHugh entering bets, and Geoff Poulson holding Terry's bookie's bag at the 2016 Birdsville Races.
Photo Michelle Havenstein.

Nurse June Andrew OAM outside the clinic in Marree, South Australia. For over thirty years she has often been the only source of immediate healthcare. *Photo Evan McHugh.*

The heritage-listed Great Northern Emporium, established in 1878, in Quorn, South Australia, near the Flinders Ranges. It now operates as Emily's Bistro. *Photo Evan McHugh.*

The proprietor of Emily's, Sally Brown, in the bistro, which mixes
memorabilia from years gone by with local produce and homewares.
Photo Michelle Havenstein.

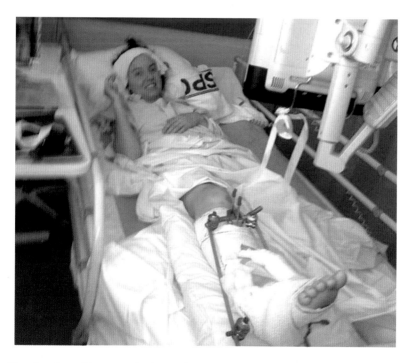

Shortly after taking over the bistro from Emily, her sister, Sally was involved in
a car accident. At the busiest time of the year, Sally returned to Emily's as soon
as she was able, working while still in a wheelchair. *Photo Sally Brown.*

Two-time world champion shearer Shannon Warnest OAM. *Photo Evan McHugh.*

Giving back to the industry that has given him so much, Shannon teaches learner Stephen Brooker Jones at a shearing school at Pinindi, in south-east South Australia, in 2016. *Photo Evan McHugh.*

Poet Murray Hartin at home on his small holding near Moree, New South Wales, surrounded by the memorabilia that has inspired many of his greatest works, including 'Rain From Nowhere' and 'Turbulence'.
Photo Michelle Havenstein.

Murray performing at a cotton growers' dinner at Moree in 2016. While some of his poetry touches on the sensitive issues affecting rural Australia, it also incorporates a huge dose of humour and relates directly to contemporary bush life. *Photo Michelle Havenstein.*

Bronco branders Peter Kleinschmidt (left) and Hughie McMillan swapping stories at the Camooweal Drovers' Festival in 2016. *Photo Michelle Havenstein.*

Drover Keith Luscombe recalling his experiences with Drovers' Festival MC John Nutting. *Photo Michelle Havenstein.*

Old drovers, horse tailers and cooks from all over Australia gather each year in Camooweal to recall the days when stock routes crisscrossed the country and were vital in bringing stock to market. *Photo Michelle Havenstein.*

Former convenor of the Barkly Women's Group, Bernadette Burke, with her husband, Henry, AACo's general manager, pastoral, in 2011. Bernadette spent decades on the Barkly while Henry managed Brunette Downs.
Photo Evan McHugh.

Current convenor of the Barkly Women's Group, Danielle Doyle, from Mittiebah Station, with the author at Camooweal in 2016.
Photo Michelle Havenstein.

Danielle (left) with guest-speaker bloggers Amanda Smyth (*Cooker and a Looker*), Kayte Murphy (*Mrs Woog @ Woogsworld*), Nikki Parkinson (*Styling You*) and Beth MacDonald (*BabyMac*) at the Barkly Women's Day in 2016. *Photo Danielle Doyle.*

The women of the Barkly take the opportunity to dress up for some 'me time' away from the male-dominated cattle industry that is the mainstay of the Barkly economy. *Photo Danielle Doyle.*

Boxing impresario Fred Brophy OAM spruiking his show at Birdsville in 2016.
Photo Michelle Havenstein.

Fred's show is unique in allowing members of the public to challenge his trained boxers. Many bouts are an opportunity for an amateur to prove their ability. Some can produce surprising results, as when this young Sydney woman, fresh from a day at the races, challenged The Beaver, Brettlyn Neal. The match was a draw. *Photos Michelle Havenstein.*

Park ranger and indigenous leader Don Rowlands OAM has sole responsibility for the largest national park in Queensland, Munga-Thirri. The desert park lies in country for which his language group has successfully made a native title claim. *Photo Michelle Havenstein.*

While Don believes the only turn you should make in the desert is the right one, this is one of the few occasions, in 2009, when he made a right turn that was wrong. A second vehicle and some digging extricated us in no time. *Photo (and digging) Evan McHugh.*

Outback recovery specialist Peter Barnes, 'Barnesy', has been rescuing bogged and broken-down vehicles from the Birdsville Track, Simpson Desert and surrounding areas since the 1990s. *Photo Michelle Havenstein.*

Barnesy 'hot dogging' on Big Red, the giant sand hill west of Birdsville, in 1990. *Photo Peter Barnes.*

Truck shearer and museum curator Trevor Keating preserves the memories of the days in the north-west of Western Australia (from the early years of the last century to the 1970s) when shearers were transported from shed to shed in trucks that became known as ring pounders. *Photo Michelle Havenstein.*

Valerie Hobson OAM has gathered the memories of many truck shearers in her book *Across the Board*. The book inspired the formation of the Shearers and Pastoral Workers Social Group. Valerie is seated in the cab of the oldest surviving ring pounder of that era, a 1934 Bedford. *Photo Michelle Havenstein.*

The last ring pounder on the road in the Pilbara region, in the 1950s.
Photo Valerie Hobson.

The truck shearers are struggling to find a permanent place to present their extraordinary history. The last ring pounder is temporarily in the Revolutions Transport Museum warehouse in Perth. *Photo Michelle Havenstein.*

A miracle in the desert at the 2016 Birdsville Races. Friday: the race track was a quagmire, following 50 millimetres of rain. Saturday: council graders levelled the track after earth movers had peeled off the muddy surface. Sunday: racing. *Photos Michelle Havenstein.*

they were gonna let go of the competition. Anyway, that's how it went.'

In 1990 Murray was in Sydney doing shifts on the subs desk of the *Telegraph,* while living in a pub across the road from the Touch of Class brothel. In 1990 he took a redundancy and went back to work in Tamworth. It was then that the poetry planets started to align.

'Marco Gliori had turned up around that time, 1989 or '90, and the poetry side of things, the competition, started to grow legs. Marco came along and won everything – the traditional, the original and the yarn-spinning – all with his own stuff. I don't think it was traditional with his own stuff, but that's how it went. He just sort of had a different benchmark in a sense.

'Then Bobby Miller appeared and he was brilliant. And then Ray Essery turned up. He was an old dairy farmer whose rhythms . . . he'd jam an extra bloody eight syllables into the bloody rhyming lines, but it would get there.

'And there was boffins who were sayin', "Hey Ray, that's no good. You've got to fix up your bloody metre there mate."

'And Marco and I said, "Ray, don't you change a thing, mate."

'He was an old dairy farmer so it made sense that he didn't quite get it. If it was someone like us: no good. Ray could get away with it because hey, that's part of the charm.

'And then Shirley Friend turned up. She's eighty-six this year [2016]. And Shirley probably taught us all more about timing and, a bit like Mrs Brown in a sense, well not that language, but double entendres. People thought she didn't know what she was talkin' about and she did. She was so clever and so funny with poems and stand-up.

'One of the things that was important for me, with regard to how I view myself, is that we were really lucky that we got that group of people together. It was just one of those perfect storms. We're all still friends. We lost Bobby, but we're all still very, very, very close. We had a little team environment and we all knew that the team was more important than the individual.'

In 1991, Murray's old coach, Alan Jones, attended a testimonial for rugby player David Brooks, held near Tamworth. By then, Alan was becoming a prominent radio personality and was also coaching Balmain rugby league club.

'I'd been asked to come and perform a poem or two. [Country singer] Felicity Urquhart was about fourteen or fifteen and she came and sang. Alan made reference to me and then the next morning, the Monday morning, I got a phone call from a mate of mine.

'He said, "Muz, I was just driving to work and listening to Alan Jones and he started talkin' about you. Then he started reciting this poem of yours. Five minutes later, he's still talkin' about you". He recited the "Fishing for Cod" [1990] poem on air, which is a five-and-a-half minute poem. And that did a fair bit of good.'

Murray was also on the lookout for good places in Tamworth for his growing circle of poets to perform their work. Then one winter's day he was assigned to do a story on the Tamworth Dramatic Society. They'd got hold of a church and were staging their latest production in it. When Murray saw the place: 'Gee, this would be great.'

An audience of about 110 could be seated in the body of the church and the choir loft upstairs. The wooden construction meant the acoustics were so good you didn't need a microphone. Murray was sure it would be perfect for putting on poetry shows.

'I made a bit of a mistake in two areas. One was that in July it was a bit cool. In January, that place was about a thousand degrees. People were losing weight in the audience. Plus, the first thing we did, we had nine people. So there wasn't any time. You went up and did this. You went up and did that. And if you had time you did it through again sort of thing.'

With some lessons learned, Murray still booked the place the following year, but limited it to himself, Marco, Bobby and Shirley, with Dingo Dryden doing some songs. Then he got another lesson in the entertainment business. Another poet asked if he could do some of his shows at the venue as well.

'No worries,' he said.

'When I went to re-book again for the third year, they said, "Oh, it's already been booked."'

'This bloke had gone and booked the whole thing and wanted to sub-let it back to us. I told him to shove it.'

While Murray was looking for another venue, Bobby attended another country music festival in Tamworth that July. While he was there, someone from the Tamworth Golf Club asked: 'Where's Muz? I want to see if he's interested in doing anything at the Golf Club.'

Apparently, there'd been no live entertainment at the club for thirteen years, not since a rock 'n' roll show had got out of hand. The golfers were hoping bush poets might be a bit less rowdy. It may not have been as atmospheric as the old church, but it did have air conditioning.

'That's when I brought Ray back into it and brought [singer/songwriter] Pat Drummond in, who'd stayed at my place the year before, because that Matt Wynn bloke who ran the Imperial double-booked all his accommodation, so Pat actually stayed at my place.'

The group called themselves 'The Naked Poets', and from the mid-1990s onwards they did a new show every year.

'We did mad skits and we'd write these little mini-plays. We could never practise till we got there, the night before we did our first show, so invariably the first shows were always way too long. You had to cut something out. 'I'll take that out; I'll take that out.' See, we had this team environment that meant the show was bigger than any individual in it.'

Not long after, Murray decided to give up working as a journalist and dedicate himself to poetry full time. It's notoriously hard to make a living as a writer. For poets, it's nigh on impossible. However, in 1996, aged thirty-three and unencumbered by a relationship, mortgage (he'd just sold a house) or kids, he decided to take the plunge.

'It was one of those things where I felt, I don't wanna die wonderin'. I've got nothing holding me back. I didn't say "I want to be a poet", I just didn't want to miss the chance of not being a poet – if that makes any sense.'

At the time, very few people, if any, were making a living as a bush poet.

'I just had no idea, no-one who'd gone before me like this. Marco had done stuff; he got a lot of good regular work through the Arts Council, through the schools. It was just one of those things really: go down and have a crack.'

He had some income from The Naked Poets shows and CDs. He had some income from the occasional corporate gig. In 1994, he'd found out how lucrative they could be when he was contacted to fill in for revered actor and poetry performer Leonard Teale, who'd just passed away.

Despite that, having made the decision, and having moved

to Sydney, the work, and enough money to live on, didn't come flooding in the door. Once again, though, rugby came to Murray's rescue.

'I was havin' a few drinks at the rugby club at Manly with Dave Williams – Steve Williams' brother – and the late Bernie Bergelin, who played first grade for Manly before I got there. And a bloke walked in and his name was Ronnie Hughes. Now Ronnie was previously the secretary/manager for the Manly club and now he was the secretary/manager for the rugby club in town, you know, which had all the functions and was sort of the home of rugby in New South Wales.

'And they said, "Ronnie, you should get this bloke for your next monthly lunch over there."

'And Ronnie said, "What's he do?"

'They said, "He's a poet."

'And he said, "Fuck off."

'Then they got me to recite the "Fishin' for Cod" poem, and he said, "Right-o, first Tuesday of next month, you're on."'

Murray went over and did a couple of poems. They were so well received he got asked back the next month. Then he was asked to the welcome lunch for the visiting Welsh rugby team. Murray still has the program, dated 19 June 1996.

'I'd been down there for six months and nothin' much was happenin'. Things were bein' chewed up pretty well. So they said, "Well, you'd better come over for this."

'And that was at the Regent, 800 people. I was nervously havin' a cigarette or something, and I met [Australian rugby great] Tom Lawton.

'He said, "G'day mate. How you goin'?"

'Tom Lawton!

'I said, "Oh, g'day Tom, Murray Hartin."'

'He said, "What's goin' on?"'

'And I said, "Just runnin' a few things through my head here. I'm speakin' today and this could be my big chance."'

'He said, "Oh, yeah. What do you do?"'

'I said, "I'm a poet."'

'And he said, "Good luck." And walked off.'

It wasn't 'Fuck off' but it was similar territory.

'My two big pieces then were the "Fishin' for Cod" poem and Archie Campbell's "Rindercella" – the Cinderella back-to-front story – and I did those. It went down really well. Tom sought me out afterwards. His wife, Jill, was there and by the end of the night I had Jill playin' pool against [then New Zealand captain] Sean Fitzpatrick, and Tom, Jill and I have been best mates ever since.

'That event exposed me to a lot of people in the rugby fraternity, and a lot of those people were decision-makers, bosses of rugby clubs and things like that.

'They'd say, "Oh, we'll get Hartin."'

They helped deal with the stigma attached to the word 'poet'.

'"Get 'im. I've seen him. He's good. I make the decisions. He's comin' on board."'

That just left one hurdle: getting bush poetry to resonate with city people. One of the challenges was helping people understand what he was talking about. Eventually Murray came up with a way of introducing his poetry that explained anything that needed explaining, then blended it into the beginning of the poem.

'I often get a comment, "Geez, you were four lines into the poem before I realised the poem was started."'

Success led to success. Not long after the welcome lunch for

Wales, he was invited to perform at the Peats Bite Restaurant on the Hawkesbury River, north-west of Sydney, run by Tammy and Rod Miljoen. Tammy had been famous in the Ricky and Tammy brother and sister country-music act.

After seeing Murray perform, Tammy and Rod invited Murray back for a function with a rugby league team, the Canterbury-Bankstown Bulldogs. Also attending the function was the king of talkback radio, John Laws.

'I met Lawsy and then we started doing a semi-weekly spot. There were times when it didn't happen, but over a period of over three years I probably did seventy, eighty spots on Lawsy. A lot of it was just for an event, for the moment. So if you didn't get on, you couldn't probably do it the following week or the week after.'

The bush poet was doing well in the big city, continuing to blur the line between bushie and townie just as he had when he was a kid growing up in Moree. Yet living, working and perform-ing in the city hadn't severed his connections with the bush.

In 1998, virtually by accident, he made one of those connec-tions with legendary Northern Territory stockman and property owner Billy Hayes, who'd be in this book if he hadn't been killed in a quad-bike accident in 2011.

'It was a brokers' insurance tour of central Australia that took me out there. One of the nights was out at Ooraminna, on prob-ably the worst part of Billy's property at Deep Well – some tourist stuff to help supplement the income. There's some dry times out there, as you well know.

'It was a black-tie-and-sandshoes type of event and I got up and did a few poems and then sat down and had a few drinks with Billy's son-in-law, Sal [Steven Hearn, nicknamed "Sal"].

'At one o'clock in the morning he's gone and found Bill and said, "Billy, you gotta come and have a chat with this bloke."

'We sat down and we drank till about four o'clock. They had to get up at five to cook breakfast (or it might have been three to get up at four). Anyway, I went down and snored me head off in a swag and next day Billy's got me sittin' backwards on a horse reciting poetry to some of these city people that were on the tour.

'I knew I'd met a marvellous family – not just Billy. I just loved it.

'And Roger McFarlane – who I've just been speaking to now because he's so close to my dad and my step-mum – was a wild boy. He was a wonderful horseman but he was a bloody rogue, and Dad helped him out a bit and he never forgot it. He was twenty years younger than my dad and Dad loved him.

'Rog went over – he was married with two very young kids – in a truck by himself to the Kimberley to go bull-catching, and he didn't have enough money really to get there. He tells the story about pulling up at Barcaldine or Blackall or something like that and he was starvin' and he was a long way from the Kimberley. He had a couple of drums of diesel on the back of his truck. He's filled up at the front of this pub and then walked in hoping he might see someone he knows – knowin' that he wouldn't.

'And this bloke come up and says, "How ya goin' mate?"

'"Yeah, right."

'Rog said, "I just saw you fillin' up at the front there. Where you off to?"

'He said, "I'm going over chasing bulls."

'And he said, "Well, come in and I'll buy you a beer."

'And he said, "Oh mate, I can't buy you one back."

'The only reason I'm getting emotional, I've never seen Roger cry before in his life. When he told me the story . . .

'He said, "Don't worry about that mate, you'll be right." He bought him a beer, and he said, "Come round to my place for a feed."

'And he slipped him some money. He was the local union rep there at Blackall or wherever it was. And Rog never forgot it.

'He went over to go bull-catching and ended up ownin' half a station. And I've got a poem called "Big Jack" (1990) and part of it goes:

> And the time of the Derby rodeo
> On a strange horse cos his had gone lame
> On this thing called the Noggin
> He won the ropin' and doggin',
> Yeah Jack was the best in the game.

'Big Jack is a bit of a compilation of different people, and that bit was Rog.

'So Rog wanted me to go over to the Kimberley, because by this time his youngest daughter was five and was speaking in fluent Aboriginal tongue with a bit of colourful language thrown in at the right places as well. He sold up but he wanted to get me back over there to take some photos, write some stories and maybe write some poems before all the old yards got knocked down, because with the helicopter age all of the romance was goin' out of it.

'He had his own plane and we were gonna have a night with Billy and [his wife] Jan Hayes [in central Australia] and then go to the Kimberley. So the thing was, he had a place just out of Tamworth. It was dry, so he had cattle on agistment up here [in

Moree]. He had irrigation with lucerne on his place at Nemingha, and we were shiftin' pipes in the morning and afternoon. Then we'd drive up here [to Moree].

'And at the end of a week he said, "Oh, I can't go."

'I said, "What the hell?"

'He said, "Don't get angry, just ring those people in Alice Springs and tell 'em you're comin' there for two weeks. You'll find something to write about there."

'So I went out there, having met these people once. Jan picked me up from the airport. So I was with Billy and Billy Boy [his son, killed in a plane crash while mustering in July 2016] and Kenny Napier – he was the son-in-law – and a German girl called Sarah. I was watching them pull windmills and do this for a couple of days and I thought, "Geez, I'd better write something."

'At this stage I'd been doing my regular spot on John Laws on a Friday. I think I arrived on the Tuesday. I'd been absorbing this character Billy Hayes I'd been first introduced to earlier that year, and I thought, "Well, what am I gonna write?"

'And I'd always had this idea, through rodeo – 1975, third in an under-thirteen poddy-calf ride – but if I was in a plane we'd hit a bit of turbulence and I'd think, "Whoa, outside."

'All of a sudden, I had this wonderful character. I spoke to Jan about him and that's where I got all the information about the rodeo, campdrafting, he won three Alice Springs Cups as a jockey, and all this other stuff. Once I got that information – a bit like Billy Birmingham with "Australiana" – I wrote "Turbulence" in under three hours and did it on John Laws the next day.'

It's hard to understand how you can connect someone you've just met with something you did twenty-three years earlier to produce one of the most memorable (and hilarious) bush poems written in years. Where does that come from?

'I heard Noel Gallagher from Oasis being interviewed and he said, "Well, it's just like songs are droppin' out of the air and if I don't grab 'em and use 'em, Bono's gonna get 'em."

'It's the same, you know, if you don't act on a poem. Sometimes it might be years before one hits you. It's up to the individual but it's very hard to force yourself to write and come up with something good. There's got to be an initial spark that just goes "whoomp". With songwriters they might get one line – it might be in the chorus – but it's just somethin' that goes "bang".

'A lot of times for me it happens early in the morning. I'll wake up early – maybe five or six – and I'll be lying there and somethin' will go in. That, for me, is probably one of the most creative times. There's nothing else to bother you and things just jump in your head and you can't explain why. Or if you've woken up on the lounge, which I do a lot, and then go to bed. All of a sudden you can't get to sleep and these things happen.'

'Turbulence' rapidly became Murray's most popular and best-known poem. However, as bush poetry goes, it's as outback as it gets – rodeo, the way people talk – and can take a lot of explaining.

'If I'm introducing "Turbulence", I talk about how I met [Billy] and how he speaks and how the people speak out there; my childhood love of condensed milk in a tube, which I see all the old stockmen are addicted to still; that he was a great rodeo rider in his day, bareback, saddle bronc and bull-riding. I say, "You gotta stay on for eight seconds until the bell rings and get off the best way you can."

'I talk about how he was a top campdrafter, which I have to explain to city people is a horse and cattle sport, in case they think he's a gay architect. If I don't tell them that – and when I do, the country people are laughing because city people just don't know and I have to explain this to them – if I don't tell them about "eight seconds till the bell rings", when I get to "For Christ's sake ring the bell", they don't get the line.

'The introduction, which is a good story in itself, and that sort of accidental way it goes into the poem – all of a sudden it's rhyming and it just runs – that wasn't something I sat down and did. It just . . . there's no experience better than being on stage. No matter how bad it can be sometimes, you learn stuff all the time and some things happen accidentally.'

The poem was recorded live at a Naked Poets gig in Tamworth in January 1999. The CD of the show went close to becoming a gold record. Another CD, *Muz!*, that contained the poem also sold well. What helped audiences identify with 'Turbulence' was that the voice reciting it was authentic.

'My accent isn't nearly as thick and broad or as Territorian as theirs but it certainly stands out in a city audience. There's nothing about me pretendin' to be from the bush. I've got that connection in the way I speak. The connection has always been there. I love the stories. I mean, I love the parties and stuff, but if I had the chance I would have been there.'

In 2000, Murray's relationship with the John Laws show came to an end.

'He got a new producer and he wouldn't let me on. John never tried to get back on to me. I tried to contact him and he said a few nasty things about me on air, about being unappreciative and all this sort of stuff. I thought that was a bit unfair.'

It may not have helped that Murray had a connection with John Laws' rival, Alan Jones. After his radio spots dried up on the John Laws program, he still got to do occasional spots on Alan's show.

'Not near as much as I appeared on Lawsy, but yeah. He's been very good to me and the political poem I sent to him recently he read out, which is a pretty cool poem. We've actually got him fired up about this current education system with the spelling and the maths and all that sort of stuff. So Alan has been a good ally. As I said, I don't agree with everything he says – a lot of it I do – but I respect his right to say it and he does a helluva lot of good for people behind the scenes which he doesn't trumpet; he just does it.'

A decade later, large parts of Australia were in the grip of drought once again. By 2007, areas of New South Wales, Queensland and South Australia were severely affected.

In January, Murray got a call from Russell Workman, a Scottish mate he hadn't spoken to for seven years. Russell was working with the Salvation Army to produce a documentary about mental health in rural Australia, in particular farmers committing suicide.

Russell wanted to tap into Murray's knowledge of 'the boosh' – meaning the bush. Murray then had some meetings with the Salvos, in particular with Captain Paul Moulds, to talk about the impact the drought was having. As June Andrew detailed in chapter two, when times are good, farmers are happy. When times are bad, the rate of suicide rises. In a severe drought, the cost in human life can be unbearable.

Murray didn't have first-hand experience of rural suicide but he knew all about the consequences of drought. He'd met Billy Hayes when Billy opened his station to tourists to supplement his on-farm income during a drought. In 1983, he'd been prompted to write a poem about the drought that affected the cattlemen of the Australian high country. A few years before that, Murray now realises, his father had struggled to pay his board at Barker College during another drought. He hadn't thought much about the sacrifices his family had made at the time, but he hadn't forgotten them either.

While talking to the Salvos, Murray came up with the expression 'rain from nowhere'.

As he wrote on his website: 'Through my experience, my rural background and constant contact with mates and relatives in the bush, it always seemed the best rain was rarely forecast. It came out of nowhere.'

Murray also had a recollection of an unverified story of a farmer who took his life after trying to sell his cattle. When he took them to the saleyards, they were in such poor condition they didn't get a single bid. The farmer's only option was to shoot them. He did that – and then he shot himself.

In February 2007, Murray woke up early one morning. He had a few lines in his head. He got up, went to his computer and started writing. Three hours later, the first draft of 'Rain from Nowhere' was written.

He comments on his website, murrayhartin.com: 'I knew it was special. There's no arrogance or self-importance there, you just know when something feels right.'

Murray might have thought the poem was good but he wasn't expecting it to 'go viral'.

'I sent it to a mate, Shane Stafford at Richmond, and he sent it to his mate, Budo Grant, who's got trucks in Winton, who sent it on to ten people, and it got out within two days of me writing it. It went pretty berserk and I got emails from everywhere.

'Within a couple of days, a girl from Victoria emailed me to see if she could use the poem at a convention or something.

'I said, "Look, I'm not being precious here but I've only just written the poem, I've just got to get my head around it. There's been pretty strong reaction to it quite accidentally after it got out. I just wouldn't mind if you could hang on for a bit because there may be stuff I've got to touch up on this yet."

'She emailed back and said, "Oh, that's okay, it didn't scan very well anyway. I would have had to re-write it."'

It was an extremely presumptuous thing to say but it emphasised that the poem had taken on a life of its own. There was a more positive response a few weeks later, when he got a phone call from a man in Melbourne.

He said, 'Murray, my name is Bob Lloyd and I invented *Squatter* in 1962.'

Bob was ringing to say how much he enjoyed 'Rain from Nowhere'.

Later that year, the poem was cited in the New South Wales Parliament by member for Barwon, Kevin Humphries, during discussion of the impact the drought was having:

> Ten years ago a medical workforce advisory committee reported serious maldistribution of psychiatrists, with one psychiatrist per 6600 people in capital cities, one per 20 000 in large rural centres and one per 40 000 in rural and remote areas. With the loss of key staff in many of our rural areas, the focus on mental health in extremely difficult times could not be more paramount.

Every day five Australian men commit suicide. In rural Australia alone twenty people commit suicide each week. There are more than 1000 deaths per year. One farmer in rural Australia takes his life every four days. There are particular pockets where this has been exacerbated – areas such as the Riverina and Sunraysia – over this drought period as sections of the agricultural sector have not coped with water shortages to keep permanent plantings alive, let alone productive. In my home area of Moree the suicide rate is more than double the State average: 29 per 100 000 compared to 11 per 100 000.

A good friend of mine, Murray Hartin, a bush poet from Pallamallawa, east of Moree, summed up the drought earlier this year when he penned the poem *Rain from Nowhere*. Murray has become today's Henry Lawson. I will conclude by reading his poem because it sums up the drought situation, and Murray is happy for me to do so.

After the poem became a permanent part of the New South Wales parliamentary record, Acting-Speaker Thomas George said, 'I add my thanks to Murray Hartin. He is a great Australian, and he certainly struck a chord when he penned that poem.'

During the discussion, the Minister for Local Government Paul Lynch also mentioned two incidents from one of his trips outback. At Bourke he was meeting mayors and general managers from the region, all of whom were clamouring for his ear. Paul Lynch said: 'The only time there was absolute silence during that meeting was when the rain started. One can read about these things intellectually and academically, but that sort of exposure leaves an impression on you; it stays in your mind.'

Minister Lynch then had a private meeting with one of the mayors, who also happened to be a farmer. The mayor explained how tough he was doing it and how he was coping. He pulled a packet of antidepressants out of his pocket. They were what was getting him through the day.

Not long after, Murray was the subject of a front-page story in *The Sydney Morning Herald* titled 'Drought, the black dog and the bard who inspired hope'. In October 2008, then Minister for Agriculture, Fisheries and Forestry Tony Burke referenced the poem in Federal Parliament.

The reaction to the poem is almost always the same. The first person he recited it to after writing it, fellow Naked Poet Shirley Friend, said, 'Muz, it's going to make your funny stuff a whole lot funnier.'

It was a strange observation that proved to be entirely accurate. At functions where Murray performs 'Rain from Nowhere', after choking back tears, audiences roar with laughter at the first joke he tells afterwards. It's like releasing a pressure valve. Afterwards, people come up to tell him their experiences with rural suicide, depression and the pressures of working the land.

Not all of those stories are sad. Murray related an old joke about when a local farmer won a million dollars in a lottery. When asked what he was going to do now that he had all that money, he said, 'Oh, reckon I'll keep on farming till it's gone.'

In the evening after our interview, Murray MC-ed a function for the Moree region's cotton growers. The organisers kindly allowed me to watch him perform. What struck me was the ability Murray had to make people smile. As he was yarning and versing, he was making everyone happy. He told me that after I left (I didn't want to wear out my welcome and Terry and Bethelle were keeping dinner for Michelle and I), he did 'Rain from Nowhere'.

Afterwards, a sheep farmer who now does talks on depression came up and told him how he used to pretend everything was normal until his wife left for work. Then he'd just sit on the verandah all day. If a neighbour came over and said, 'I'll give you a hand with those sheep', he'd do whatever the neighbour wanted to do. The rest of the time, he was mastered by depression. It was only when he sought help that things got back on track.

The Naked Poets shows ran for thirteen years until 2009. By then, Bobby Miller had passed away.

'We were doing CDs, and once we had no more material of Bobby's recorded, we were never gonna do another CD without Bobby on it.'

Murray, Marco Gliori and other poets occasionally get together to do shows, but no longer as The Naked Poets.

As mentioned earlier, in 2011, Billy Hayes Snr was killed after an accident on a quad bike. Thousands turned up for his funeral in Alice Springs, including Murray.

'He was well known without the poem. He was that quintessential cattleman. He had that wonderful Territorian accent and called me "Murrayartin" – all one word. There was just somethin' special about him.

'I suppose if you look at it, say, in rugby or sporting terms, where you've got a kid who can do stuff – why? Because he can. Who taught him? No-one taught him, he just does it. And Billy was who he was because of that, because he was Billy Hayes.

'One of the magic things about him was, Billy had no concept that he was held in awe. When they had these big functions out at Ooraminna, 800 people under the stars, and the Hayes family catered it all themselves, Billy would be doing the damper and the tea and they'd be coming over, and Billy thought they were just comin' over to get some damper and tea. They were comin' over to see Billy Hayes but that never entered his head. He didn't have an ego that would allow him to think that.

'And he'd say, "Murrayartin, where's my royalties, Murray-artin?"

'I said, "I don't get any royalties."

'I'm down probably forty to fifty grand on radio play because they don't collect for spoken word.'

Not long after Billy died, 'Turbulence' was read to the Northern Territory Parliament by the member for Greatorex, Matt Conlan. In his introduction, he said:

> It was written by Murray Hartin, also a great friend of Bill and Jan's. I was at Ooraminna on my birthday a few years ago – we had a party there. Murray was there and recited the poem. Bill and Jan were so proud Murray had written this poem about Billy Hayes. I would like to read that now and, Madam Deputy Speaker, there is some very mild language in this poem. I hope you will allow me to complete it in the spirit of the Territory, in the spirit it was written and, indeed, the spirit of Bill and Central Australia.

Murray is still making a living as a poet, although he admits things have slowed down a bit. Nevertheless, his poetry has taken him all over Australia and brought him into contact with thousands of people in the city, bush and outback.

He's been surprised by the generosity he's been shown, such as a Western Australian couple lending him a car to use during a visit. When Murray gave a CD to an army officer who couldn't get to one of his shows, he was invited to Duntroon, where he was given a tour and presented with an Australian Army slouch hat.

Up to that point, Murray hadn't felt qualified to write poetry about Australia's military traditions, but he found a way to express his feelings in a poem about what that gift meant to him. 'Slouch Hat' has subsequently been recited widely, in particular at Anzac Day ceremonies.

These days, Murray isn't keen on the direction bush poetry is going. He hasn't entered the Tamworth Poetry Competition for years.

'People are still writing about camp fires and billies, but there's plenty to be writing about now. These people have taken over and made the competition so pedantic that they've cut all the life out of it by "you've gotta have this in and it's gotta scan properly and it's gotta be precise rhyme, and you can't be doin' this".

'Well, come on, it's entertainment. They forget that side of it. You stand up in front of 'em, your obligation's entertainment. You can't just say, "Here, look what I remembered, or listen to my interpretation of something that hasn't happened in 150 years."

When it comes to nostalgia versus relevance, traditional versus modern, poems like 'Turbulence' and 'Rain from Nowhere' win hands down. They acknowledge contemporary heroes, problems, hopes and aspirations. Significantly, they don't just resonate with people from the bush: they speak to something all Australians understand.

'Australia's voice comes from the bush. Who cares about people in suits? We connect to the stories of bush life.'

Murray's books and CDs, and the words to his poems, can be accessed at his website, www.murrayhartin.com.
Beyondblue 1300 22 4636
Lifeline 13 11 14

Leg Seven

We took a different route for the drive home: over to Warialda for coffee and a pie, then lunch at a restaurant by the river in Inverell. Then came a spectacular drive through the towns of Uralla and Walcha in the high country of the New England Plateau. The winter sun was getting low as we descended the rugged mountains and valleys of the Barrington Range to the town of Gloucester. It was dark when we finally reached Lake Macquarie.

A month later, Michelle and I were on our way again. This trip was the biggie for this book: research on five chapters, plus launching *Outback Cop*, the book that started as a chapter for this one but quickly became a project in its own right. Not only was the Truckasaurus carrying camping gear, as we'd be roughing it for parts of our journey, but for the first two days we had to carry 600 copies of the book for the launch.

We drove up through the Hunter Valley, a scenic trip that I enjoy every time I make it. Coffee and another excellent chunky beef pie at Dunedoo's White Rose. After our regular overnight at Nyngan caravan park, we headed on to Bourke for coffee. Across the Queensland border, the winter rains had brought on flowers that stretched to the horizon. There were endless fields of yellow, purple and white. In places there were bouquets of colour.

The roads had little traffic but we managed to get stuck behind one grey nomad towing the obligatory caravan. We were on a major highway, two lanes wide, but for some reason, when we accelerated to overtake, old mate pulled over so half his vehicle and trailer were on the gravel verge. Trucka, with its brand new windscreen, was showered with rocks.

CRACK!

A big one got us. The language that came out of my mouth is unprintable; it had been an effort to bottle up my road rage in the car. I was sure I was going to be up for yet another windscreen.

We paused in Cunnamulla for lunch (where I searched for a stone chip but couldn't find one) and then drove to Charleville for the night. There we stayed with the subject of *Outback Cop*, Neale McShane, and his wife Sandra.

In the morning we transferred the books to Neale's 80 Series LandCruiser for the trip out to Birdsville. Then we set off for Tambo, where we had morning coffee and a pretty decent chunky beef pie. We refuelled in Barcaldine, lunched in Longreach and headed on towards Winton. The country was greener than I'd ever seen it. If it was always like this, this country would be the food bowl of the world.

At Winton, we stayed at the famous North Gregory Hotel, site of the first public performance of 'Waltzing Matilda' in 1895. We'd booked online, but there was a mix-up and there was no room available when we got there. However, one of the staff, Vanessa, gave up her room so we could have a bed for the night.

We got talking with her and she told us that the country around Winton was the greenest it had been for fifty years.

Unfortunately, the rains had come at the end of five years of drought, and most of the properties in the region had been forced to destock. Almost half were facing the prospect of losing their properties. It felt like a variation on the theme of *Rain from Nowhere.*

When Vanessa heard about the project I was working on, she said, 'If you're in Birdsville, you've got to talk to Don Rowlands.' She thought he was one of the most remarkable people she'd ever met and was pleased to learn that he was already on my list.

We had morning coffee in the Cloncurry bakery, where I gave the chunky beef the thumbs up, then it was on to Mount Isa for enough supplies to cover our stay for several days in Camooweal. We got the makings for sandwiches and lunched at a rest stop that had signage about the first sealed road that was built in World War II, the remnants of which could still be seen. It was explained that the road was replaced in the 1980s – but I can remember driving it, or sections of it, in the mid-1990s. My recollection was that it was narrow, rough and a nightmare when it came to road trains (overtaking them or meeting them coming the other way). It was an interesting piece of history, but I doubt anyone regrets its replacement.

In the mid-afternoon, we rolled into Camooweal with plenty of time to set up camp before it got dark. There was plenty of time, too, to catch up with some of the people who were setting up camp around us, many of whom are the subjects of the next chapter.

6.

Larger Than Life

Camooweal Drover's Camp

(1996–)

'Is Stumpy here?'

'No, he's not well.'

'Geoff Simpson?'

'Recovering from an operation.'

'Dave Allworth?'

'Yeah, he's camped over near the shower block.'

'Bob Savage?'

'He's getting on. Ninety. His daughter brought him over from Alice Springs.'

At least some of the old drovers I already knew were going to be at the twentieth annual Camooweal Drover's Camp Festival.

Another old drover who couldn't make it was Geoff Simpson's brother, Bruce. At one of the ceremonies that was part of the event, another drover shared his favourite story about him:

> I've been asked to say a few words about a fella called Bruce
> Simpson. Bruce is about ninety-two years old now and lives at
> Caboolture but he was drovin' out here for a few years and he'd

been known as 'Twenty-One'. And I'll tell ya how he got his name, Twenty-One.

Bruce was always a very baby-faced fella and he hadn't had a shave I think until he was about thirty-five, but of course all these drovers from out here, at the end of the season, they'd head to Brisbane, get on the grog, blow their cheques and they used to all meet at the Australian Hotel.

Anyway, this morning there was about five or six of them in the Australian and they're groggin' on and Bruce walked in and this barmaid took one look at him and said, 'Sorry mate, we don't serve minors here.'

And Bruce says, 'Oh come on. I'm twenty-one.'

And she says, 'Yeah, they all say that.'

And it happened to Bruce that often that he always carried his birth certificate with him. So he pulled his birth certificate out and he said, 'Here.'

And she had a look at it and read it and said, 'Right-o, what'll you have?'

He said, 'I only drink sarsaparilla.'

If you wanted to hear stories about the days when drovers criss-crossed the country with stock, this was the place to be. Every year at the end of August, drovers from across Australia gather in Camooweal for a reunion that includes exhibitions, music and remembering the days that made them the stuff of legends.

The mayor of the City of Mount Isa, which encompasses Camooweal as well, emphasised that point when she opened the festival the following morning.

I'm a wee bit biased because I was brought up in the outback, in the Northern Territory and Queensland, but I always say that the bush is what made Australia. The bush is the backbone of Australia and I feel very sad for people that live in the city areas that don't get the opportunity to come out here and see what the outback is and what Australia is made from. More than that, to meet the people. They've worked very hard all their lives to create Australia and droving is a big part of Australia. There's a lot of history here and a lot of interesting people to have a yarn to and to learn what our history is.

I'd already done that with the drovers I knew, and a few others besides. Owen Alloway was an eighty-nine-year-old from Charters Towers who'd been born and raised in a bough shed.

'Three sheets of iron to keep out the wind. Mum had eight kids, which stopped her from realising her talents. She recited poetry all the time. That's how I learned Banjo Paterson's *Lost*. I've remembered it all me life.'

Owen knew six other old drovers in Charters Towers who weren't coming – most were getting too old to make the journey. Owen had only made it because he knew a woman in Victoria who was prepared to drive all the way to Charters Towers to pick him up, then drive him to Camooweal. It was about 3500 kilometres each way.

Dave Allworth pointed out an old bushie with a big grey beard. 'He was a brilliant horse tailer [the drover responsible for the team's horses],' Dave said. 'I've known him since he was fourteen. I hired him at seventeen. He was great at his job. We lost touch for fifty years, then we were reunited here at Camooweal.'

Other drovers I knew not to ask after. Scrubba Watkins had passed away a few years before. Charlie Rayment, a true gentleman of the outback I had immense respect for, had also died.

Capturing and preserving the old drovers' memories before they were lost forever was one of the primary functions of the festival and of the Camooweal Drover's Camp, the volunteer-run museum where the festival was held.

Despite being very busy running the festival, one of the founders made time to detail its twenty-year community-based history.

Back in 1996, Aidan Day and her husband, David, were leasing the Camooweal roadhouse. They'd been there for about eight years, almost long enough to be counted as locals, when, during a flood, there was an issue involving the town's policeman. He regarded the flood, in a town where floods are a common occurrence, as an emergency – and he started distributing emergency relief money. That promptly led to drunkenness and domestic violence, which was even harder than usual to deal with at a time when the town was isolated. A town meeting was called to coordinate a response to the policeman's actions; while they had everyone together, Aidan said, 'While we're here, let's try to find a way to promote Camooweal.'

She knew there were a few old drovers around town from the days when it was a centre of droving, so she said, 'Let's have a droving festival.'

Camooweal wasn't so much *a* centre as *the* centre. Before the construction of 'beef roads' and the wide-spread use of truck transport killed large-scale droving in the 1960s, Camooweal was the crossroads for stock being walked across from the Northern Territory and the Kimberley to markets to the east (Brisbane and Sydney) and south (Melbourne and Adelaide). In good years, a river of cattle flowed down the Channel Country of western Queensland.

Camooweal was on one of the major rivers of the Channel Country, the Georgina. A large, semi-permanent chain of waterholes at the edge of town made an ideal camping spot for drovers and their horses while they waited for their next job.

As Aidan recalled: 'I said, "Our goal is it's a droving festival. We're not going to take from the Stockman's Hall of Fame in Longreach. We're going to create our own." Then I looked at what all the old drovers did, like camp down the river, so our first festival was down on the river. We did lots of things that revolved around that.

'Bronco branding was important. Everyone looked at this girl who's a schoolteacher and said "What does she know about bronco branding?" but I'm an avid reader and I grew up in the Territory, so I was sure it was important.'

That first year, they had no way of knowing how successful the event would be, but they had to prepare for hundreds to turn up. In a town with a population of less than 200, it was all hands on deck.

'Everyone just took a role. You can't think, "Someone else is going to do it."'

Some of the challenges were quite novel.

The first year, my husband – who's still my husband – I said [to him], "Can you build a stage?"'

For someone whose career was in the trucking industry, the correct answer may have been, 'Don't know. Never tried.' However, he was soon pleasantly surprised to discover that he could.

One of the most important elements in the success of the first event was word of mouth.

'I was given a painting and I looked on the back of it and there was a thing from Jack Gardiner. And I tracked Jack Gardiner down. He was a journalist on the Sunshine Coast. So I rang Jack, who then got onto Bruce Simpson, who then got onto . . . And all of a sudden we had a hundred drovers. Whoosh! Just like that. It was really amazing how that came together.'

As well as the drovers, 600 other people turned up who had heard about the festival and wanted to be part of it.

It was immediately clear that it couldn't be a one-off. The strong response from the drovers meant that whether it was a reunion, a celebration or part of something larger, the event had to continue. A committee was formed to organise the next year and start looking at developing a venue to support it.

Eventually, a 30-hectare site was secured on the eastern side of the town and an information hut was built, as well as a permanent stage, bronco branding yards, a shed for a permanent exhibition and a house for a caretaker. Toilet and shower blocks were constructed and camping areas were set out. And it was all done by volunteers, many of them drovers. A few years ago I did a bit of fencing and whipper-snipping myself.

Says Aidan, 'The second or third year we really got serious about applying for government funding. That was a lot of hard work. I think we met anybody who would meet us. State Development were really good. They gave us lots of ideas.

'[Country singer] John Williamson was [saying to us] "great, doing the right thing". He used to come through and go fishing out at [adjacent station] Rocklands. He came in and gave us lots of stuff. Posters and stuff like that.

'This is something that, if we could get massive funding, could really be a great icon for Australia.'

Out in front of the main stage, the value of what Aidan was talking about was made clear when the master of ceremonies got the assembled drovers to talk about some of their experiences. Some were reluctant to speak; a few weren't accustomed to talking at the best of times. Fortunately, there were plenty of drovers who had tales to share.

For someone who'd just spent three days driving to get here, this was what I was hoping for. Pull up a chair, open your ears and let living outback legends take you back to the larger-than-life times that shaped them. And that, indirectly, shaped me and the couple of hundred people sitting in the shade of the big marquee.

Terry Prowson started droving as a kid.

'My family were drovers; grandfather did droving. Then I did a couple of years as a stock inspector in the Territory and was tangled up with a few of these old drovers from 1968 to 1988. I was born in Derby during the war. My grandfather was buried at Wave Hill [in the Northern Territory]. My father was part of the history. I enjoy coming out here, but nowadays I like to have all of my horses under my right foot.'

Keith Luscombe started droving as a youngster in 1956.

'I worked with Stan Fowler, Ian McBean, Dave Allworth and a few others. Did four trips from Auvergne down to Brighton Downs and South Galway with old Stan. It used to take five weeks to walk the horses out. Then all that way to South Galway and on to Quilpie and then back again. It's gotta be probably eight or nine months.

'The boss drover was me family. It was all male, not like it is now. Might have been more drovers then if there was more females.

'Quite often a couple of men would leave and you'd be stuck with just the three of you with probably 1250 head of cattle and about forty or fifty horses, so you had to work then.'

When he was asked if the youth of today could replicate such a feat, his answer wasn't a predictable disparagement of the younger generation.

'I suppose they would. Well they're over bronco branding there and they're still working on the properties, still working horses.'

Jeff Hill went droving around 1952. He reckoned the country around Camooweal was easy to drove in.

'I was down in the scrub country between Clermont and Charters Towers, six years. Fairly short trips, but because they were short, your cattle were never broken in properly. You had to watch the cattle all the time. One thing I remember was that's when I learnt to drink rum. The camps were dry but when you knocked off you used to have one or two. You always had a little bottle in case of snake bite.'

Women have been and still are part of the droving scene. The best known, perhaps, was the late Edna Zigenbine, a supporter of the Drover's Camp. Eileen Lanagan is another. In 1940 she became the first woman to drove cattle down the toughest and most remote stock route in the world, the Canning. Among the personal items she was allowed to take were a pot of face cream, a diary and a revolver. (My book *The Drovers* [2010] goes into more detail about Lanagan.)

At Camooweal, Ruth Bradshaw was one of the women drovers present. She'd done a bit of droving with her family.

'I did three-day trips, taking cattle into Roma Saleyards. Nothing like these fellas out here. It was droving but not like this out here. About 1952, '53, '54. It was good. It was fun but hard work.'

Not all drovers enjoyed the experience. One such was John 'The Pom' Flint.

'I did a few trips with Pic Willetts and them. I arrived in Australia in 1955. I learned to ride in Grenfell, New South Wales. Got thrown off a few horses The thing about drovin', there was no romance in it. It was seventeen hours a bloody day. Talk about it now – oh dear, so tired, I used to get behind the cattle and put me head on the horse and go to sleep. Had to. You just can't keep it up.'

Had he dreamed of becoming a drover when he came out from England?

'No dream,' he said. 'A nightmare.'

Others may not have had romantic notions either, but had been enriched by the experience. One of them, Ian McBean, now a pastoralist who has been made a member of the Order of Australia for services to the cattle industry, spent ten years in Camooweal, almost all of them droving.

'I had the good fortune to come to Alice Springs in the early 1950s and I worked for a couple of old-time drovers, Don and George Booth, for a couple of years, and Max Shepley. I was taught the art then I got a plant [the horses and equipment required to run a droving operation] and put in the next ten years drovin'.

'Keith Luscombe just told ya he did a couple of trips out to Auvergne. We come back into Avon and down to Headingly. Before that I drove off Brunette down to Quilpie, a couple of times down there, also a couple of times into Mount Isa.

'I've got no chance of doing it again. I'm too bloody old and crippled up. It was a terrific life and I did it because I loved it. You learned every day of your life, the skills of workin' stock and stock management. You never stop learnin'.'

Another drover who loved the life was Ben Trindall. His experiences echoed Shannon Warnest's comments in chapter four about the way learning has changed. Ben got his education in the school of hard knocks.

'I was born here in Camooweal just out on a station called Herbertvale. I've been ringin' around here all me life and drovin' and enjoyed every damn minute of it. I'm eighty-five now and if I could go back drovin' tomorrow, I would, because I really enjoyed it. If I could, I'd do nothin' else.

'I never grew up here. I went to school for twelve months in my life and then I was back out ringin'. I went with me dad. He took me out to Lake Nash because he worked out there for years and I was with him. I started out on the stations when I was twelve and grew up in the stock camp with all the old dark people in those days. They never talked much but they kicked my arse and flogged me and made me learn whatever they told me. If they told you something, you had to do it or they would flog you. And it never done me harm. It done me the world of good because I learnt a lot about cattle and horses, because I've been breakin' in horses for years.

'When we come in from out west it'd take about twelve weeks to come in, but mostly we drove from here with the Finlays and Pedwells and all them. You'd take the cattle from Morestone to Dajarra and truck 'em [load them onto cattle trains], or to Kajabbi and truck 'em, but that only took about three weeks. We always enjoyed it and come back, and you might do four trips or five trips a year. That was your work and you grew up and did it otherwise the old fella would give you . . .'

While most other drovers hadn't ridden for years, or only rarely, Ben was still in the saddle. In fact, he'd ridden a horse the night before, in the parade in the main street of Camooweal.

Errol Connolly regarded himself as a short-distance drover,

but he had managed to spend more than a year going nowhere.

'I started droving in the mid-fifties when I should have been at school more. Mostly going to the truckin' yards: the nearest truckin' yards or a bit further. The longest distance was the one that came from out of the bottom end of Queensland and went down as far as Wodonga in Victoria, and that was about nine months it took to go down there. When I left school in '58 I did a bit of drovin' with other people: still only short, a couple of hundred miles or so.

'The longest distance droving I done was in the eighties. We had young cattle on the road. It was going around in circles, anywhere I could find grass, thirteen months straight. That's a lot of mornings to get up and saddle your horse and go again, hoping it might rain. And it did rain after thirteen months and I was able to return home.'

Like a lot of his generation, Wally Sanderson was only in his early teens when he gave up sitting behind a school desk in favour of sitting behind a mob of cattle.

'I started to ride a pony at four, and we rode to school most of the time. I just loved horses and cattle. I started droving when I was about fourteen. A fella that wasn't that far from home rung my dad and wanted to know if he had a spare man there to help him unload a mob of cattle off a train and take them out on a trip that was only four days. We pulled the mob off the train, settled them down, so that was an experience. First big trip.

'As I grew older we did quite a lot of droving one way or another. We didn't do the big jobs, like the other fellas. I was more like a jackaroo, but we used to drove the cattle from Eidsvold for about a week, with packs, so we got to know what droving was all about.

'I rode about six months ago. Visiting rellies and went mustering and I was in the ute and I said, "I'd just love to get back on a horse." I hadn't been on a horse for the best part of ten years. Then young Peter [Wally's son] picked me out a young horse, his son got on 'im and trotted 'im around the yard, and I got up there and it felt good. A bit like Benny, I'd just love to be doin' it again: going places and doing things I shouldn't. I really enjoyed droving of any sort, any sort of stock work, horses. It's been the love of my life.'

While we were enjoying the memories of a way of life that few get to experience today, the drovers also recalled mates and their stories that have long since gone to the grave.

The Drover's Camp has captured some of those memories before they were lost, with a series of recorded interviews. The challenge now is to convert the interviews, which are on analogue tape, into digital files that can be made widely available.

Aidan Day explained: 'When you talk to those old fellas, they all have a story, so we need to make it so people can come and learn, "Yeah, we did do the droving". I'd like to see more displays on how they did it, like set up the camp. There's a lot to do but it takes time, money and people, and that's the hardest part.

'The old drovers have got some very interesting tales when you talk to them. The quietest ones are the ones that have probably done the biggest and the most.'

Her comment prompted me to mention the loss of Charlie Rayment, one of the long-time supporters of the Drover's Camp. He was still riding and competing in the bronco branding in Camooweal a couple of years before his death, in 2013, at the age of eighty-eight.

'Ah, Charlie,' she sighed. 'He was my . . . he was bronco branding. When I got onto Jack Gardiner, we said, "We're going to do bronco branding."

'And he said, "You've got to get onto Charlie."

'Well, Charlie came every year. Always there. And Clargie Saltmere. At eighty-something still throwing himself on a horse. And Charlie was eighty-three. When you see those types of men doing that you think, "Amazing. Really strong, good, salt of the earth."

'Charlie was a stalwart. He was here the first year. They're amazing men: quiet, unassuming, and get on with it.'

That night, the Saturday of the festival, Anne Kirkpatrick and her family were performing as the headline act in the musical entertainment. Anne is the daughter of country singer Slim Dusty and a major force in music in her own right.

The festival has always attracted big names, including John Williamson, Ted Egan and Sara Storer. Many perform because they understand and support what the Drover's Camp is trying to do, but Sara has a much closer connection. Says Aidan: 'Sara Storer used to work for us. Her best friend, Faye, worked on Mittiebah Station and we knew her really well.

'And Faye said, "Can I work with you in the off season, the wet season?"

'We said, "Yeah."

'Then she came to me and said, "My best friend, who just finished teachers' college, can't get a job. Can she come and flip burgers?"

'So I said, "Yep."

'We always needed staff. So Sara turned up and she was as quiet as a mouse. At that stage, I had my daughter and we had a little two-year-old there, my granddaughter, and Sara used to sit up the back and Courtney was on the big rock and she'd sing, very quietly. She'd sing nursery rhymes. The only time she got a little bit vocal was when she went to the pub and had a skinful.

'In the time she was with us, Old Harry – her first song was *Buffalo Bill* [based on Harry] – well Old Harry and her were really good mates. She wrote a lot of songs while she was here. Really, really lovely. Then, as I do, I got her a job teaching in Katherine.

'I said, "You know, you've just done three years of teachers' college. You are going to put that into work."

'"Oh."

'I used to teach in the Territory. I rang a friend who was in charge of Katherine. I said, "I've got a young girl here, very talented, very good with children."

'I faxed all the paperwork through and he rang back, had a talk to her, and said, "Can you get her up here?"

'So we stuck her in a truck and sent her to Katherine. The rest is history. Faye, her best mate, had done twelve months of nursing. Same with her. Sent her to Townsville, made her finish her nursing. So we've had a lot of interesting people in Camooweal.'

Not for the first time in this book, I'm being told how 'legends' of the outback have inspired younger generations. Sara has gone on to become one of our finest singer/songwriters, and a genuine voice of Australia, not just the outback.

Aidan ran the festival from 1997 until 2001, although she actually left Camooweal in December 2000.

'It really broke my heart. I wasn't ready to go. Once you've come across the Thomson [near Longreach], you're always going to come back. We were from the Territory but we ended up going over to the Queensland coast.

'I said, "Now that we're retired, we'll be able to go and do things", but those that came after us have done an amazing job. They took it on.'

Subsequent presidents of the Drover's Camp committee included Bill Petrie, a former Vestey's manager. He organised acquiring the lease to the current site and found the house that's been put on it. When he became ill, he handed over to Liz Flood, who ran and developed the place for eight years.

The current president is Paul Finlay who, with his partner Ellen, has been involved in the Drover's Camp 'for yonks'. Paul and Ellen have connections to Camooweal that go back over a century.

'My grandfather came out here in 1882. In 1884 he was the first settler and Grandma Fin was the first child born here in 1884. My grandmother was the first kid born at Camooweal. Finlay Park is named after her.'

His family were involved in droving on his and his wife's side. Paul maintains that he only did short trips himself.

'It's good to keep it going,' he says. 'All the previous presidents did a mighty job to keep it going because Camooweal was a big drovers' town.'

While there have been concerns that a lot of old drovers are passing away, the experience at the Drover's Camp is that they've got more drovers than ever.

'They've come from all over. Not only drovers but people who were stock inspectors, cooks and anyone who's had anything to do with droving, that's got a droving story. One old bloke, when he's up where he lives, he's a former station manager. When he comes to Camooweal, he's a drover.'

As previous presidents have found, one of the greatest challenges is staffing a museum and festival that's all volunteers.

He acknowledges the support of government, especially Mount Isa Council, noting that now the mayor is the daughter of a drover, there might be even more help. What he needs more of, though, is drovers who can work at the museum.

'Drovers take tourists around,' he says, referring to the presentation of the exhibits. 'Tom Green's been doing a lot, I've been doing some, but Stumpy Adams has been sick, Geoff Simpson isn't well enough to come. You've gotta have someone who can explain it to 'em. If you just look around, it's not worth ten bucks, but if you get Tom to explain it to you, then it is worth ten bucks.

'Tom's working his guts out. It can be two hours. I'm trying to line up a couple of other blokes. The main part is when the tourists are here: May, June and July. That's when we're busy. Everyone wants to come for the festival but we need them right through the season.'

Tom Green, who's been with the Drover's Camp for much of its existence, is running back and forth but takes a moment to echo Paul's remarks.

'I do a two-hour tour but I don't like the sound of my own voice. I like it when people ask questions. I'm not like the big-time drovers; just a few small trips.'

There's no question that a lot of people, from a range of backgrounds and age groups, appreciate what's at Camooweal. It gives people a chance to appreciate real outback legends before they're gone. They can rub shoulders and swap yarns with living history.

Near where we were camped, a family and their friends from South Africa had a blazing camp fire. They worked in the mines at Mount Isa but came out to Camooweal whenever they had visitors 'so they can see real Australian history'. Some of their friends told them it was the best-value experience in the outback.

Then, of course, there are the serendipitous moments that are beyond value. On our last night in Camooweal, we were having a throw-everything-in-the-pot dinner with Dave Allworth and his partner when Paul Finlay popped over to give us a tip. 'Bob Savage and a couple of the others are singing some of the old songs over at the kitchen.'

Bob, aged ninety, was another of the outback legends I much admired. I remember him telling me for my book *The Drovers* about a time he was droving and the mob was settled for the night. All was well until they rushed [or stampeded, if your knowledge of droving derives solely from American cowboy movies] – and rushed. And rushed. Bob and the other drovers tried everything to head them but nothing could pull them up. They rushed all night. It was only when the sun came up that they stopped, put their heads down and started feeding as if nothing had happened.

Bob wanted me to do a book about his life – or possibly three. One about his life as a jockey in the eastern states with legends such as Bruce Smith and George Moore; a second about his experience trying to grow bananas in Broome; and the third about Suplejack, the station he pioneered in the middle of the Tanami Desert, 500 miles (730 kilometres) from the Alice Springs post office. It's on my 'to-do' list.

After dinner, we went around to the camp kitchen to see if they were still singing. It was late, but they were. Song after song: some recognisable, others from an entirely different era. Sometimes they could play the whole song through. Sometimes they remembered just a few bars. Tom Green was singing along, and Paul Finlay and his wife, Ellen, and Bob's daughter, Lette Cook.

At one point Bob broke off and said, 'I haven't played the harmonica for thirty years', but it was as if he'd never put it down. It was the end of the festival and everyone was tired, but they sang long into the night. They were still singing when we left and went back to our swags with the songs of the old-time drovers echoing in our ears.

Leg Eight

After so much driving for this project, the next leg was a welcome relief. For once, the next person I wanted to meet was coming to me. In fact, she was already in Camooweal for the race meeting that was held in conjunction with the Drover's Camp Festival. So all we had to do was drive from the Camp to the race track. If we'd wanted, we could have walked it.

Before we did, though, we did a bit of exploring around Camooweal. When we went to have some lunch on the Georgina River, we discovered that, in a way, Camooweal is still a cross-roads. Now, though, the drovers have been replaced by wandering travellers of a different kind – grey nomads. All along the river where the drovers once camped, there were now four-wheel drives with caravans and camper trailers, motorhomes and RVs. There were dozens of nomads dotted along a couple of kilometres of waterfront, camping for free, having first spent a sizeable chunk of their kids' inheritance on their mobile accommodation. Apart from the quarter-million-dollar price tags for some of it, the set-up was like old times.

The Georgina was pretty idyllic. Its coolabah-lined waterholes were thronged with birdlife – brolgas, ducks and waterhens – swimming and wading among the water lilies. Who could blame the nomads for pulling up on the riverbank for an extended stay?

7.

The League of Extraordinary Women

The Barkly Women's Group
(1995–)

Head west from Camooweal on the Barkly Highway for 261 kilometres and, with another 187 kilometres before you reach Tennant Creek, you're pretty close to the middle of nowhere. Conveniently, the Barkly Homestead Roadhouse is located there, so you can refuel your vehicle and get a burger or pie, as most travellers and long-distance truck drivers do.

It's just like roadhouses anywhere else in the outback, except for twice a year when, if you're there at the right time, you'll be able to witness an extraordinary scene. Instead of grey nomads in T-shirts and thongs, and truckies in high-vis shirts and work boots, there'll be dozens and dozens of women, of all ages, in their best frocks and high heels. There'll be stalls selling clothing, jewellery, crafts and food. There'll be people doing hairdressing and makeup. There'll be other women talking about everything from health care to the latest book they read.

Sometimes there'll be as many as sixty or seventy women. This in a place where you haven't passed a single house for more than a hundred kilometres on that long, lonely highway.

Who are they? Where have they all come from?

They're members of what could be the largest women's net-work in the world. Forget the phone or the internet. These women drive and fly to the roadhouse from across a region that spans 500 000 square kilometres. That's twice the size of Victoria. It's the United Kingdom and New Zealand combined. They call themselves the Barkly Women's Group.

'Women come out of the woodwork,' says Danielle Doyle, the group's convenor since 2010. 'Some travel eight hours to come, ten hours. The minimum people probably travel is one or two hours.

'Women have travelled from as far away as Alice Springs to come,' says Bernadette Burke, convenor from 2002 to 2010. 'They've travelled from as far away as up on the flood plain near Darwin. So it is a wide expanse of country that they travel. A lot of them have to have an overnight stay before they even reach there. It's lovely once they get there just to see them be so happy to be with other women and be away from the day-to-day activities and having something new to think about.'

It may seem like remarkable behaviour, but not to anyone who has even a passing understanding of the challenges of living in the outback. At one time, isolation was the main issue, as poignantly described by Henry Lawson in *The Drovers' Wife*, a short story about a woman left to fend for herself in a remote bush shack.

In the 1920s, the formation of the Country Women's Association was in part a response to that isolation, with one of the founders painfully recounting how she'd visited a woman who hadn't spoken to anyone of her gender for six months. At the end of the visit the woman tearfully said, 'I feel I cannot let you leave.'

Just a few years later, more tears were shed as the pedal radio, then voice radio, broke down the sense of isolation as never before, with instantaneous communication to many places where messages and news formerly took weeks to arrive.

In modern times, to all appearances, outback stations are neither isolated nor lonely. There's a constant circulation of staff and contractors to carry out the myriad jobs required to breed, feed, water, fence, muster and transport stock. However, the cattle industry is still a man's world and as the song goes, 'Sometimes it's hard to be a woman'. Or, at least, it was.

Says Bernadette, 'There's a lot of women coming into the industry. In the Northern Territory the CEO of the Northern [Territory] Cattlemen's Association is a female [Tracey Hayes], which is a good thing. I know the Consolidated Pastoral Company have their first female station manager and AACo [where Bernadette's husband is the company's general manager, pastoral] have their first female station manager [Kelly Ennis]. So they're very big steps for the industry.

'Women are generally becoming more confident and are generally following their passion. Before I think they might have been a little bit afraid to speak up. I don't know that it's our women's days that are doing that, but women are definitely more confident and are taking on more of those roles.

'In the Kimberley they've just got their Cattlemen's Association; they've got a female CEO as well [Catherine Marriott]. So I think there's a lot of women going into the agricultural field and doing a good job of it.'

'I always thought Ladies' Day was a little bit of navel-gazing: taking the time to actually have a look at yourself and think a little bit about yourself for twenty-four hours is pretty rare when you're in the bush. Normally you have to think of everyone else.'

My road to the Barkly Women's Group extends back to 2011, when I visited the Barkly Tableland researching my book *Outback Stations* (2012). On Brunette Downs, I'd met and been deeply impressed by Bernadette Burke, wife of the station's then manager (and general manager of AACo's northern stations), Henry.

Bernadette, or 'Bern' as she's known to many in the region, was described to me by a number of people as 'the mother of the Barkly'. However, it's a line that provokes snorts of derision from Bernadette every time I bring it up. She regards herself as being like anyone else on the Barkly who's simply good at getting on with things.

Still, when it came to this project, she was an automatic contender. I hoped with a mix of arm-twisting and cunning manoeuvring, I'd get my 'mother of the Barkly' story. The spanner in the ointment, though, was that Bernadette was no longer on the Barkly. With the opening of AACo's abattoir in Katherine, the Top End town had become the hub of the company's northern operations, so she and Henry had transferred there.

Bernadette was happy to focus on the Barkly Women's Group, though, in particular how it was part of the changes that are underway in the Barkly and the cattle industry generally.

The group was founded in 1995 by Carmel Wagstaff, wife of the previous manager of Brunette Downs. Her foresight was matched by the passion of the women back then to have a day for themselves. Originally there was just one women's day per year, held on the verandah of the Brunette Downs Guest House. The Barkly may have been the first outback region to hold such days, although other regions (such as Western Australia's Kimberley and Queensland's Channel Country) now hold them as well.

Says Bernadette: 'Carmel was always a leader in working towards better opportunities and recognition for women in the bush. She did a lot for women in the bush during her time with AACo, while living at Brunette. She continued doing that during her time as human resources manager in AACo Brisbane head office.'

When Carmel and her husband were transferred to AACo's head office in Brisbane, Bernadette, the wife of the new station manager at Brunette, 'inherited' the job of convening the women's days.

'It was part of the package. I was asked by Carmel if I would continue on the role of coordinating the Barkly Ladies' Day. Due to the overwhelming support and success of the day, it was only a couple of years after I took over the role that we moved to holding two ladies' days per year.'

The events also moved to the Barkly Homestead Roadhouse.

Bernadette sees the group's primary function as providing an opportunity to bring the women of the area together to network, support each other, form friendships and spend a day with other women.

'The stations on the Barkly Tablelands are large land masses, mostly owned by corporates. Therefore the management of the stations and the staff on the stations changes regularly; there's always new people moving to the Barkly each year. You don't have a town as such on the Barkly, so the Barkly Homestead is the most central meeting point for all station women to get together.

"It's also a day where childcare is provided and the mothers have a rare opportunity to have someone else looking after their kids, while they enjoy some time out for themselves, some uninterrupted adult conversation.'

Guest speakers are invited to present on topics ranging from women's health and mental health to laughter therapy and the latest bestsellers. Representatives from a range of community services in Tennant Creek attend, as do a fair number of women from the town.

Says Bernadette: 'During my time as coordinator I was always on the lookout for interesting people to bring something new into the women's lives, something that was unique to what we were experiencing.'

The value of the day has been recognised with sponsorship to help run the event. That means it doesn't have to rely on government assistance, which is scarcer and scarcer the further you are from the centres of power. And the Barkly is a terribly long way from the centres of power.

More importantly, each day is eagerly awaited by the women of the Barkly.

'It's a day where the young jillaroos from the stock camps frock up and don their heels and discard their jeans and work-shirts and hats for a day of glamour.'

And not just the jillaroos.

'During my time on the Barkly, the thing I loved about it, and always will, is that everyone is treated as an equal. There are no airs and graces on the Barkly Tablelands. It's a unique place to live and one of the most caring and compassionate communities I have ever lived in. It doesn't matter if you're the grader driver's wife or the manager's wife. We're all treated as equals on the Barkly.'

Bernadette's comment touches on one of the most important functions of the Barkly Women's Group: support. In the outback, as several chapters of this book show, times can be very tough indeed. Nevertheless, it can take courage to admit you're struggling with the demands of a staff of twenty to fifty people, or raising a young family, or living a few states apart from your own family.

'These are just a few issues that women face regularly,' Bernadette says, 'having the courage to ask for help and share your story and also, when you can, to be the person to listen and offer advice. Being a mentor and support person to someone new to the area was something that I enjoyed during my time on the Barkly. It was a privilege and a pleasure to be able to share my knowledge and be of assistance to someone who asked for HELP.'

The capital letters are Bernadette's.

Sometimes, organising the women's days themselves, or attending them, can be the challenge. Weather can be a factor, as it was to prove in getting to meet face to face with Bernadette. The closest we got was about 500 kilometres of impassable roads. We ended up talking on the phone and emailing.

By then, I'd pretty much given up on a 'mother of the Barkly' profile. That was mainly because Bernadette wouldn't have a bar of it, but also because I'd found out that June Andrew was right back in chapter two when she said: 'I think all outback people are inspiring'. In other words, I'd met Bernadette's successor.

Says Bernadette: 'Danielle is young, vibrant, full of fun, and has put her own stamp on the Ladies' Days during her time as coordinator. She is more savvy with social media and has promoted the day through her blog and other social media networks.'

Danielle is Danielle Doyle. Mother of the Barkly? Not so much. For starters, her blog is written under the pen name of Miss Chardy – 'Chardy' being short for chardonnay. In her blog (misschardy.com), she discloses that her husband, Martin Doyle, manager of Napco's Mittiebah station, refers to her as an 'inside cat'. Her blog juxtaposes a photo of how she sees herself (glamorous 1950s housewife posing confidently in her kitchen) with her reality (shorts, T-shirt, sunhat and boots, out in a paddock somewhere). And when I ask her about her relationship with horses, she says, 'No, no, no. You lost me at "hor".'

We're pretty much talking the last kind of person you'd expect to find out on the Barkly. I couldn't help thinking of Sally Brown's line from chapter three, 'the hostess with the mostess'. There was, however, one quality she shared with Bernadette. She makes a lasting impression.

We had arranged to rendezvous at the Camooweal race track, where the town's annual races were held in conjunction with the Drover's Festival. Danielle was thirty-something, with straight blonde hair, and had a style that, if it wasn't quite *McLeod's Daughters*, was one of the cousins. She also had a get-on-with-it directness that suggested if I didn't make a decent impression in the first minute, I'd be shown the shortest route out of Camooweal, and thanks for coming.

Danielle grew up in the central New South Wales town of Mudgee but always looked forward to moving to Sydney. That is, until she got there.

'So many people and just so busy and on a packed train every day. I was, "Oh, get me outta here."

She did a year of business college then worked for two years, until a friend told her about being a governess. Keen to leave the rat-race, in 2000 she headed for the back of Bourke for a year. When her time was up, she planned to return to country New South Wales, but then she and her friend saw an opportunity to go to the Northern Territory.

'I'd led a very sheltered life in Mudgee and had basically not even been out of New South Wales. So I went up to the Territory, drove my little Corolla to Alroy Downs, 50 kilometres north of the Barkly Homestead, and governessed there. A few months later I met my husband here at the Camooweal Campdraft, my first ever campdraft, on that dance floor.'

She could actually point at the spot where she met him. He was then an overseer on Alexandria Station, next door to Alroy.

'The rest is history. I did a year and a half at Alroy and then a bookkeeper's job came up over at Alex so I moved over there with Marty. Then we moved down to Kynuna with Napco – we got the manager's job down there – and in 2008 we came back up to Mittiebah and we've been here ever since. My husband has been with Napco since he left school.'

They'd driven down to Mudgee and married in 2004. The first of three boys arrived a year later.

'I've got a five-, a nine- and an eleven-year-old – all boys. Had all of them down in Dubbo. I go and hang out with Mum and then go over to Dubbo and have the baby. It works out well.'

She encountered the Barkly Women's Day shortly after arriving at Alroy Downs.

'I went down with Sue, my boss, and I've only missed a few since then. Even when we were at Kynuna [800 kilometres east] I'd come back up for it. If it wasn't for that – that was when Carmel was still running it – that's how I met friends. There's two a year and we'd all look forward to going over there, getting dressed up, meeting new people, catching up with old friends. Sometimes it's the only chance you get to catch up. We don't really live that close but we kind of do, but sometimes it's the only chance you get to catch up with each other.

'The year gets busy with campdrafts or mustering or when the kids start school then you've got school weeks. Everyone is doing their own thing and it just fills up, there's not a spare weekend.'

Two of the people Danielle met through the group were its convenors, Carmel and Bernadette.

'I first saw Carmel when I was a guvvy back in 2001. That was at the first one and the second one and I thought, "Wow." I was twenty-two, and I used to look at her and think, "Oh, my gosh, you're amazing. Imagine getting up there and speaking in front of all these people."

'I've gotten to know Carmel – there's my friend Shelly [she points] – who is good friends with Carmel's daughter, Megan. We went to Megan's wedding a couple of years ago and I've gotten to know Carmel a bit better through Meegs. She's so wise, so calm. You ask anyone who's worked up at Brunette for Carmel. They'd tell you the same thing.

'You can be saying, "Oh, my kids, they've been so naughty or they've been this . . ."

'And she would just be very calm. "Oh, they'll be fine. They're only children."

'She's a really lovely lady.

'I got to know Bernadette when she took over. I just love Bernadette. I always tell her she's my secret mentor and I think the world of her.

'As she even says, "Oh, I could talk to anyone. It wouldn't matter if it was the Queen of England. I just talk to them."

'And she can. She can make anyone feel good about them-selves. Bernadette and I are the same personality type. We both love people but the way she deals with staff – she's really good dealing with people, delegating or organising. And she's always happy.

'They [Carmel and Bernadette] worked on stations for years. They managed Brunette for many years – I don't know if it was twenty years – and that's a big place to manage and you see a lot of staff and you deal with a lot of people and, yeah, they would have seen it all and had to deal with everything.'

In 2010, Bernadette succeeded in convincing Danielle to take over the job of organising the days. When I asked why she was chosen, Danielle said, 'Oh, because I'm a wild social butterfly.'

We both laughed, but it wasn't a bad answer.

'Well, I do like a party. I used to look at Bernadette and think, "Oh, imagine being able to get up there and do that. How does she do that?"'

'And then here I am. How did I end up doing that?'

Maybe it wasn't as hard as she thought.

'Fake it till you make it,' she laughingly admits. 'Don't let people know how nervous you are.'

It turns out her social skills are a valuable pre-requisite for the position.

'I like to bring people together and make them feel comfortable. I hate for someone to turn up there and think, "Oh, these women are very cliquey." We're just a big bunch of friendly women; it doesn't matter who you are.'

Danielle is also very savvy when it comes to social media. The group has a Facebook page and people are encouraged to share notices of upcoming women's days widely. They're also emailed to all the stations on the Barkly. There's normally one in May and another in October. None are held over the hotter months, as much of the Barkly experiences a wet season and effectively closes down.

'We were really lucky in May this year: we had about seventy women, which is a really good turnout. Sometimes it can be thirty, forty, fifty – it just depends on what the stations are doing. If they're mustering and they're busy, some people mightn't be able to come, but normally it's about fifty, sixty, seventy.

'Anybody who has a hobby or a craft, anything that anyone has to sell, they can just bring it and set up a table. I have necklaces that I make so I take them and set up a table. Sally Town from Helen Springs Station, she's got a company called Gumnut Designz – beautiful shirts and skirts – she brings them. I've got another friend who does necklaces and clothes. These women, often they might be jillaroos or they work, work, work, but they don't get a chance to get off the place and go shopping. So it's just a good chance for them to have a little browse and do a bit of shopping. We had a lady with a skincare range there in May. We had a hairdresser, a lady from up at Borroloola [500 kilometres north].

'I'm like, "Oh, bring your stuff and do some haircuts."'

While there are only two women's days a year, when someone needs help, the women's network they reinforce swings into action. That was the case in early 2016 for the mother of a newborn [Thomas] with extremely serious health problems.

'They've left the Barkly,' Danielle says, 'they're over in Cloncurry. Poor baby, he was only born in December [2015] but he's in Lady Cilento Hospital [the children's hospital in Brisbane; he's since been allowed home], she's been there with him since February and it's gonna be a bit of a long haul. It's costly and she's got a one- and a three-year-old still at home.

'With our day in May, I got up and told everybody about them – she was a long-time resident and did a lot for the Barkly – so we did a bit of a fundraiser for her. Another of her friends started up a Facebook page, the Thomas Walsh Support Network. At the Brunette Races [held in June], Bernadette and some other women organised an auction and raised about $17 000 for this family.

'Krystal [a friend of Cindy, Thomas's mother] had organised a Facebook sale to raise money. She got lots of people to donate gear. So I thought, "I'll write a blog post to try and make everybody aware that this sale is happening and tell them what's happened to Cindy."

'I have a lot of readers down in Brisbane and that area. I thought, "If someone could pop in or bring her a cup of coffee or give her a voucher for a day spa or something so that Cindy could just go and have a bit of down time."

'People are so generous. They're happy to help. So I did this blog post and put it on Facebook and thought, "Can you share this, guys, with . . .?"

'Well, oh my Lordy, I can't even remember what it was but it was shared something like 200 times and it had 50 000 views.'

Danielle didn't think anyone was reading her blog.

'I thought, "Well that just shows you."

'And my readers were, like, "Oh, we really wanna help this family."

'So I had the bank details so they could donate or if they just wanted to pop in and see Cindy. I went and saw her the other week down in Brisbane and she just does the same thing every day. Goes in, poor little boy's attached to tubes and stuff. I don't know how she does it every day.'

———

The Miss Chardy blog is another surprising aspect of Danielle's busy life. It was one of the first things I found about her when I started my research. It's well-written, sometimes humorous, sometimes heartfelt, and gives a real sense of life on an outback station.

'I started that at the beginning of 2014. I'd never really read a blog and then my good friend Felicity – who's lived up here for years and years and years and has probably never missed a ladies' day in her life – got me onto this blog called 'BabyMac'. It's just so honest and didn't sugar-coat anything, didn't make out she was some domestic goddess mother of the year.

'I just needed something real. At that time I think I'd been on the station for three months without going anywhere. December, January, February. I might have been the only girl on the station, because everyone had gone away and there was just me, my husband and kids and a few other blokes. I was just starting to go batty because I'm an extrovert. I need to get out and see people. So then I started reading this BabyMac, and the posts I was reading, it was like she was writing them for me.

'And then I thought, "Oh, maybe I could write a blog."

'I had no idea what I was doing. Still don't. You can google it: how to write a blog.'

It wasn't like Danielle could enrol in a course at the Barkly TAFE.

'I fumbled my way through and thought, "Yep, no, I'm gonna do this."

'I thought I had to research everything and do it perfectly, and in the end I was, like, "You know what, I've just got to figure it out as I go."

'Started with one post and thought, "Oh, nobody will read this."'

'I started a Facebook page, too, and I think Bernadette was one of my first likes. "Oh, somebody's read it. Oh, fifty people." Now I think I've got 3774 likes.

'At the start I don't really know what I was writing – I'd probably go back and think they were pretty terrible. Now I do a lot of blog posts about what people do on the station. I've done one about the grader driver, what he does, and photos, then one about our bore runner. It might be one about what's happening – my boring day on the station or my kids are driving me mental – all different things.

'I've got a lot of country readers. There's quite a few from Western Australia, farm ladies, but all over. There's also city ladies – Sydney, Brisbane – but a fair chunk are country people. I've got a few overseas, too, from America, Canada. There's one lady in Africa I think, there's New Zealand, there's Europe.

'I've got one lady, Heidi from Missouri, but I think she lives on a ranch, and she's one who's always like, "Oh, great read, Miss Chardy, loved it, ra ra ra."

'Sometimes I'll ask her what she's doing: "How's things over in Missouri?"

'And she'll tell me. There's another lady from up in Canada, I think she's an ex-pat living in Canada.

'A lot of people have their own blog as well. I've actually made some really good friends. I just caught up with two of my blogging friends down in Brisbane. I go to a ProBlogger conference; I've only met them through that but I count them as really good friends now. One of them – [who lives] where my son is going to boarding school next year – Nikki, her blog's called Styling You. Her little boy started there this year so we're gonna be school mums. It's just such a small world. And they're amazing. They're like, "Oh, if Tom needs to come out on the weekend."'

'Of course, to have a blog, you have to have the internet,' I say, knowing that in the outback, internet speeds and data allowances are a constant frustration.

'Yeah,' Danielle laughs. 'Mmm. The internet's a bit dodgy because at the moment we're on-peak and off-peak. Well, we've just switched to Sky Muster [a new internet satellite] and it is a bit faster, but I generally get up at five in the morning to do my blog post because it's fast, the internet is reliable. I think your peak kicks in at maybe six or seven, so I get that one hour of internet where I can upload photos quick, because otherwise it takes forever.

'We were the sixth house to have this new Sky Muster installed but there were teething issues with that. We were without internet for about two-and-a-half weeks. We just think, "Oh, that's just how it is", but it isn't until you read my blog comments saying, "Oh, gosh! Can't believe!"

'People in cities, if they didn't have internet – can you imagine if someone in the middle of Sydney didn't have mobile phone coverage and their internet didn't work?'

It raises the question, what would she do if they took away the internet and the community in the Barkly?

'I think I'd have to move. I'd go batty. I'd probably be depressed. I'd be talking to myself.'

She can't imagine the days when women suffered incredible isolation. No communication at all. No air conditioning, for that matter. Danielle is quite open about the fact that she prefers the comforts of home to the rugged outback life.

'Now that Clancy, my youngest, has started school, I'm getting out more. I've learnt how to drive the Manitou – the loader-thingy. I've started a garden and I'm getting out.

'Somehow all my friends are outdoorsy horsey people. They're all outdoorsy women but they need me to organise their social life – organise a party. They don't want to leave their station or their horses or their house, so they need me to organise the get-togethers for them.'

While the internet allows the Barkly network to extend well beyond the region, and in Danielle's case to the whole planet, it also helps women to stay connected with the region after they move on. Bernadette does just that.

'I don't think you leave the network behind,' she says. 'I feel it's there and I am still friends with so many of those people. Many of those young women that go there still ring me up at different times and ask me things, if they're having troubles with a difficult staff member and things like that. I think it's a good solid network that stays with you.

'We were at Brunette for thirteen years. It went by in a flash, though. We went with a five-year plan and before we knew it, we'd extended that. Once you get busy you don't really focus on getting out of somewhere.

'People used to say, "Do you enjoy it here?"

'And I said, "I haven't really had time to think otherwise. We're still here and we're doing what we're doing."

'When I get back to the Barkly I mostly go back in a work capacity: I'm still a lifetime member of the ABC Amateur Race Club which is held at Brunette. I'm still on the committee for that and help out where I can. I do some HR work and look after some of the injured workers' claims.'

The challenge, after living in a close-knit but far-flung

community, has been adjusting to life in town.

'I had to make a huge adjustment to my life when I left Brunette, after living and working with so many people and being responsible for so many people's health and well-being on a daily basis – making sure everyone was fed and watered. It was a big transition to move into town and just be a two-person family. It's taken me until now, and we're in our third year, to really adapt to it, but, luckily, I'm still involved in the industry through my work and still working for AACo.

'I was never lonely at Brunette but I found it quite lonely moving in here. At Brunette you just walked out your door and there was someone there all the time. I think we [she and husband Henry] are both a bit like that. He's normally got a lot of people around, too, but he's away a lot of the time travelling.'

While Bernadette rejects the notion of being the mother of the Barkly, as well as looking after injured AACo workers and fundraising for Thomas Walsh, she was helping organise the hundredth anniversary celebrations for Headingly Station. However, she wasn't going to be able to get to the Women's Day in November 2016 because of family commitments.

'My children, this year, three of them are having babies. They're all having them in Katherine so I haven't got away too much for the last half of the year. They all come home and live here for the month before they have the baby. I think Henry probably thinks it's a good reason to go away. I think I'll go back next year. I've got no weddings and no babies.'

Back in Camooweal, Danielle talks about how inspiring the previous convenors of the Barkly Women's Group have been, but she doesn't see herself as being in their league.

'How could I ever be like Bernadette and Carmel?' she says. 'I can just type fast. That year at business college paid off. Dad wants his money back but it's paid off.' She laughs.

I persist. Does she aspire to be like them?

'Oh, absolutely. There's a lot of women up here you look at and think, "Yeah, gosh, I'd love to be like that." I just think I'm organising a ladies' day. And you know, Evan, sometimes I think, "Oh, maybe I can't be bothered doing a second ladies' day this year. Nobody's going to come. They're all too busy."

'I think, "I've got to get funding, I feel bad trying to get sponsorship out of people. I feel bad asking people."

'Then Sue – who I also admire, who I used to work for at Alroy – and Robyn Peatling, who used to run Alex, say, "Dan, what you're doing is very important for the community. Don't forget how important it is."

'Because I'm organising it, I forget that it's actually a really important day for the women of the region. I forget that it's really important for mental health, for isolated women, to get out – especially women with little babies – to get off their station. It's a day where they're like, "Right, we're going."

'And a lot of the stations, they put it on their calendar. They know the women are going that day. They're not gonna be mustering. They're going to Barkly Homestead. Sometimes I forget, but without those days I wouldn't have made friends. And I think, "Oh, well, yeah, it actually is really important."'

I suggest that, in a circular way, she's answered my question.

'Have I?' she laughs. 'Like a politician.'

No, like a woman of the Barkly.

Leg Nine

It's one of the privileges of writing books like this that, while most people regard Camooweal as a little fly-speck town you pass through quickly, I'd spent half a week there and been enriched by the experience. Not for the first time and hopefully not for the last.

From there, Michelle and I headed back into Mount Isa, bought enough food and wine for the next week, then headed south. We were bound for Birdsville, 700 kilometres away, but we'd set off at lunchtime and didn't relish covering all that distance in one hit, which would mean driving on unfenced roads at night. So we pulled up in Boulia, 300 kilometres down the track, and spent the night in a motel, much to Michelle's relief.

We noted that rain, and plenty of it, was expected in Birdsville. Around there, 25 millimetres will cut all the roads. The forecast for Thursday, the day before the races, was in the region of 60 millimetres. We reviewed our supplies, contemplating the possibility that we might have to spend an extra few days in a little outback town with a few thousand others. We decided that, between what we had and a few meals from the vendors who would be in town for the Birdsville Races, we'd have enough to cover ourselves if we were stuck for a few days.

Next morning, we poked down the road to Bedourie, had a coffee and microwaved packet pie at the roadhouse, then continued on to Birdsville. I was expecting the road around Lake Machattie to be a chain of pools, as it had been a month before, but it turned out to have been completely remade and ballroom smooth, thanks to the roadworks skills of the Diamantina Shire Council. Further south, there were some new crossings where the water was quite deep. In places, the countryside was pooled with water. There had already been quite a bit of rain. More was coming.

In Birdsville, we went around to the house of former Birdsville policeman Neale McShane. As mentioned earlier, he'd been slated as a potential subject for this book until it was decided he'd make a book in his own right. Neale agreed to do it and together, in just four hectic months, we'd written the colourful story of his adventurous decade on the most remote beat in the country. The plan was to launch the book, *Outback Cop*, on the Wednesday before the 2016 Birdsville Races, the day after Michelle and I arrived.

At the house Neale has bought in the town, he generously gave up his comfortable double bed for us and moved into one of the rooms with a couple of single beds. His son Robbie was also coming out for the races, arriving Thursday (weather permitting), and was going to take the other bedroom. Out in the yard, Bob and Marion, newly installed proprietors of the iconic Hotel Corones in Charleville, had parked their caravan. The following day, bookmaker David 'Crockett' Power and two of his colleagues were arriving, weather permitting. Crockett (the nickname derives from Davy Crockett) was a Charleville celebrity of Neale's acquaintance who'd been swagging in Neale's yard at the races for years. He'd been coming to the races since Prime Minister Malcolm Fraser's visit in 1978.

Birdsville was a great place to work on a book like this, as the Birdsville Races draw people from all over the outback. Three of them were 'legends' I wanted to catch up with. The downside is that, during the races, everyone is too busy to take time out for a yarn. After the races, it's a different story, but then people can be up and gone like smoke.

The next day, the book launch went well. The community hall was filled with people, quite a few of them staff from Fred Brophy's Boxing Troupe, including Fred, and we sold nearly a hundred copies. We'd have sold more, but the weather prediction meant a lot of people with memories of being trapped by floods in 2010 decided not to risk it.

With good cause. It started raining that night; the following day, it really came down. Crockett and his crew made it in. Then the roads closed, meaning Neale's son could only get to Windorah, 400 kilometres east).

The camping areas around town rapidly became quagmires. To make matters worse, towards evening a howling gale blew up, collapsing tents and awnings. Neale's warm, cosy, dry house was buffeted all Thursday night, the noise and shaking keeping us awake. I lay there for some hours thinking how bad it must be for the campers on the town common.

By Friday morning, 50 millimetres had fallen and the races for that day were cancelled. Driving around town, there were scenes of devastation. The marquees for many stallholders had been flattened. Brophy's boxing tent and stage had partially collapsed. Many of the rows of tents for bus tours were rows of bent and broken canvas. Everywhere that wasn't surfaced with asphalt or concrete was mud.

The council and police started evacuating people from the

camping quagmires on the common, directing them to any firm surface they could find in town. Every side street became a campground. Around Neale's house, there were camper trailers, RVs, caravans. When people started lighting camp fires, the place took on the aspect of a refugee camp.

By then, Neale and I had set up a desk in the Information Centre and were selling more copies of *Outback Cop* to people who realised they were going to be stuck for a few days. Dusty Miller let us do the same on the verandah of the Birdsville Bakery that afternoon.

During the day, I managed to speak to Terry Picone (the subject of chapter one) on the phone. I told him we were thinking about him, camped on the common, during the wind and rain the night before.

'Ev,' he said, 'I once had dysentery in Thailand and I remember thinking it was the worst night of my life. Let me tell you. Last night was worse.'

He refused to abandon his camp, though. I told him the good news that, according to the weather bureau's website, from here on, the weather was going to improve. Neither of us thought there was much chance of horse racing. Terry noted that the same thing had happened at Betoota's race meeting (200 kilometres east of Birdsville) the week before, and the council had miraculously managed to get the track back in order in a couple of days.

The trouble was, it was already Friday. The last day they could conceivably hold the Birdsville Races was Sunday, and there was no way they could get the track dry by then. Not only that, quite a few of the horses were still up in Bedourie (200 kilometres north) cut off by the floodwater.

That afternoon, the weather forecast proved correct. The sun came out. The wind started to ease. The water drained away. Unfortunately, the mud was going to take a long time to dry.

On Saturday morning, conditions had improved enough that we could actually drive into the race track. There were a few people camped in the buildings, including the other half of the Odds Couple, Gordo, with his far-less-taciturn wife.

Outback caterer Dogger Dare was there, too. A month or so earlier, there'd been plenty of talk about Dogger selling 1.3 tonnes of chips during the Big Red Bash. He wasn't selling many chips now.

Around the track, Diamantina Shire Council staff were trying to do something about the water that was still lying on the surface. Where there wasn't any water, there was mud. As far as I could see, there was no hope of racing that day, that weekend, or for the next week.

There was a lake where the track made the turn onto the finishing straight. On the outside of the turn, I noticed an excavator was busy attempting to do some earthworks. I spotted a slightly elevated route through the mud and coerced Michelle to follow me down there for some photos. It was a couple of hundred very squelchy metres but we made it.

Who should be operating the excavator but Colgate? He was digging an enormous hole in an effort to drain the water off the track. While we watched, he used the excavator bucket to press down the ground between the hole and the lake. It was just a small furrow, but soon the water started to move and the lake began to ebb. When he shut down the excavator he posed for a picture, giving Michelle a smile that explained his nickname.

He'd solved one problem, but the real problems were the main straight and horse marshalling areas. They were inches deep in mud. There was hardly anywhere you could safely walk, let alone race a horse. The motto of the races was 'The dust never settles'. Looking around, I thought, 'Oh yes it does.'

There was one silver lining to this cloud – none of the people I wanted to talk to was going anywhere. With every road out of Birdsville closed, it wasn't hard to track them down.

8

Last Man Standing

Fred Brophy, OAM

(1952–)

There's a photograph of Sandy Moore's boxing troupe, taken in the 1950s, that bears a striking resemblance to the set-up for Fred Brophy's Boxing Troupe at Birdsville in modern times. On a raised board, Sandy is spruiking to the crowd and someone is beating a drum, while boxers are lined up on one side and challengers are lined up on the other. Behind Sandy and the fighters, banners display the top stars of his show, in fighting poses.

The resemblance is no accident. Not only was Fred born into the showman life as the son of sideshow operator Mick Brophy, his mother, Goldie, was also once involved with Sandy Moore (who was married at the time). In fact, after Mick had a nervous breakdown (caused by post-traumatic stress from being caught in the bombing of Darwin in 1942, and by the shock of Goldie dumping him for Sandy), Sandy became Fred's stepfather for the next few years.

At the time, boxing tents were a common sight around Australia, often travelling from town to town as part of the agricultural shows. Boxing was more popular than it is today, and while some tents staged exhibitions or planted boxers in the crowd to challenge the professionals, others encouraged members of the public to demonstrate their prowess.

Born in Western Australia in 1952, Fred grew up with the sound of the drums, the ringing of the bells and the spruiking of men like Sandy Moore, Sandy's brother Selby and George Stewart. From his earliest years he hung around their tents, doing odd jobs, telling anyone who'd listen that he would one day have a boxing tent of his own. When he was about five he stepped into the ring for the first time to box against other youngsters in warm-up bouts.

Fred was the fourth generation of his family to be involved in shows, and they were always on the move. As such, his education was sketchy at best and it would be some years before he learned to read or write.

Well before then, Goldie and Sandy had split, and his mother took up with a violent man named Max McIntyre. He took a particular dislike to Fred. In Fred's teens, when he got his first proper job, Goldie and Max ignored him until Friday, pay day, when they turned up to collect his pay packet.

The rest of the time, Fred ran wild, drinking and fighting around Perth, which was booming as mining and construction took off around the state.

At the age of sixteen, Fred married a twenty-one-year-old named Sandy Beattie, who already had a child by a previous relationship. He was working the show circuit with his father, Mick, spruiking a variety of acts of dubious merit. Some were little more than practical jokes played on unsuspecting members of the public. 'The Ruins of China' was sold with banners of the Great Wall snaking over misty mountains. Inside, punters were shown a tea chest full of broken cups, saucers, plates and other ruined china. 'The Man-Eating Shark' promised a ravenous monster of the deep devouring a swimmer. Inside, there was a person eating flake, a species of shark used in fish and chips.

In 1970, Fred was the centre (literally) of a brawl at a nightclub called the Green Cockatoo. It was Fred with a baseball bat versus twenty assailants. His combatants only gained the upper hand when Fred started tiring. It was then that the police, who'd been observing events from nearby, intervened to save his life.

The police then threatened him with twenty charges of grievous bodily harm, plus charges for other petty crimes, whereupon Fred hired a car and fled to Victoria. He was arrested in Melbourne three days later, remanded to Pentridge Prison and extradited back to Perth.

In October 1970, he pleaded guilty to charges of assault, breaking and entering, stealing a car and absconding. He was sentenced to three years in Fremantle Prison.

When he was released four years later (having been given extra time for drunkenness), he'd gained a daughter (Christina, by Sandy) and lost a little finger. He'd tried to escape by cutting it off so he'd be sent to hospital. There was no chance: the doctors took only two hours to sew up the stump and send him back to prison.

He still harboured an ambition to have his own boxing troupe, but at the age of twenty-two, he still had a lot to learn. He went back to the show circuit but his first act, a mouse circus, was promptly shut down when it was discovered he'd glued mice to the props.

He had more success running striptease shows. There were limits to how far the artistes could go but Fred found ways around the restrictions. When Fred promised that one of his most glamorous strippers would bare all, the place was packed. As advertised, the artiste took off all her clothing and the audience left happy. Then the police moved in. Fred then revealed that she had not, in fact, bared anything. What appeared to be pubic hair was a kangaroo-fur merkin.

By 1978, Fred was doing well, and had three more children, daughter Annie (born in 1973), son Levi (1975) and daughter Rocky (1977). His last daughter's name also described his relationship with Sandy. He was coming to realise that the person he was when he was sixteen wasn't the same as the twenty-six-year-old who was approaching a turning point in his life.

In 1978, Fred attended his first Birdsville Races. For a lot of people it was the first of many, due to the attendance of then Prime Minister Malcolm Fraser. The impact of that visit still hasn't worn off. Before Fraser's trip, attendance was like most other outback races: a few hundred. These days, it's several thousand.

Fred was extremely taken by the people of the town – he'd never met a more friendly, sociable group of people. He told them he'd be back the following year, with a boxing tent and striptease show.

Never mind that he didn't have a boxing tent: the planets were about to align. At gunpoint. When a dispute with another showie escalated, Fred was confronted with a shotgun, and shot. He survived, despite taking eighty-five pellets in his right leg, seventeen in his left. He vowed that, now he knew what it felt like, he'd never shoot a duck again. While his legs healed, he worked in a ticket booth on the show circuit and pondered his options.

The days of old-style boxing tents appeared to be all but over, especially since the 1974 death of a young man in a boxing tent in Victoria had led to tighter regulation in Victoria and New South Wales. It wasn't a total ban, but the rules and the fines for breaking them amounted to much the same thing.

While Fred was wondering how he could overcome such obstacles, Trevor Leach, son of former boxing-tent owner Bill Leach, wandered up to his booth to say g'day. Fred asked Trevor if his father still had his tent. The answer was yes – it was stored in a shed – and after a conversation, Bill was prepared to sell it to Fred on 'circus terms', meaning he could pay for the tent as he earned money with it.

In October 1978, Fred held his first boxing show, at Mount Gambier in less-regulated South Australia. The choice of location was significant. It was the place where the boxing troupe of Fred's stepfather Sandy and step-uncle Selby did their last show, in 1969. By then the troupe was being run by Selby's son, Alan, who drew the curtain on a show that had run since 1941.

'Holda! Holda! Holda! Ladies and gentlemen, my name's Fred Brophy and I'm the fairest referee in the outback!'

From the start, Fred knew perfectly how to deliver the almost hypnotic patter to spruik his show.

'Give 'em a rally on the bells and drums!

'Ding a-ding a-ding a-ding a-ding a-ding ding!

'Tum te-tum te-tum te-tum te-tum te-tum tum!'

Fred then introduced his boxers with their evocative nicknames: the Tattooed Man, the Black Lizard, the Ape Man and the Maori Cannibal.

Fred had a lot to live up to. As he wrote in his 2014 book *The Last Showman*:

The boxing tent tradition is such an important part of Australian folklore and of our national identity, and I desperately wanted to add to the honour roll rather than detract from it. The tents have a long and glorious history and, they say, helped shape our national identity as much as they reflect it. We Australians have always loved outlaws, underdogs, heroes, sport and the idea of a fair go, and the tents were great levellers. From the very earliest days they pitched free settlers against convicts or their descendants, the rich against the poor, white against black – all without fear or favour. *(Reproduced by kind permission.)*

He had plenty of support from other showies, and from an unexpected quarter. Country singer Chad Morgan, one of rural Australia's great characters, said he'd help out with refereeing the show. When it came to the final bout, between a local cray fisherman and the Maori Cannibal (a heavyweight who actually worked as a showie), Chad stepped up to officiate, brandishing a guitar. The three one-minute rounds were conducted over, under and around him, nearly resulting in the guitar getting KO-ed.

From there, Fred headed to Casterton in Victoria, where he did another successful show, little knowing it would be that state's last-ever boxing tent of its kind. He travelled on to New South Wales and did a successful show at Blacktown, on the outskirts of Sydney.

At the Hawkesbury Show, also near Sydney, there was trouble. He'd just taken the audience's money and let them into the tent when a show official and a policeman turned up.

The official insisted that if he went ahead with the show, he'd be in breach of the regulations. In particular, his boxers, who had just fought at Blacktown, couldn't fight again for a week.

If they'd been knocked out, they couldn't fight for a month. All the challengers had to have medical certificates saying they were fit to compete.

As the crowd in the tent grew restless, Fred's pleas that the show must go on were in vain. If he went ahead, he faced a $20 000 fine. He was forced to refund the money of a lot of unhappy customers.

It was a blow for Fred, emotionally and financially, and he retreated inland, risking a show at Lithgow to get enough money to pay for fuel to get out of New South Wales. He never took his show there again.

His treatment there still rankles: 'I was the last boxing tent to work in Victoria and New South Wales about thirty-seven years ago. I could work there if I want to change to their rules. They class me down there as professional boxing – professional fighters and they're only allowed to fight so much – once a month or something. And you've gotta have a ring and all that sort of stuff gets away from what I'm doin' traditionally. The boxing tent is a show and there's no show like it. It's not like TV ringside. You ask someone to explain what it's like when they come outta there and it's pretty hard to explain. It's different than boxing. It is boxing but not the same. We get people to laugh in there and they enjoy it, and there's some real tough fights as well.

'So I said, "Well, if that's the case" – and they were gonna fine me, you know, $20 000 or something if I worked it again – "I'm not working in these states anymore: Victoria, New South Wales."'

He was hoping things would be better in Queensland and stopped just over the border, in Goondiwindi. It didn't start well. While he was setting up the boxing tent, a police officer appeared.

'Where's your licence?'

'What licence?'

'Your licence to operate a boxing tent.'

'I haven't got one.'

'Well you can't have a boxing tent without one.'

'Where can I get one?'

'Go down to the courthouse and get one there.'

So he went down to the courthouse where, after some stand-ard-issue bureaucratic blank looks, he was given a form to apply for a licence to operate a tent at the show. In answer to the question about the type of amusement he was operating, he wrote: 'Fred Brophy's Boxing Troupe'.

The young bureaucrat at the front desk took the form and, probably not really knowing what he was doing, typed out a licence and charged Fred $125. Not only had Fred just been issued an official licence to operate his boxing tent in Queensland, when he looked closer, there was no expiry date. He's taken very good care of that piece of paper ever since.

'I was the first boxing tent in Australia to actually get a permit for it – legally.

'And the policeman that comes up the north run, he said, "They've given you a permit but they wasn't supposed to."

'And I said, "Well, I've got one."

'He said, "Look, I've had a talk to the Commissioner" – or whatever it was – "and they said they'll let you go up to Cairns. After the Cairns Show they're gonna review it and see what happens."

'And they did. Then he come and see me after Cairns.

'He said, "Fred, they're gonna let you keep it because you run a good show."

'And that's the reason why they let me have it. Then after about ten years I didn't need one anymore.

'They said, "Well, you're the only one doin' it. You don't have to pay the money for it."

'It had been so much a year or somethin'.'

It was a stroke of good fortune that meant Fred's tent wouldn't close down after a handful of shows. He could also operate the way he wanted: locals as challengers, three one-minute rounds fought on a floor at the same level as the audience, with no ropes to lean on. One-minute rounds might not sound very long, but for amateur boxers, they can be an eternity.

It was the beginning of an epic journey criss-crossing Australia that has extended over four decades. For much of that time Fred has done it tough, sometimes barely covering costs, and keeping them down by camping out and supplementing his supplies with fish and donations from stations. He's come to love that aspect of the lifestyle, as he wrote in *The Last Showman*:

> It might not have been the most luxurious surroundings we were all living in – sleeping in our swags under the stars or in the back of the truck, and showering under sprinklers or taking a quick dip in the rivers when we couldn't see any crocs – but no-one minded. They [his boxers] were often from different backgrounds, some Aboriginal, some whitefellas, but they were all hard workers, ready to pitch in with whatever needed to be done, and party afterwards.

By 1982, Fred still hadn't managed to get his boxing troupe to Birdsville, but this was to be the year. By then, he and his wife were mostly living apart. She'd set up house at Beenleigh; he was mostly on the road. Just before he left for Birdsville, he was doing a show in Brisbane when he met a woman he realised was much more his type. Her name: Sandi.

Their relationship got off to a rocky start. They had a few meals together but Fred kept standing her up, distracted by work, parties or a mixture of both. However, he wanted to get to know her better, so he invited her to Birdsville. It was only after she'd agreed to go that he revealed what she was in for. He picked her up in a truck full of boxers. The strippers were flying out later. It was a hell of a 'first date'.

Birdsville welcomed Fred and Sandi with open arms, marking the beginning of Fred's two greatest relationships: with Sandi and with the town, both thirty-four years and counting.

Unfortunately, Birdsville can be a hard place to get to or home from. On the way back, 200 kilometres from town, his truck's engine threw in the towel. Another showie towed the troupe 450 kilometres to Quilpie, where Sandi took a bus to Brisbane. Fred and company got towed down to Thargomindah, another 200 kilometres, then Cunnamulla, another 200 kilometres. Weeks passed, during which Fred realised he was missing Sandi. He rang her and asked her to join him on the road (or stuck beside it) permanently. She thought for a moment, then said she and her daughter, Josie, would be on the next train.

Eventually, with help from friends, showmen Des Wittingslow and his father, Tom, Fred got rolling again.

Fred may have a head for show business, but Sandi proved a valuable asset in finance. That was especially so in the years when the boxing troupe struggled from show to show, and town to town. Often, Fred and Sandi would have his kids, her daughter and the daughter they had together, Emerald, in tow. The children had an upbringing that echoes *Huckleberry Finn*. As Fred wrote:

Usually when we were camping, we'd bathe the kids, then cook
and give them their tea, and read them stories around the fire
before tucking them up in their swags, or in the big bus [they'd
acquired] if it looked like rain. They all say now those times
are among their most precious memories. Growing up like
that, they didn't have any of the material things most kids have
today – most obviously a house! – but they say now they loved
the travel and the kinds of experiences money can't buy.

The same could be said for Fred's boxers. Some stayed for a
few weeks, others stayed with him for years. Many, such as the
Belgian Bomber, joined the troupe after fighting as challengers.
In the case of the Bomber, who'd competed for Belgium in the
Olympics, he'd won his bout in seven seconds, with a knockout.

Sometimes people joined Fred's troupe who couldn't box.
He picked up hitchhikers who needed a meal and a shower, gave
them some work and helped them on their way. On one occasion he was approached by a Dutchman named Jacques Gregoire.
He wanted to join the troupe, hoping there would be opportunities to photograph scenery and wildlife. Jacques couldn't box so
Fred put him in the dagwood dog van, cooking hot dogs dipped
in batter.

Fred found out later that Jacques was an internationally
renowned artist. He and Jacques did a painting together (Fred
having learned to paint and cook while in prison), and it now
hangs in the Kilkivan Hotel, which Fred and Sandi own. Jacques
also gave Fred a two-panel painting of his boxing troupe in the
style of Rembrandt's *The Night Watch*.

By 1986, Fred Brophy's Boxing Troupe was starting to gain
recognition as something more than pugs slugging it out in a tent.

When *60 Minutes* approached him to do a story, Fred was concerned that he'd be subjected to a hatchet job – but the opposite was the case. He was recognised as someone who was preserving an aspect of the Australian character that didn't need to be wrapped in cotton wool.

'It's part of Australia, and the difference between this boxing tent – I've done exactly the opposite to any other boxing tent that's ever operated, and that's me family and everything – they used to have a lot of their own fighters in the crowd and they'd virtually be puttin' a show on.

'Well ever since I've had it, I've had none of that. If there's no-one to fight, I'll take the gloves off. And people pay their money to get in that boxing tent and if they've paid the money, they deserve to see what they've paid for. I've always told them that. I've said, "Listen, if you don't like the show, I'll give you your money back."

'And no-one has ever said that before. As a matter of fact, a bloke came out and give me $50. He said, "Mate, it's worth more than that."

'I play me own drum. In all the other boxing tents they never played their own drums. They had a bloke playin' a drum for 'em. Hardly any of them refereed the fight. Some of them did, some of them didn't.

'Everyone when I started said, "You won't last doin' it like that, Fred; you should do it this way. Oh, you should do it like [famed boxing-tent impresario Jimmy] Sharman," or whatever.

'I said, "Well you do it your way, I'm doin' it my way."

'And it's proved – there it is there.'

'I'm right, you're wrong,' I suggest.

'That's right. And it's the only thing I've ever wanted to do in my life since I've been five years of age, is have a boxing tent, and I got one.'

Unfortunately, recognition such as that from *60 Minutes* led many show committees to ask for more money from him to set up his tent. He was becoming a major drawcard but all they saw was a cash cow. The only place where that wasn't the case was the outback.

Accordingly, in 1986, the year Sandi gave birth to their second child, Fred Jnr, Fred made the momentous decision to turn his back on the cities and towns and focus exclusively on the place that still made him feel welcome: remote Australia. For anyone who's spent much time there, it wasn't hard to understand why.

'I think it's the people. That's the reason why I keep goin', too, because I just come here thirty-seven years ago and there was only 400 people coming to the [Birdsville] Races. And they asked me to come out and bring the boxing tent out here and I did. People said, "She's a long way up there and it's a hard road."

'Roads were like that [he points to the chopped-up mud that surrounds us], not like it is today. There's was none of that built here, none of them service stations.

'I used to pull up in the middle of the street opposite the pub there. There's not a lot of people here but they said, "If you come out Fred, if you break down, we'll get you goin', and we'll get you a bit of meat."

'You could live on sausages in those days. And that's why I kept coming back. And I had an account over the shop here. Windorah [400 kilometres east] would book me fuel up. I could pay it on the way back. I did, I kept doing that. Even to this day I go in and, "No, you'll be right, Fred, off you go."

'I said, "No, I can pay."

'"Nah, nah, you're right."

'That's the reason why you keep comin' back. I could go to the Brisbane Exhibition or the Adelaide Show when this is on but I'd rather be here because of the people. Well, you've lived out here, you know what they're like.

'You don't get people like that anywhere else except out in the outback. And people ask me, "When do you reckon – when are you in the outback?"

'I say, "Well, you'll find out when you get into the outback, when a car goes past you and waves to you, they come from the outback."

We agree it's not an actual wave, it's a single finger lifted off the steering wheel in acknowledgement.

'If you're down in the city in Melbourne or Brisbane, you go like that, they go like that to you. Two fingers.

'The people in the outback are – well, you know – there's no-one like it. There's blokes out here that walk around with, like, old clothes, could buy or sell anyone. Average people out here but they don't care. They don't put on side or anything.

'All my kids went to school here. My kids have grown up with all these blokes that own the stations here.'

While Birdsville became a regular fixture, Fred headed even further north and west. In Mount Isa, he thought he was in the toughest town in Australia, with some very hard people coming from the mining, cattle station and Indigenous communities. In the Northern Territory and the Gulf Country of Queensland, he visited some of the wildest towns there are, including Normanton, Karumba, Burketown, Doomadgee, Mornington Island and Borroloola. Fred didn't discriminate when it came to Australia's Aboriginal communities. He wrote:

We'd shown that the boxing tent could entertain the crowds at some of Australia's most remote and toughest Aboriginal communities as well as at the rodeos, shows and towns in the middle of Australia. We wanted to treat everyone equally and we'd shown we could.

It was the same when it came to his boxers. It didn't matter what colour you were. What mattered was whether you could box and fit in with the extended family that was the troupe.

That attitude may explain his reaction when, on the death of his mother in 1991, his father Mick revealed that she had been part-Aboriginal. She'd kept her origins hidden for decades. Fred wrote: 'While it was a shock to know I had Aboriginal blood in me, it wasn't a nasty shock. It was just a surprise.'

His heritage might explain some of his nomadic existence, although not long after, Sandi negotiated a low-income government loan that allowed the couple to buy their first house.

For Fred, it took a bit of getting used to: 'When I first got my house I used to just leave the doors open and that and I didn't know to cut the lawn or anything like that.

'Sandi would say, "Why don't you shut the fucken door? Was you born in a tent?"

'And I didn't know about houses and all that. I always lived in a caravan or tent. And I didn't have to have any lawn to mow.

'I reckon the best living room in the world is the outback. That's the best, you know, with a camp fire going. What better scenery? And if you light a fire, you're never lonely. They get around there.

'Years ago when I first stayed here, [Birdsville] people used to look down on us. I'd arrive here with six, seven Aboriginal blokes, I had all Holden cars, old vehicles and they used to sort of, "Oh, look at that bloke out there."

'I had all me kids with me and the dogs. They sort of thought I was a gypsy or something, but I'm not a gypsy. And anyway I proved them that I just kept comin' back and comin' back and always done the right thing. Never burned a bridge in me life. It was hard all the time uphill – it levelled out in the last ten years – and I earned the reputation so now I have no problem with life. I can put that tent up anywhere – on the land or on a block in town – and people come in.

'I'd go to South Australia, Western Australia, Northern Territory, Queensland, ACT. I didn't have enough time to do the other ones anyway. Now I only do Queensland and that's why a lot of people come up here all the way over the border just to see the boxing tent. I mean, they'll go to the races too but . . . I've had two people just come up from over the border just to say they've had a fight. That's what their main purpose was.'

The 1990s also saw Fred joined by a group of boxers who have remained part of the troupe ever since. They include the Friendly Mauler, Glynn Johnston, so named because Sandi differentiated him from all Fred's other 'Maulers' as 'the friendly one'. The Digger, Darryl Burley, is an aeronautical engineer in the Australian Army who now keeps the troupe organised.

Blair Wilson, the Cowboy, is one of the few boxers who has taken Fred unawares. Normally, Fred can pick a boxer from the way they stand and the marks on their faces. The Cowboy's face was unmarked when they met, and he turned out to be one of Fred's best. There was a simple explanation: he didn't like being hit and did everything he could to avoid it.

In 1997, Fred and Sandi bought a half-share in a small pub

in the town of Cracow, in Queensland. Sandi thought it was a good doer-upper and might attract filmmakers with the outback scenery, much as the scenery around Quorn has done, as detailed in Leg Three. Cracow and its pub were a sleepy little place until just after the Brophys bought it. Then mining started to boom, gold prices rose, and a moth-balled mine nearby was reopened. Suddenly, there were well-paid miners everywhere and the Cracow pub became a gold mine of its own.

Fred and Sandi haven't looked back. Not long after, Fred decided it was time to wind back the boxing troupe. He settled on a dozen favourite outback places that it would visit every year, and it's been doing so ever since. Of course, that includes Birdsville and Mount Isa, which he thinks is still the toughest town in the outback.

'I get all me boys together and we work out where we're going to go and they take time off work and we go and do it, and we enjoy doin' it. I don't have to do it anymore but I'm just passionate about it and I love it and that's why I'm doin' it.

'I do a lot of football clubs, the shows get me and all that sort of stuff. They pay me. But I just love Queensland and I don't even really feel like going out of the state. I do a bit of guest speaking and that here and there. I won't be retired for a long time but that's what I was gonna do, just guest speaking.

'When I can't get up on that board, then it'll be too late to do that I suppose. Yeah, that'll be all I do all me life.'

In 2010, Fred and Sandi bought another pub, at Kilkivan, between Cracow and a holiday house they bought near Noosa. That year, having run his boxing tent for more than three decades, Fred was inducted into the Boxing Hall of Fame. The following year, with Fred Brophy's Boxing Troupe the subject of a documentary series, *Outback Fight Club*, the Australian Government honoured Fred with a Medal of the Order of Australia. (He was eligible for the award despite going to prison as he was a juvenile at the time.)

The reasons for the award were his services to charity and to the entertainment industry in keeping old-style tent boxing alive. No-one seemed to notice the irony of a government acknowledging Fred's contribution despite having done everything it could to kill off old-style tent boxing years before. Where once there'd been up to thirty shows all around Australia, the only one who'd survived was Fred.

What does it feel like to be the last man standing?

'That's sad, but I'm lucky to have seen all the good old days. Everywhere in Australia's changed. It doesn't matter what business you're in. The government is killin' it. It's a shame really but that's what's happened. Nothin' we can do about it. I'm not goin' to change for any politician or bureaucrat until it comes to the day when they say . . . Well, when I go I think that'll be the last of it because I'm in a "too hard" basket and I make it too hard for anyone else. You know what I mean?'

Some years ago, Fred frequently suggested that each year might be the boxing troupe's last. He'd done well in life and didn't need to keep going on the road. In 2016, though, he was still visiting Birdsville every year. He loves the place so much that he hopes, when he dies, that his ashes will be scattered in the dusty patch where he's pitched his boxing tent since 1982. As it happens, it's the very spot where we're having our conversation.

Fred Brophy's Boxing Troupe is now like a living museum. It's an expression of an Australia that's disappeared almost everywhere else. If it goes, the whole country will be poorer for its loss.

In its way, when Fred's boxing troupe finally takes off the gloves, it'll be the end of an era.

'It will. When that goes, a part of Australia goes, and it belongs to everyone in Australia. I'm only running it. I'm the figurehead. It'll be a bit of a pity when it goes. My son doesn't want to take it over. If me son wanted to take it over, they'd let that go. I'll most probably leave it to someone and see what happens.

'Me wife will be around, I suppose. I don't know. Not many people can do that. There's only one bloke who wants to do it and that's the Friendly Mauler – Bronco Johnston – he's here. That's about the only one that I'd sort of – well I was supposed to have given him the old tent anyway – you know, he's got the one at Mount Isa.'

I suggest to Fred that the Birdsville Races wouldn't be the same without Fred Brophy's Boxing Troupe.

'Of course it would be. The races was here before I was here, you know. Okay, they might miss it for a year or two but time goes quick and nah, the races will always go on, yeah? Even if the pub wasn't here, the races would still be on. And that'll never change. It was the races that made me.

'This is the town that made my name. In the outback with Birdsville, people think of me and there's Birdsville, and I've always mentioned Birdsville. I'm known at the races.

However, a lot of people that come to the races also want to go to the boxing tent.

'I think that's on the cards. You go to the pub, you go to the races and you come to the boxin' tent. And there's a lot of old people in there now, people seventy years of age, sixty, women and that – never seen a fight before and they just love it. Couldn't believe it.

'First time they said, "We've gotta go there."

'And they all bought their tickets and all come in and loved it. They said, "It's not like we thought it was gonna be."

'I said, "I told you that."'

Fred now wants the show to go on for as long as he can put it on. It's already the longest-running boxing tent ever, at thirty-eight years.

'If I can get up on that board, I'll be runnin' that show. The council said to me, the Diamantina Shire said, Colgate said, "Fred, look, when you can't get up on that board, we're gonna go and get a forklift and put a pallet on for ya and lift ya up."'

They will, too.

'Yeah, they will do that. That – touch wood – will be a long time from now. I've got still plenty left in me.'

Leg Ten

Later that day we joined the procession of vehicles with nowhere to go, driving around town like bees in a bottle. It was late afternoon and we decided to check out how Colgate and his crew were getting on out at the race track.

The sight that met us was astonishing. Not only had all the water been drained from the track, the entire muddy surface had been picked up by earth-movers and dumped over the inside rail of the course. As the sun set, two graders were circling the course, levelling and smoothing the dry ground that was exposed underneath. Over in the tighter spaces of the marshalling areas, road-building contractor Nigel Gilby was using a bobcat to remove the mud and bring in fresh dry soil. In short, a miracle was being worked.

'They're gonna do it,' I said to Michelle. 'If they go all night, the track will be ready tomorrow.'

The next day, Sunday, I had a chat with David Brook, secretary of the Birdsville Race Club and a major landholder, who would have been a candidate for inclusion in this book if I hadn't already written about him extensively in *Birdsville* and *Outback Stations*. He's someone I'm proud to consider a friend. He told me Colgate and the crew had knocked off around eight o'clock at night. They were starting to get testy, having worked a sixteen-hour day, and Colgate could hear the tension building in the radio chatter. So he sent everyone home and they were back, fresh, at daylight the next morning. The track was ready half an hour before the first race. In fact, some jockeys reckoned the surface was a bit hard!

David pointed out the only damage that had occurred as a result of the furious activity: a dent in a post in the marshalling area. Later, I was talking to Nigel Gilby, who'd hit the post with his bobcat, and he explained that he had still been working in the yards when the horses came in. At one point he'd faced a choice between hitting a horse or the post. He chose the post.

I spent race day behind the computer screen, pencilling for Terry Picone. Late in the day, he gave me a bit of a run carrying the bookie's bag and taking bets (very closely supervised). I was taken aback moments after putting on the bag: locals came from everywhere to get photos of me being a bookie.

I also discovered how much money bookies carry. At one point, I had to stand on the right side of Terry's stand, with the bag on the side where the punters were thronging. It would be nothing for someone to reach inside the bag while I was distracted and scoop themselves a big win. Terry showed me how to shove all the fifties and hundreds up under a pocket so they couldn't easily be reached. It reminded me of a practice Fred Brophy once used to stop anyone stealing from his moneybag: he put a python inside so would-be thieves got more than they bargained for.

Back in town we headed for Fred's tent to watch the huge charity auction he runs from the board each year. After that, we watched one of his shows. A glamorous young Sydney woman, stylishly outfitted for the races, had volunteered to fight the

Beaver, female boxer Brettlyn Neal. The Beaver is so tough, Fred says, 'she has hairs on her legs strong enough to spear a rat'.

When Fred wouldn't let the contender fight, she turned to the crowd for support. She prevailed but Fred managed to turn the bout into a tag-team affair that pitted two against the Beaver. The fight became a study in Fred's approach to ensuring would-be boxers don't get badly hurt: his fighters will only hit you as hard as you hit them.

The young woman had some moves that suggested she'd done boxercise. Accordingly, the Beaver covered up each time her opponent came at her, took a few hits, then popped one at her to let her know she was in a boxing ring. Her reaction suggested that Sydney fitness trainers never punch their clients in the face; the young woman didn't need much encouragement to tag her teammate (a bar worker from the pub). Interestingly, while her face was reddened, she hadn't got a cut or a bloody nose. It was pretty clear the Beaver was damming up a lot of her firepower.

The bout, as with the other five or so, was thoroughly entertaining, and to their credit, the female challengers lasted the whole three rounds.

9.

A Voice in the Wilderness

Don Rowlands, OAM
(c.1948–)

In a land of soaring red and yellow sand dunes etched against an arid blue sky, of sun-scorched gibber plains that stretch to the horizon and far beyond, where plants wither and turn to dust in the relentless, killing heat and water has turned to vapour so long ago there's no sign that it ever was, there are many places I would never go alone. Death would be tracking me from the moment I set foot in them. There is, however, one person I would follow into the wastelands of central Australia without a moment's hesitation.

Back in 2009, I got to know Don Rowlands while living in and writing about Birdsville. I've gotten to know him and his wife Lyn a lot better since. Over the years, I've picked up snippets, enough to know that he is a remarkable person on many levels. As with others in that rough and tumble outback community, he could do things that people might argue with but he always had the interests of his community at heart.

He was also very accessible; whenever I needed something, he was always ready to help. He's taken Michelle and I out into the desert and shown us his country. He's demonstrated incredible knowledge when navigating flooded country without getting stuck. As former Birdsville cop Neale McShane put it, 'He's a GPS on two legs'.

One of my favourite memories of Don is a trip to camp on a sand dune between the Muncoonie Lakes, on Adria Downs Station (with the permission of its owner David Brook and manager Don Rayment, son of Charlie (mentioned in chapter six)). On the way we stopped for lunch in the shade of a coolabah beside a large pool of water. Its roots were soaking up the first abundant water in years and its leaves were green and glossy.

'This is a very happy tree,' Don. said, gently patting its trunk. He was smiling, too.

Don was not just born and raised in the Birdsville district, his connection with it goes back thousands of years. And for the last twenty-two years, he's been the ranger with sole responsibility for Munga-Thirri (Simpson Desert) National Park, the largest national park in Queensland. He's one of the strongest voices for the Wangkangurru Yarluyandi people, one of the most prosperous Indigenous groups in the country. Yet he started with nothing, or less than that, considering the Indigenous disadvantage and entrenched discrimination he grew up in.

Typically, Don didn't hesitate when I asked if he'd participate in this book. Getting together during the Birdsville Races was a bit problematic, though, with so many people coming and going – and quite a few of them were at his house. We eventually retreated to the ranger station. What followed was one of those interviews where asking questions ran a distant second to simply listening.

'I was born in Hawker, South Australia, but we were at Clifton Hills [190 kilometres south of Birdsville]. My mum was working at Clifton Hills station at the time as housemaid. Artie Rowlands was head stockman; he was living with an Aboriginal girl who came from Mundowdna station near Marree. Henry, my father, drowned while swimming a mob of Queensland "fats" (cattle) at the Nine-Mile Crossing on Coopers Creek.

'There's some stuff – I'll tell you but I don't know if I want it in the book – I'd like it to be in there, but I don't know. There is another twist to my story. Recently there have been suggestions that someone else is my biological father. You know Mrs Smith in Bedourie?'

Mrs Jean Smith (nee Scobie) is the much-loved late publican and post-mistress from the town 200 kilometres north of Birdsville. The Scobie family (of Scobie whip fame) is one of the extended pioneering families of the Birdsville track.

'I've been hearing snippets here and there. Her brother. They all knew about it and they're all tellin' me that now, but I don't know whether I wanna talk about that too, mate. I don't know why I shouldn't, but anyway. So he was driving cattle and stuff past the place [Clifton Hills] and my mother was workin' there and so in the back of the paddock there somewhere I was conceived, way back in May 1948.

'Once we came back from the hospital we travelled to Davenport Downs Station [150 kilometres east of Bedourie] because Mrs Smith's sister's husband was managing it – Frank Donellan and his wife, Ethel. All this is startin' to fall into place for me, you know.

'We lived there for a while and my mother was getting crook and that's when they [the Smiths] started writing to the government to adopt me, because they knew who I was, really. I've got letters from them to the government asking can they keep me. They called me "My Donald", "We love our little Donald."

'Due to her illness Mum and me travelled to Cuddapan Station. Mum needed to be with her mum and dad. Back in those days, before Aboriginals could travel from one place to another, they had to get "permission", sort of like a passport, which was arranged by the Protector of Aborigines. Or the government could send you to any station they decided and you had to go.

'In the last half a dozen years perhaps it just started to come out. Mrs Smith's boys, Roy and all them, they tell me now that they know that I am their cousin, kind of thing.'

Don subsequently decided that he wanted this part of his story to be public. His cousins also said, 'Go for it.'

'So when my mother got sick, my grandparents was over at Cuddapan Station [250 kilometres east of Birdsville], so we got across there and the doctor flew her out and that was it. She died while we were there.

'I was two. I still remember these little vague things. It's a funny thing. Before she passed away, I had my other cousins and they used to towel me up a bit. Then all of a sudden everybody was lovin' me and huggin' me and I couldn't work it out but I have now – it was because she'd passed away.

'Well all the letters to and from the government, they wrote back and said, "No, we think it's in the best interests of the boy that he stays with his grandparents."

'And I'm sort of thinkin', I wouldn't be who I am today had I gone and stayed with the Donellans at Davenport Downs. I'd probably go away to college and learn to be some bloody thing and never be part of this country anymore. So, that's the downside. The upside of that might have been you had more opportunities in terms of education and work. Although there's nothing wrong with being a ringer, that's the best job.

'After we left there, we lived at Betoota [170 kilometres east of Birdsville] for twelve months. Across from the pub there was an old customs house, built out of bricks; a bit fallen down but we lived there and the oldies worked in the station across the road, Mount Leonard. We'd swim in the waterhole and fish and carry on there. I can remember swimmin' across the river [Teeta-Teeta or Betoota Hole] to go and get some meat. A couple of milk tins with a bit of rope in the middle. Get in there and swim across. It's a bloody long way across.

'They used to have corroborees there, down at the waterhole. We'd go down and all the people from all around the country would come there. We weren't allowed to see anything, we had to be covered up, but, you know, a bit of blanket slides up sometimes – you see them all with their paintings on and carrying on.

'After that we moved to Durrie Station [100 kilometres east of Birdsville], and I grew up there. We came to Durrie just after the 1950s flood. The manager had two boys, Bill and Don, and we had some good times together.

'There was a little old brown and white donkey and we learnt to ride on this bastard. He'd let you get on and kick, kick, kick, and all of a sudden he'd take off 400 mile an hour and you'd get left behind. We'd chase him all up in the hills and catch him and do the same thing, and he does the same thing every time. Then you learnt to hang on to the mane and stay with him for a bit longer.

'Jesus learned to ride a donkey, so I thought, "All right for me to do it, too."

'I didn't have sandals. I had nothin'.

'We'd go out to the stock camp there – we weren't goin' to school – so from about eight . . . and I remember the boss saying, "We'll give you sixpence a week."

'I never ever got the fucken sixpence, but anyway.

'So then the flying doctor flew my grandfather out. One night Grandmother comes in screaming and carrying on – I don't know how she knew – and she told us he'd passed away. That was about '56 or something like that, '57.

'Then we came to Birdsville. We used to have them humpies we used to live in, with rags and shit all over it. I've got photos of that. We used to live there for a long time. When it rained you all kept together and built a bit of dirt up so you didn't get in the wet.

'Goin' to school was another issue altogether. I was ten years old when I started school. I had one of the worst schoolteachers you'd ever find. He used to mess with some of the boys. Being older I was a bit lucky. We didn't think about it, really, but we knew what was goin' on when we saw him. Some folks turned up here a couple of years ago. They knew and we're havin' a yarn.

'"Oh, you know this bloody schoolteacher?"

'"Yeah."

'"Oh, he was a mongrel" – started telling me the story.

'They said he just died of AIDS. He was a serious bloody predator. We did tell our parents, in my case my grandmother; we did tell the police and he give you a floggin' for talkin' about this man with the high status in the community. You can't spread rumours. And we get a fucken floggin'. And the old people, they'd get locked up, for drinkin'.

'We weren't allowed to tell, you see. And it just went on and on. I don't know about any girls but certainly . . . he used to do it in front of you. Make you lay with your head on the desk but everybody would get a look. So that was a real horrid period, it really was. We were in a bad place and couldn't do anything.

'We'd build gardens. "This is yours, Don, and this is yours." If you ate one of your carrots or your cabbage or whatever, you'd get the bashing of a lifetime because you're stealing. But he said it's yours. We'd clean the school and he'd give us all a lolly each. He'd a big lolly tin up there: you know them old boiled lollies. We'd just sit there all day droolin'. He'd give us one each, and he'd come back the next morning and bash us for stealing it. He was a real terrible bastard. Really was. Then he left, then we got good schoolteachers after that.

'Then I went to work. I remember that day. I think it was July. I was year five but I was doin' six with Barry [Gaffney, who now runs one of Birdsville's two petrol stations]. The day I left we had to do a bloody presentation to the minister, a Mr Pizzey.

'The teacher picked me, Joyce Crombie and Eileen Butler.

'He said, "You three go home and write something and I'll pick the best one and you can do the presentation".

'So I done the bodgiest one I could do and still won. I wasn't gonna get out of it at all. That was a bit of a bloody smoke-and-mirrors kind of stuff I think now.

'I was leaving soon after. The boss came to town, parked in front of the school because he was from the council and he had to be part of this presentation. I carried my swag to school and my boots and a bit of crap and laid it at the gate. And jumped in the car and away we went to the mustering camp.'

The camp was on Roseberth Station, which surrounds Birdsville.

'Went out to the camp at Moonie's Grave [a locality where a contractor had drunk himself to death years before]. All the other ringers were there. I'd already done a bit of ringin' on Durrie so I had a bit of experience in mustering and driving cattle. I was sort of half ahead of the game anyway.

'But, mate, I don't wanna tell it like it is but Lyle . . .'

Don's silence left unspoken many of his experiences working for Lyle Morton, then owner of Roseberth. Eventually, he went on.

'And because I was a kid I just got pummelled. Oh my God. But you know, there's still some good that comes out of it. It teaches you inside to have these kind of work ethics.

'Sadly, that's the truth of that. The other thing it does – and we were taught all through our lives – to not be bold or whatever with white people. They were superior, you know. Everyone was "Mrs" or "Miss". If they came out, you just cowered in the corner. Even when you got to be a young man, all these good-lookin' daughters, you weren't allowed to even look at 'em. It just was pumped into you. You were totally, totally scared of it all.

'That still happens a bit today, funny enough. There's a bit of a façade goin' on but you have to keep reminding yourself, "Fuck it. I'm just as good or just as equal, whatever". I don't know about other people who grew up in my time but you still really have to remind yourself about who you are today.

'That's why I believe places like Birdsville – and all around Australia I suppose, but this place in particular – we can't come together as a group because we have all that subservient kind of thing that's ruling us still. Some people still won't disappoint the white fellas. So all the stuff I do, all the arguments I have, is still on my own, but everyone else is the recipient of the outcome in the end.

'Mustering camp was all Aboriginal ringers, and as we were "under the act" [the *Aboriginal Protection Act*] we were basically contracted to the station, controlled by the Protector of Aborigines, in this case the local policeman. As a ward of the state I had to sign a contract with the station and government. My number was D472. The repercussions for breaking the contract were very dire. In the Australian constitution Aboriginal people were listed as flora and fauna and we were treated as such.

'Anyway, I was "promised" six quid a week. The idea was to bank three quid into a government account and I'll have three quid spending money from the station. There wasn't much left in either [account] when I finally was able to move on. "Sorry. You don't have any funds left." It got taken out from under the hat, as they call it. I had a penny in my pocket when I started work but nothing when I left after five years of hell.

'You'd come to town – the station wouldn't give you your pay – and you go to the cop, which was a scary thing in itself. You'd want five quid for the weekend, races or something, and he'd give you two.

'Some of my mates [black uncles], they'd come in and only use their thumb [to sign for their pay].

'The copper would say, "Oh, you've fucked that up."

'And he'd throw it in the bin. But you can't fuck up a thumbprint. He'd give him another one, but the other one's in the bin till they leave. So he'd get his cut, too. A lot of that went on all over the place, and some of the stations, when the blokes left, after working for [long periods] and he's owed 2000, 1000, 500 pound, whatever it might be, he'd end up with fifty or eighty because he bought all this stuff: saddles and bridles and Christ knows what. When he lands in town he's got his swag. No saddle, no bridle.

'So all that happened but that didn't happen to me 'cos I could read a bit. We just never got the money, really. They'd just bully you.

'Even asking Lyle for money for the weekend – "How much do you want?"

'"Oh, ten quid."

'"Nah, you don't want fucken ten but here's five."

'You're always short-changed but that's what you had to take.

'So we were under the Act and some of the real dark fellas, they couldn't even eat at the same fire. They'd light another fire. Come across here and Lyle would hand out their curry or whatever and they'd go and sit down over there, pour their tea. I don't know where it gets contaminated. I don't know where that process would've happened.

'Sometimes they'd get to the camp first and they'd cook the damn thing. They'd cook the curry but didn't get served. So contamination could have happened in the process of makin' it, in the process of cooking. Oh, man, that was so funny.

'Us brown-skinned fellas, at the station we were allowed inside of the building. We'd still have to go to a kitchen to get served ours, but our black uncles, they'd sit out on the wood heap. Rain, hail or shine you'll see 'em sitting out, rain's pourin' off their hat, but they were havin' to eat. Then he gets up and jumps on a horse and goes and musters just as good as anyone else. It just seemed odd but that's the way it was.

'This was in the sixties. When I was at Durrie, I didn't notice it, but Kidmans [the family company that owned the station] were a lot better, really, back then. That was the station to be on.

239

I finished up workin' for Kidman in the end but it was a rough time, mate, I tell ya.

'I was contracted or signed on for five years so I couldn't leave. Just wasn't allowed to walk off the place or anything. I remember one Christmas, I come to town and they gave me six weeks off or whatever. Two weeks out they'd come and get me and leave the rest of the men in town.

'I said, "Nah, fuck this, I'm not fucken goin' back."

'Somehow I got back to town and the next fucken thing, the copper turns up with the lights and took me back. Then they both got to me in the huts and give me a good fucken towlin', a blastin', you know, so you don't do that again. I was property.'

When his five years expired, Don went to work for the council, driving a truck.

'That was more fun 'cos every fortnight they brought a brown envelope with all your pay in it, cash. All of a sudden I've got money, you know. It was good. Yeah, they actually paid you but first time we had money. Then I went to Kidmans.

'When we were working at bloody Durrie, we're there for the '74 flood. You shoulda seen the snakes, mate. That tree there would have fifty or sixty in it. You'd shift up on the hill and camp, and slept on a bed with a mosquito net. You get up in the morning and there'd be a snake or two sleeping under the bed. Then you go to the islands and they're just chock-a-block with snakes and lizards and God only knows what. In the trees there'd be snakes right up the end of the thing, and all these little rats, the snake just layin' there, waiting till he gets hungry again.

'We had to stay out there for fucken three months livin' on the hill. We had a few head of cattle on there, so we'd shoot one of them, and Sandy Kidd [an outback pilot who reputedly pioneered aerial mustering] had to fly out some bread from Windorah, chuck it from a plane. Nobody really cared about you, but you just grew up with that. It's funny, isn't it?

'I went to Kidmans, then back to Roseberth.'

At this point I interrupted to check I'd heard Don correctly. This was the place where he'd been treated so badly.

'Just sort of gone back to those places where you were, and there was bad times but there's something about the country that you get used to in your life. Roseberth, I just liked the country, kind of thing. Then when you're more mature and . . . I had a couple of biff-ups in the pub so you start . . . [getting] a little bit of more respect.

'I often think about old Lyle. For all the bad things, he did teach me this work ethic. When you look at it, you can fix motorcars, pull bores, windmills, build tanks. You had to do the lot – cut posts, build fences and you just learnt a lot. Trial and error, you get better and better, and when you go and work some-where else you take all that with ya.

'I wrote the tribute for Lyle, which Bruce Scott read at the funeral.

'So when I went to Durrie, they're more laid back but 'cos we had this other thing goin' on with us [from Lyle], you'd be the first person up every day, you'd be the first person to saddle your horse, throw your swag on a pack horse and you'd be the first bloke to do all this though 'cos that's what you're . . . So that was all the good side.

'And there was no résumés back them days but it happened in the camps, before their eyes. They saw you, your abilities and when you landed in town . . . Like when I left Durrie, by the time I got into Birdsville, there was other fellas waiting to take me again.

'"Mate, I just got here, give me a break."'

The other thing working on stations gave Don was an intimate knowledge of, and love for, his country.

'It's my home. Like I said, we lived in humpies, we lived down at Jardine's [a waterhole near Birdsville] in the brush humpies and run around fishing and doing all that stuff to start with, so the land was kinda giving me water, giving me a fish for dinner and all that stuff right from the get-go.

'Then you go out ringing, you have to get to know that country. When you go onto a new place they take you out and muster a mob of cattle for branding or the markets and say, "Right-o boy, take him that way. You go past that big sandhill point and when you look thata way [pointing], you'll see a big high tree on a creek line. You can't miss it. Go there."

'So you go there and that big tree will be stickin' out, no matter what direction you come from. So that stays in there. The next time you come from the other direction you look for that big tree. All those little gaps in the trees or the high ridges, they're all part of the internal map. When you started on a property, after about two or three weeks mustering, you know the whole place. It's all in there and I think that's pretty neat. And that's how we learn. It's like Aboriginal song lines that describe the natural features and how and why they were created in the Dreamtime.

'For me I never forget where north is. You go to bed at night knowing where north is. I don't know if you've been lost, but if you drive at night you've got to keep your wits about you. I've done it a couple of times: all of a sudden the headlights blind out the natural features. You pull up and you go to bed thinkin' north is there. You get up and the fucken sun comes up over here and that really screws with your mind. So that's why I always try to keep north in my mind and the lay of the land, at night. Sometimes you might just have to pull up, switch the lights off and let it settle and the country will come up and you'll see what you're looking for over there. If you keep driving, mate, you're fucked. Absolutely.'

As already mentioned, Don has been called a GPS on legs, but I wonder if he actually uses one.

'I do now. It's more about when you're goin' up searching places, you need to find a gap between the sand dunes, so that's good for that. And if you find a [significant Indigenous] site, you can record it. Up until recent times I always had one but I never used it. That's why I still can't use 'em properly. But like I said before, once it's put in there it's there forever.

In his thirties, Don went out on his own, fencing and yard building.

'Sounded romantic at the time but fucken Christ, hard work and for very little. You got your own tractor or your own motor-car and a couple of blokes, you then become – I don't know what the word is. I'd make $250 a mile or kilometre, whatever, but they can nail you down making sure you're in debt. Paticularly, they'd sell you a drum of fuel. So you're in debt to have this, you're in debt for food and shit. So all of a sudden he's in control of ya and the price that you got initially, it comes right back down, just enough to pay it off.'

'Anyway you struggle on for a few years doin' that, then back on the council for ten years I think it was. Looked after the power station and looked after fixin' cars and things.

'I was just doing some contract work up in Pandie . . . This is your country, this is where you live, so you just keep goin' back to these bastards. Anyhow I was in town and we used to bank with Westpac – what was it called back then? – Bank of New South Wales – and the manager he rings me up and he says, "Hey, there's a job going with National Parks."

'"Yeah, okay."

'He said, "You should put in for it."

'"Oh, I wouldn't have a clue how."

'He said, "Look, I'll write up the fucken résumé."

'So he did. I don't know why. I only knew him from just on the phone. He wrote it out. I've still got it. It's way out of kilter now, though.

'I always tell people, when they ask me how I got the job, "Well, normal process, 600 applicants". That's a bit of bullshit. There was only two of us but I tell everyone else it's 600. Both lived in Birdsville. Me and a farmer down here.

'So Chris Mitchell and Mike Chuck came to interview us. The other bloke goes in and they ask him, "Now, do you want this job?"

'"Yeah, I will kill all them fucken cats."

'He kept saying that. "I will shoot the fucken cats."

'And they walked out and said – you can ask Chris – "What the fuck's goin' on there?"

'So I think if I was drunk as a monkey, I would've still got it.'

Don started work on 9 March 1994. He was responsible for the Simpson Desert National Park, now known as Munga-Thirri ('Land of sandhills') National Park, the biggest park in Queensland.

'And I'm the only Indigenous ranger that manages his own traditional land.

244

'It was, to start with, like comin' from a stockman's background: "Don't shoot the dingo. Don't shoot this. Don't kill that."

'And lucky enough, they provided so much training that sort of gets you over that but, mate, initially, I just couldn't understand why they'd want to do this, why they'd want to do that. Gotta burn to protect the plants. "Burn the fucken thing? Why do you wanna do that for?"

'It was, I reckon five years it took me to get my mind around protecting. And the dingo when I was on the stations was number-one enemy. Shoot every fucken dog you saw. It took a while to change my mindset, honestly.'

Don soon found out that protection didn't extend to feral animals. He was involved in animal counts and eradication programs, particularly rabbits and camels.

'There was no way we were gonna get rid of the rabbits. There were zillions, you know. There was just no way. We'd try fumigation and bombing and all sorts of stuff but not a chance in hell. And one year, in August 1996, along comes this calicivirus. Actually, we were driving out there and you come over the sandhill and all you see is all these little white bellies in the valley. Dead rabbits everywhere. Dead in their holes. Wiped 'em out.

'So down goes one problem but it created another one with the eagles and other raptors. They had to come to town then. Initially, the rubbish tip was chocka with bloody birds, hovering around. And the dingoes, they starved, too, you know. Before, you'd go there and there's dingoes everywhere. Now you might see a track or three, very seldom see a dingo.'

He also became a ranger just when four-wheel drive adventure tourism was taking off. Crossing the Simpson Desert (as it's still referred to on the Northern Territory side of the border) is one of the must-do trips for many but it can be too challenging for some.

'When I first started in '94 I was the only rescue operation in Birdsville. No-one else did it. Now it's a commercial thing [operated by Peter Barnes, the subject of the following chapter] and thankfully we don't have to do it anymore. I was the number-one person and I'd get called all hours of the day and night. I loved doin' it so I'd just jump in the car and go. Anything and everything – breakdowns, bogging – I'd be out there. If you called a cop, he wasn't even interested back then: "You deal with it, don't even wanna go there."

'Although, back then, there's probably 300, 400, 500 people a year. The numbers were down, so it was manageable in that sense, but it gave me the opportunity to get out there and hone the skills, the driving, the knowledge of what to look for when you're travelling and recognising places, and reading the sand dunes, where the road's been buried. I was out there all the time, which was a lot of fun. HF radio, call in twice a day. Worked perfect.'

Don invited me on a trip out to Poeppel Corner back in 2009, to do some repairs to the boardwalk. Poeppel is about 160 kilometres west of Birdsville. All the way there and all the way back, all we did was pick up rubbish left by tourists. They'd driven thousands of kilometres to see the pristine desert only to trash it when they got there. Some thought they could 'bash, burn and bury' things, not realising dingoes would dig them up again.

'Man it was in a mess. Initially, we'd bring out wool bale loads. Now it's half a bale, for the whole place. My grandkids reminded me the other day, I took them out – two cars, Lyn and

I and the grandkids – and we got out there and I said, "Right-o, you've gotta run along now and pick up all this rubbish."

'They still remember that.

'"Poppa, you would sit in the car while we ran and threw all the rubbish."

'Well, that's all right. That's what poppies are for.'

When it comes to natural phenomena, like fire, there's a blend of new knowledge and old.

'We have a plan but we haven't put it into action, and that is mosaic burns. We talk about that but the last big fire burnt the whole bloody desert out and you can't compete with that. The plan is to go out there and do these mosaic burns to control it. Like I was saying, I never would have dreamt that a fire is a good thing for the country, but it totally is.

'Aboriginal people, you hear 'em say "fire-stick farming" and that's true. They'd have all these areas to burn and they'd burn this area, and all the animals would come out into this place and of course they'll be there waiting.

'We talked the other day with the national parks in South Australia, particularly on their side down towards Kallakoopah Creek [north of Lake Eyre], we should find a place that we can do these trial burns. The vegetation that was there that was taken out by the rabbits may need regular burns. You might bring it back because without a fire a lot of that stuff won't come back.

'So my mindset has changed totally now. I wanna try to get into this land recovery stuff. I can see the benefit of it all. Where initially: "Burn a fucken fire 'cos I wanna boil a billy."'

If the challenge isn't fire, it's floods.

'That falls back on the coppers and myself to try and find safe tracks to negotiate the flood country [in a vehicle]. It's easy sometimes and not so easy the next. It depends on how much local rain you get, and you must be able to recognise terrain where it's wet, or wetter. For me the giveaway is the grass: small young grass or more established. Sometimes it's better to go for the old grass because it's been there longer so it's got established roots and stuff. Other fella, just sittin' on the top and you fall through it. If you don't know the country, sometimes it's better to go upstream to find a place to cross.

'You've got to read that as you come towards it. Take the right turn. And that's the only turn you should take in the desert. The right turn. You do that at night, too. You've still gotta be able to read it. If there's water, you still gotta read it. I would choose most times to go through water but you still gotta read that, gotta know that country. If there's a black-soil swamp, don't go near it. And the trick with goin' through water is not fast. Just come in and take your foot off and let it roll. When it rolls, it clears all the mud out of the treads. When you sneak your foot back on, all the treads doin' the work. If you coming screaming in it just ends up like a bloody big round Flintstone tyre.

'It gets really slippery. You can rev all day and just . . . you gotta jump one part of the car out so it pulls the other part out. All those little things you learn as you go along. I travel with other people sometimes and it makes you think, "Why do you do this?"

'And when that bloody tyre is shined up like that, it's a no-go.'

I had first-hand experience of what Don was talking about, as detailed in Leg Two.

While Don has been getting all this experience, he's also developed a unique understanding of the human presence in one of the most challenging landscapes on the planet.

'I'm probably the only person living that knows that country and knows all those special places – but you can't pass it on. Nobody wants to hear it. I'm gonna have to try and record it myself and I haven't. I just keep it all in here, and that's what Aborigine people do – and when they die it turns into ash – it turns into ash.

'Those places are all special in their own way, from the point of view that they connect not only with each other but with the people. It's a DNA, for our people. Early in the piece I've heard people say, "No idiot would live out there."

'But man-o-man . . . that's why it's so important to protect these places – because there's more out there than you'd believe.

'I've got special places in my own heart where my grandmother is from and it's only me and the information that the [National Park] Department's got. Now, I'm trying to go back out there and record it all so that it can help people later on. People at the moment are not all that interested. There's still that stigma there so it's a tough battle.

'Working for the Department's easy because they wanna see it all. They want everything. They want you to go and do it.

'My lot, they just . . . that's the word, no engagement with it. I don't know. We found all the humpies, we've found those mourning caps [detailed below] and all those wells, and grinding stones everywhere out there.

'For people to say, "How could you live out there?"

'They did live out there.'

One of the most fascinating finds is the large collection of mourning caps.

'The mourning caps are for the women to wear after the death of their partner or husband. They do get married; the fire-stick marriage. When their husband dies, you've got gypsum, put it in the fire and it turns to powder and you can mix it with water and it turns into something like plaster of Paris. You gotta be quick though 'cos it sets pretty quick. Shave her head and stick it on and when the hair grows it away, it's time you can take it off and look for another partner. That's the mourning period, you know.

'When you think about it, it's no different to other mourning periods in other cultures. Everything is pretty much the same, isn't it? Like a wake for instance. I guess everything we have today would have come from that culture because it's the oldest culture on the planet. And these are the things that kept people not interbreeding and all that. You know, you're born into a moiety. They had it pretty much sorted and if anyone did break the rules they would be maimed or killed.

'Then there's this one site where there were many mourning caps. I don't know whether we've reached a real conclusion, but one of them is that somebody really important is buried there. So, we were going back out with one of those machines that can scan underground without digging it up. Maybe there's more than one in there is the other thought.

'Nothing conclusive. We took all the experts there from [anthropologists and archaeologists] Luise Hercus, Phillip Jones, Mike Smith – they're all top at their jobs – and they're the only two conclusions. It's all interesting.'

For Don, working for Queensland's national parks has had unexpected benefits.

'National Parks is probably the mechanism that gave me my independence and a voice. I was able to say what I wanted to say against the odds or whatever, and still have a job. It gave me that independence that I probably should have had earlier.

No-one locally was in charge of my employment. It gave me status as well, which I could use to help people. And all this training taught you other levels, too, you know, so you could work at all these other levels. You wasn't just some dummy, you had a voice, and I had a job that they couldn't interfere with. They could if they wanted, but there's a process. So, that set me then to try and improve other Aboriginal people's situations.'

The remarkable thing about Don's country is that, while he has responsibility for the part of it covered by Queensland's largest national park (10 120 square kilometres), the total area is much larger.

'North of Birdsville right down to the top end of Lake Eyre, which is the northern part of Lake Eyre across to Mungerannie, across to Dalhousie Springs, it's a really big area. There's some unclaimed land out there and I think we're in the process of trying to get that on the boil and see where that ends up.

'I'm from the Wangkangurru Yarluyandi group through my mother and my grandparents.'

He's also connected to the region south of his through his wife, Lyn, who is Dieri Arrabunna.

'They're neighbours, obviously. Earlier this year we went down to Killalpaninna [an abandoned mission 400 kilometres south of Birdsville] for the Easter break. A group came up. All their families came up and spent three or four days relivin' the old stories. Some of the missionary people turned up, older ones. They told their stories – Lutherans, that's the buggers, yeah – and showed all their photos and some of the older people knew a lot of the people. That's the sort of thing we need to do I reckon, our mob.'

In 2014, his mob obtained a Native Title determination for a large part of the Wangkangurru Yarluyandi country.

'A federal judge flew out here. We had the ceremony down here on Pelican Point [a strip of land on the billabong adjacent to Birdsville]. I was the man on the mike. As part of my opening address I said, 'My happy batteries are fully charged.' It was a good day and pretty significant in the whole scheme of things.

'But the stigma's still there. It still feels like you're doing something wrong. You still feel that you're on stage with all these eyes lookin' at ya, thinking all these nasty thoughts. Honestly. So you have to brave the wave and go forward and make it your special day.

'There's two different states, two different things. South Australia we've got ILUAs, Indigenous Land Use Agreements. With permission we can go there, we can go hunting, fishing, camping. Any new roads or structures, they must notify us and get clearance. I think this helps bridge the gap. You can lose your lease if it's serious enough. In Queensland, we haven't yet got ILUAs.

'In getting that decision I worked my butt off. A lot of hard work, lot of hard driving, lot of searching, it's day and night. We've got to be thankful, I think, to the non-Indigenous people who first ventured into that country, like David Lindsay in 1845. He was taken to all the *mikirris* [native wells] by an Aboriginal guide – not all of them but most. Thanks to brilliant navigation by Dennis Bartell, who studied Lindsay's journal and worked out distances in camel-time, using his information we were able to go there. Then you got all those other people who wrote these books about our people, without which today we wouldn't have this collection of historical data that is so important for our mob. We have to be thankful to these people and that they had the interest in the first place.

'My memory goes back to when I was two years old, you know. I had a grandmother and a grandfather. I never knew my mother; never knew my father. So that's kind of my background. If we didn't have this work by anthropologists and others, we wouldn't have been able to do this land claim because we didn't have this knowledge. It's no fault of ours but our job would have been much harder. I don't know if too many people really appreciate what these people did. And I think it's really important. The reason I'm saying that is because somebody reads "This is what happened", they'll come to a meeting and say, "Yeah, my grandfather so-and-so was there", but they didn't know that. The researchers did all the work, recorded and told it.

'If we can break away from tryin' to be important 'cos you know something that I don't know, and just say "I read what Aiston and Horne said in 1924." That's fair enough. I might have a different view on it but these guys were there with the people. Like I said my memory can only stretch back to when I was two years old. So I have my memory and what my grandmother told me.

'Corroborees. I can say I've been to these three things – two corroboree ceremonies and one burial.

'All the stories come from those early people – anthropologists and other people – but all the early explorers were assisted, like David Lindsay was assisted by an Aboriginal called Paddy. He was a big part of the story. Without him he wouldn't have gone anywhere. And Colson came across [the desert] in 1936 with an Aboriginal guide, "companion" I think it says. I wanna try and give the story back to the person who really owns it. He doesn't get any more mention and I'd like to bring all that back and put that as his story.

'There were some good explorers. I think Mitchell was someone who recorded good stuff – there's this myth about people not farming the land – but Mitchell saw different when he happened upon a big valley and it was just all tussock grass ready for collecting the seed. They were in fact farming the land.

'If you don't bring those Aboriginal people back to the front of the story, you won't get to hear all of that. It's really important that we get to make a point of all of that.

'Burke and Wills, they were misguided and they died 'cos they were foolish and wouldn't listen or do what the Aborigines [Don's ancestors] were doing. The Aborigines were eating the fish and Burke and Wills were saying, "It looks terrible. Can't eat that." And they died. That's probably the closest we can get to someone not claiming this as a victory, because they made the fatal mistake.'

While Don's talking about the contribution his forebears made, it's hard not to remind him of the contribution he – as a ranger, traditional custodian and campaigner for Indigenous rights – is making.

'Look, I'm proud of what I've done in the last twenty-eight years in Aboriginal affairs. Slow start because I had to get my mindset changed. Big learning curve it was. But I'll drive from here to bloody Boulia tonight to save a bilby or something or other. It's just changed me so much. I'll drive from here to Winton to protect a site because I believe Aboriginal sites are so important to Australia and it needs everybody's collective effort to protect them.

'It's our heritage. Everyone's heritage, bloody oath. There'll come a time when the mining folds up: tourism's gonna be the next big thing here. Do overseas tourists want to come look at a big hole in the ground or do they wanna come to a cultural place and have a look?

'Let's get serious about all of this. Let's recognise all these things for what they are and how important they are. They're our heritage and culture but don't just make it about us. Make it about all of us, and how important it is to all of us. I'd love to see Aboriginals and non-Aboriginals get up on a soapbox saying, "We will protect our land. When do we want to? Now!"

'One thing I wanna say on that is – and this comes up a bit – our people were massacred all across the country. That's my old people. That's not me. We recognise that and we are not asking today's generation to bear the guilt. What we're saying is, "You've got to leave what he left you behind, too. You've gotta be the changed person."

'It's not about accepting the murders. It's about changing your views now. Whatever Grandfather did or Grand-aunty or whoever did, leave that, but don't have those same bloody stupid views. Don't continue with it. Why can't you change? Mostly the argument has been: that was our ancestors; we're not responsible. It's easy to say but what I am asking is for you to discontinue the bad behaviours and horrible systems left by your ancestors. Mean it if you say it.

'I think the only way that will change quicker is if the non-Aboriginal people embrace it more. My mob are not gonna change until they see . . . Then I'll bet you 5000 to one they will claim the reason for it changing. "I did it. I told so-and-so."'

In some ways, Don seems to inhabit an ambiguous space between two cultures. Is he an elder in the Indigenous community, the non-Indigenous community, or both?

'I'm not sure that "elder" is a word I would subscribe to. I would rather – and this is probably even worse – but I believe I'm a leader or something to that effect. I'm not sure what an elder is, to be honest. He's the oldest person in the room obviously, or the team, but is he the one with all the knowledge? Well, I don't think that's true anymore. There are the elders there, in those books, who ruled according to traditions. Today I don't think that's true anymore.

'A leader, in my opinion, is the person who is now leading the cause or trying to change the thinking, get rid of the old stigma. And if these other friends of mine would join me, it would change overnight. These guys are probably still sitting on the fence because they can. But if all the others joined me . . .

'If they do some clearances without permission and I go really ape . . . I'm just sayin' there's a bloody ILUA, we haven't broken a fucken thing in terms of the agreement . . . and you can still get accommodating people to tick it off. They're still doin' it. That's probably where I stand apart and alone here, because I still try to stay with the letter of the law. It will back me. Protecting our country and cultural heritage has to be paramount, in my thinking. It's best practice, I would've thought.

'When you respect our input, we'll respect yours. If I wanna go on to Adria Downs, I'll ring up, which is just a common courtesy thing around this country. I can go on a trip to South Australian stations. I've just gotta ask and it is nice to just ask. They need a reason to say "no" apparently, according to the ILUAs and stuff, which is fair enough. If they were mustering in the area, as a washed-up old ringer, I understand that.

'They might say, "Best not to take your dog because we've just baited that area."

Despite the frustrations, the Indigenous community in the Diamantina Shire has nothing like the social problems of other outback communities.

'Absolutely. It goes right back to what I said earlier with the Act and people having to work. When you came to town and the copper thought it was your turn to go out, he'd come and say, "I'll pick you up in the morning, I'm taking you to Morney [Plains Station]."

'"Oh, where's that?"

'"Oh, you just be fucken ready."

'Nobody could stay in town if you didn't have a job, kind of thing. So you learnt from that to always work. We all are very conscious of the shame of not working. You got teased. Shame job. Although it's startin' to relax, I'm noticing, with some of the younger people not willingly looking for work. Having said that, some of the romantic work like being a stockman is vanishing. In some places it's already gone. So it's self-defeating now, all this other stuff, but from my generation, mate, nobody sat down. Today, I think this community shows that – we're a responsible group of people. We had the same ethics as everyone else here and we all worked. National Park people work harder, of course. Nah, but we all have the same work values.'

I remind Don there's still zero unemployment in the Diamantina Shire.

'Yeah, mate, and that's something we're proud of, really, from our Aboriginal community point of view. I don't know if people understand that at the moment or talk about it.'

No drug problems.

'No.'

Life expectancy is much higher. Health is better. Is it all the result of a strong work ethic?

'Nothing's surer than that but it's also that people have a pride in themselves. They always present well. They always dress up.

They always attend social events and stuff well dressed. If you took the colour of their skin off them, you wouldn't see 'em in there. They would fit in perfect. There's a lot of good people here. It's just they're still struggling with that stigma side of things, with the subservience. Mate, it's good to know that this community and all of the country is healthier than all the others.

'Too often, sadly, white people get involved with blackfella business not because they care but because they want to keep the status quo: divide and rule. Sadly, it's still happening. Look, I can hold my head high; it's been a struggle, but worthwhile. It's pleasing to note Birdsville is being noticed as a showcase community.'

Don and I were talking a few weeks after the announcement that he'd been awarded the Order of Australia medal for services to conservation, the community and the environment. As it detailed:

> Ranger in Charge, Simpson Desert (now Munga-Thirri) National Park, since 1994 and contributing to the greater understanding of Indigenous culture in the Simpson Desert, researching a number of culturally significant sites in the Park, promoting the greater district and undertaking cultural tours, in particular the Great Australian Outback Cattle Drive in 2004 and 2006 and returning former Wangkangurru Elders' memorial plaques to the Desert.

I suggest the award indicates that people far and wide see him as a leader in his community and have respect for him.

'Mate, I think it comes back to what I have to say, and no matter what meeting I'm at, I just make my points of view. Wherever I go, if people don't know me, they're glad to meet me. So that gives you a bit of an injection in the right arm when you get that.

'It could be easy for me to say that it doesn't bother me that much, but the real truth is that you must be doing something all right, you must be doing something in line with what the community wants. The Order of Australia beyond doubt kinda says that I am doin' good things.'

When we'd first spoken about doing this book and he mentioned the Order of Australia, he asked if I thought he should accept it. It was an opportunity to protest the treatment of Indigenous Australians. It was also an opportunity to be recognised by all the Australians who respected him. In the end he decided to become Donald Keith Rowlands, OAM.

'If I threw it back, who would be the only person who would suffer? If it was for all the old mob, maybe it'd be worthwhile having another think. I understand some people might not wanna, but this is about what you achieve as an individual. I never set out to do anything to get anything, but if that's what you earn on the way – and it has to be earned, really, totally earned – then I don't see anything wrong with that.

'For me and Lyn, it was a magic moment. We weren't allowed to tell anyone so we snuck it out to our kids and they were equally as excited. We had to keep quiet for a couple of months. Once the official word came down and the community knew, they were surprised.

'Apart from two people in town who came round and said congratulations [David Brook, OAM, and his wife, Nell], the rest of the community went quiet on us. That's pretty sad in a lot of ways, from the point of view that I know these people. I went to school with these guys and I remember hunting and fishing and chasing bush tucker and all the rest. It really is sad. It's sad that people can't leave some of their garbage behind to recognise someone else that they've grown up with. It's water off a duck's back – you do see it and feel it – but it's their issue not mine.

'That, to me, appears to be the old keeping-down syndrome.

'"He's got a voice. He's out there. We're not gonna lend our support to that."'

'People in Winton and Longreach and all across the country – down in Adelaide, the top departments, the bloody South Australian National Park, everybody – says, "well deserved" and "very good".

'I've got more handshakes from people I've known in the last few years rather than the people I grew up with. These guys, they wanna keep that old "foot on your throat" kinda thing. They might have picked on the wrong person, to be honest.

'It's a sad indictment on their life. I don't mind that being written because the only way we're gonna change the way people think in this kind of situation is to let 'em know that they're doin' it and people can see it, 'cos they seem to think it's their right to do that while at the same time wanting respect in return.

'The OAM, from what I can read and gather, you really have to be on your game to where a lot of people notice before you get the award. I think I've done the hard yards, I must have got nominated by someone who thought I was worthy. So, I feel special about that.

'I spoke to you about when we were growin' up, having to call people Mr So-and-so, Mrs So-and-so. We were forced to do that. I still do that today but it's more out of respect. Since this OAM thing, it's thrown in this curve ball. I've stopped sayin' it. If I can't get respect returned to me, well, I don't send any more out.

'This place was called Wirrari, that's the name of the water, and someone called it Birdsville. This is our home. And those hills – like I talked about the features in the landscape there – when you're comin' down from that way or you get on that big hill and you see those two little hills, you know you're goin' the right way. They belong and can't be destroyed.

'How can we get the community to embrace everything: our culture, our existence here, why things are so important to us? How do we make this community, that's already strong from the Aboriginal point of view, stronger by being more together, more . . . respect and all that stuff . . .? "Unified" is probably a better word than "reconciliation".

'I want to help change the situation. It's not a bad situation. It's just that there's still this little stand-off. We're on two different pieces of floating timber.'

Leg Eleven

Not long after the Birdsville Races were finished, the roads started to reopen. You could get to Bedourie to the north and Windorah to the east, although there were many spots where water was flowing over the road. Word was that the Birdsville Track was submerged for many kilometres of its length and would take many days, if not weeks, to be drivable.

Under the circumstances, any hope I had of connecting with Bernadette Burke had been washed away. She was taking a commercial flight to Mount Isa to meet the AACo plane that was going to Headingly Station and we might be able to get a few minutes. However, if the plane was already there, we might not get even that. As for driving to Headingly and trying to talk there, the unsealed roads were impassable. So that was that.

Fortunately, the next person on my list was another Birdsvillean. We organised to have a chat before we hit the road for home.

10.

'Barnesy'

Peter Barnes

(1954–)

There's a sign on the wall of the mechanic's workshop in the Birdsville Roadhouse that reads, '*We don't believe in miracles, we rely on them.*'

It's just as well. Miracles are often expected of the mechanic, Peter Barnes, known in the district and far beyond as 'Barnesy'. Motorists who've broken down in the middle of nowhere demand repairs asap. Never mind that parts have to be freighted from some far-away depot to one of the remotest towns in the outback. Four-wheel drive adventurers who've rolled or wrecked their vehicle in the desert expect that vehicle to be recovered, no matter how far off the beaten track they've managed to get.

Barnesy is up to the task. He combines an ability to fix just about anything with a quiet confidence that he can get the job done. He's always busy but he never seems to be in a hurry. He often looks to be in need of a shave, is always wearing a greasy sleeveless shirt and dirty baseball cap, but never fails to leave a good impression. You may wonder what his wife, Bronwynne, who runs the shop at the roadhouse and is always stylish and neat, sees in him. Until you get to know him. Or as another sign in the workshop says, '*We may be rough but at least we're expensive.*'

Barnesy has worked for or with Birdsville land-owner David Brook for many years, but there's more to their relationship than boss and worker: there's a mutual respect for each other's abilities. People like Fred Brophy mention Barnesy as one of the 'salt of the outback' people who've ensured they come back year after year.

My first impression of Barnesy dates back to 2009, when he'd returned to the Birdsville Roadhouse after some years away. There was a rattle in the Truckasaurus that had defeated all attempts at being located and fixed.

Barnesy said, 'Let's go for a drive.'

I headed off down the Birdsville Inside Track with Barnesy crawling all over the vehicle . . . listening here . . . listening there. A few kilometres out of town, the rattle started. Stopped. Started. Barnesy got in the back seat. Rattle. No rattle. He opened the windows and stuck his head out. Rattle.

'Found it!'

A bolt holding a roof rack was loose. Back in town, an allen key had the rattle relegated to reminiscence.

'How much do I owe you?'

'How much do you reckon tightening one bolt should cost?'

It worked out to be a couple of beers at the pub.

Barnesy was born in the south-eastern South Australian town of Millicent in 1954. He grew up there and was always going to be a mechanic.

'I had a job pickin' up spanners and sweepin' the floor after school and Saturday mornings for two years – fifty cents an hour. Buggered off [from school] and did an apprenticeship; worked for him for nine years – loved it.'

In his late twenties, his first marriage ended, and in 1982, he and his new partner, Bronwynne, started looking for some life experiences further afield.

'Bronwynne and I went over to Springsure [in the Central Highlands of Queensland]. I wanted to drive a tractor but because of the drought I thought, "Nah, this isn't good 'ere, I'll go back to Millicent and do something."

'I was at the pub one night and I had about ten bucks in me pocket. I owed some money on a Holden ute I owned and I had a little bit of debt and didn't have a job. A mate of mine had just come back from Kamaran Downs [in Western Queensland, near Bedourie]. He'd just been up there visiting where his brother had once worked. And he said, "Well, you'll get a job tomorrow at Kamaran."'

Mechanics have always been in short supply in the outback. His mate's advice was spot on.

'So I said, "Well, I'll ring the bloke tomorrow." David Brook owned it. So I rang his manager and he said, "Yeah, come up for six weeks."

'I borrowed five hundred bucks off my cousin 'cos I needed to put the diff back in the ute properly and buy a tyre or two and get it going so I could come up here. I drove up, started there and loved it.

'I went up for six weeks' work and I stayed for seven months. I liked the warmth and I think the dirt smelt good. I liked the vastness. And I still like the variety in Birdsville. If it's not 50 degrees, it's blowin' a gale or rainin' or dust storm or something. Real extreme. Having said that, you get lots of lovely days, like this, in the year. So it's pretty good. I enjoyed the space.

'I enjoyed working on the cattle station because I didn't have to fill out any time sheets or anything. I just had to do the work. And there was work enough to do – those old Suzukis [they're a signature vehicle of David Brook's operations, perhaps favoured because they're so light they practically float over the sand dunes], a few motorbikes, light plant, planes. I messed around with every-thing. You had to get it goin' because if you didn't get it goin', well . . .

'I went back home to Millicent and then we come up here for the Birdsvillle Races and went to Bedourie – Bronwynne and I in the Suzuki. I went out to the station and the manager said, "What about comin' back for six weeks again in October or some-thing – late October – and look after the place while I go away on holidays?"

'Bronwynne didn't really want to go back there. Then she said, "Oh, yeah, might as well."

'I said, "I'll let you know."

'Anyhow, I went up again and stayed for another seven months.

'The first time I come up, I said to David Brook about getting a workshop going because there was no workshop in Birdsville. And David said, "Oh, yeah."

'Then the second period I did there, David seen me and said, "What about this workshop idea?"

'And I said, "Yeah. I got nothin' else to do."

'So I come down to Birdsville then and just started in the old shed there [on David's expansive Birdsville block]. Cleaned it out. It had thirty years of junk in it. Me and the Suzuki and the trailer, we took loads to the dump. Shifted stuff around. They were buildin' a bridge at the time so the cement for the floor, they mixed the cement for us. We dug a pit in it. I went to Adelaide and bought some second-hand workshop equipment and brought it home and started fiddling around. So we stayed for twelve years.'

During that time he did an increasing number of desert rescues and recoveries. While many Australians were discovering the attractions of the outback, some didn't appreciate the dangers. When I was living in Birdsville, Barnesy told me of a couple of tragedies that occurred in the early 1990s.

'I fixed this birdwatching bloke's tyres. It was the hottest time of the year and this bloke was determined to go down to Walker's Crossing [200 kilometres south-east of Birdsville]. On the way back he rolled his vehicle and spent half a day sitting there. He'd run out of water so when someone came along they gave him a drink and drove him back to Birdsville. Along the way he started complaining, "Why have you put vodka in my water?"

'The people didn't think anything of it. They just thought he might be a bit crazy. When they got into Birdsville they dropped him at the clinic. Half an hour later, he was dead. He'd thought they were making him drunk. He was actually dying from organ failure.'

Then there was a couple who took the advice on what to do if they got stuck too literally.

'They'd broken down and in the heat of summer they sat in their car. They'd been told, "Don't leave the vehicle."

'Eventually they were found and they were in a pretty bad way. They came in here [to Birdsville] and had a beer. Then they went to their room. She said she was going to have a shower. He said he didn't feel well and was going to lie down. When she came out of the shower, he was dead.'

Tales like that ensured I always carried 20 litres of water in my vehicle, and told someone where I was going and when I expected to get there. Even driving on the expressway between Sydney and Lake Macquarie, I carry water in case an accident closes the road for a few hours and it's over 40 degrees. The outback isn't the only place where heat can be fatal.

In 1995, Barnesy and Bronwynne and their young son, Sam, set out on what was intended to be a road trip round Australia.

'We drove over to Tamworth Music Festival and then Dubbo – I got a job tractor drivin' in Dubbo. Then we got a call that Bronwynne's dad was a bit crook so the family wanted us to go back to Millicent. While I was there, a mate of mine who'd worked for me in Birdsville, we were in the pub one night and he said this bloke in New Guinea rang and wanted him to go over there.

'I said, "What do you gotta do?"

'He said, "Oh, fix a few cars."

'I said, "You goin'?"

'"Nah", he said, "I can't go."

'He had young kids. I said, "I can. I'll ring him tomorrow."

'So I rang this bloke in New Guinea and he said, "Oh, I was only jokin'." Then he said, "Now I'm talkin' to you, I have got a bloody job for you."

'It took a while to get organised, a few tests, a few needles, police check and things. So we got all that ticked off and we went over there for eight months. That was fantastic for the three of us. Sam was only young; he went to school over there. People were lovely. We lived in Rabaul and we worked at a coconut oil mill. We only stayed there for eight months, because the place was lovely but just the way they ran the place was a bit . . .'

By then it was 1996, and with a young family to support, Barnesy didn't want to go home without a job.

'So I rang David [Brook]. He said, "Oh, keep comin' home. I'm thinking of buying this block of land down the road."

'Which is Mumpy [Murnpeowie Station, in South Australia near Innamincka]. The grapevine had us goin' to Mumpy but I hadn't been told, so we got to Birdsville and Dave said, "Go down to Mumpy."

'"Right-o."

'He said, "Go down there for six months and see what you can get done, as a manager."

'So we went down there and we went flat out for six-and-a-half years. Did lots of stuff.'

Lots of stuff included helping David out of his aircraft after he'd forgotten to put the wheels down for a landing.

'Yeah, well, David had a bit of bad luck there one day. I heard him say something like, "I've landed and I can't get the wheels down."

'I thought, "That's not right."

'So I went over there and saw he'd landed the plane on its belly and realised what he really said. He said after, he thought the ground was softer than he thought [he thought the undercarriage had sunk in] and he'd struggle to take off. Then he saw the ground was right there! Got him out and then there was quite a bit to do to fix the plane. A couple of blokes came up one day and I gave them a hand to pull the plane to bits and load it onto a trailer, then it was taken away for repairs.'

Not long after, Barnesy left the outback and went back to South Australia briefly. He looked after Cordillo Downs for six months and while there, he and Bronwynne bought a small block of land on the Queensland Coast and spent the next year or so there. Theo Nel, a South African, took over running the road-house and doing outback recoveries, along the way becoming something of a legend in his own right.

Birdsville cop Neale McShane recalled Theo going like a 'scalded cat'. He'd go out and get a vehicle, bring it back, then go straight out and get another one. It was a lucrative business, and by 2009 Theo had earned enough to set himself up in business nearer to the Queensland coast.

'David rang me one day to tell me that Theo was leaving and wondered if Bronwynne and I would like to come out to Birdsville for a couple of weeks, to get the place organised till someone else came along. That was about eight or nine years ago.'

In 2009, one of the biggest dust storms in recent history hit Birdsville, and everything east of it. In fact much of southern Queensland and New South Wales was covered in fine red dust. There were incredible images of the Sydney Harbour Bridge wrapped in a dull red gloom.

In the midst of the raging wind and dust, an emergency beacon or 'EPIRB' (short for 'emergency position-indicating radio beacon') was activated nearly 200 kilometres west of Birdsville.

'I went for a run [in my ute]. All we had was an EPIRB so we didn't know what was happening, just that there was an emergency. They're terrible those things. Satphones are much better because you can find out what the problem is. On this recovery, the sole occupant of the vehicle, John White, wasn't injured, but the vehicle was on its side, near Poeppel Corner.

'I went back out three days later [in my truck] to get the vehicle. The chassis was halfway down a sandy slope. I hooked a cable onto a back corner and sort of pulled it back upright, but the angle was so steep that it was just balancing. I got Hugh Brown [a photographer who went along to get some photos] to put his weight on it while I reattached, then I was able to pull it out.

'John White thought the car was a write-off. He was saying, "There's a fridge there, keep that. Compressor, keep that. It's all wrecked."

'I said, "Wait on. It's not so bad."

'Like, the mirror on the side that had dug into the sand wasn't even broken. The panels on that side were a bit depressed. If the car was five years old you wouldn't even worry about them. The cab was full of dirt and sand: cleaned that out. Cleaned the air filters, turbo and those sorts of things, and it was, "There you go. Happy holidays."'

Sometimes jobs come thick and fast. Then, people who want to be rescued have to join the queue. That's particularly so when they drive down flooded roads.

'One trip was 200 kilometres down the track. I was thirty minutes down the road when Bron called. There was another breakdown 200 kilometres out the other way.

'I said, "Tell him he'll have to wait."

'Got the first one, got back, had about an hour's sleep, went to get the other one. After a day and a half he was pleased to see someone. I'd tried to get the police [Neale McShane] to call to let him know but they didn't get through.

'Satphones are the go. They can save so much. EPIRBs give you nothing. There could be someone under the car. With phones you can say we need an ambulance or a recovery. I'm often first there because I can travel faster.

'I've talked a lot of people out of the desert. Try this or that. Let your tyres down. One bloke needed a starter motor, out at Poeppels. For a recovery I charge $400 an hour and the truck I use is slow. A typical job is $4000. So I said to this bloke, "Wait three days, we'll get the part and bring it out."

'Well, after a day, he said, "Come get me."

'I've fixed all sorts of things. I've welded trailers, I put some rear springs in a 79 Series LandCruiser in the desert one day about 190 kilometres from Birdsville. It was raining. It was okay under the vehicle but getting in and out of there was a lot of sloppin' in mud. It's pretty sticky that mud when you're rolling in it and it builds up 5 centimetres thick on your boots. I did one recovery on the other side of the desert. The diff went. It took me half a day to go to Mount Dare to weld it up and get some parts sent from Alice Springs. Plus I broke things on my vehicle getting there.

'In desert driving, my tips are, it should never be hard driving on sand. Stop before you dig in. Let your tyres down. It's easier on the vehicle and not such a rough ride. You get these people with all these fancy beadlocks and special tyres. I don't think we've ever had a tyre come off the bead. You can tell when the pressure's right because the tyres get traction and the driving gets easier.

'Don't drive too fast up or down the dunes. You don't want to launch over the top of the dune or lose control on a slope and maybe roll. If you don't think you're going to make it over, stop before you hook yourself on top. If you end up with all four wheels off the ground, beached, you need to dig a lot of sand to get them all on the ground [before] you can go again.'

When it comes to desert driving, Barnesy knows what he's talking about. He's not just a legend among bush mechanics. He's also up at the pointy end of the pack when it comes to off-road racing.

'I started racing in 1979 in Millicent Sand Buggy Club and bought an old buggy that cost me fifty bucks essentially. I swapped a second-hand motorbike for fifty bucks. It needed re-wiring and I got it goin' and flogged it around Millicent Sand Buggy Club for twelve months to two years. Then I built another buggy. I did all right in that in up to 1200 cc, Class Three.

'I raced for a few years then we got out of buggies for a little while. Then Sam wanted to ride a four-wheeler motorbike in the Finke Desert Race.

'So Bron and I thought, "Well, maybe we'd better buy a buggy. Kids have more fun with a roll-cage and seatbelts and appropriate stuff."

'So we bought another machine off a bloke in Millicent. I bought another one and then I sold that and I bought another one that I knew was good. I drove it for the first three or four years and then Sam started takin' over drivin'. We were Class Three National Champions five years out of seven, which is good. Nobody could catch us. We had a light machine and we'd move around a bit.

'Amongst all that we raced Australian Safari from Sydney to Darwin three times: in 1990, '93 and '94. First year I did it in a Suzuki Vitara, so we finished the race and that's all. In '93 we raced a LandCruiser ute with a 3F petrol engine in it and we won the National Class outright, so that was good.

'The year after that, I had a few dealings with Ford Motor Company and they offered me a Courier to drive and I thought, "Well, no, it's too hard" because that's the style of car the big boys from overseas run and they literally spend a million bucks on 'em. So I thought, "Well, there's not much point in just tagging along behind the winners."

'I said I'd race a Falcon ute, just for the hell of it. So we got a new Longreach ute, outfitted it for the safari and did well. I can't quite remember how many cars started in our class in Sydney – maybe eight – and we were the only one to get to Darwin. We won the international two-wheel drive class. Once they all dropped out, we could concentrate on what we were doing. One of the cars was like a brand new Ford Mustang or some bloody thing from America. It looked like it had nearly a million bucks spent on it.

'It was a bit of a challenge drivin' that event but it was fun. I knew the director of the event: he used to come here a bit looking for track. I wasn't gonna race in '94 – he come here late and I showed him a bit of track out here, up around the desert, and then next thing I'm racin' in two-wheel drive and I straight away thought, "Well what about those bloody big sandhills I've put in there?"

'Me navigator down in Sydney said, "What about these big sandhills?"

'I said, "I'll tell you where we gotta worry about 'em. When we get to the bottom of 'em."

'We had no trouble. Drove over 'em. The leader of the event, I seen on video – the winner outright of the race – he had about ten goes on some of the sandhills.

'What else did I do? I don't know how many times I raced, at Finke, now – probably ten or fifteen. Varying results. I raced a Suzuki Sierra down in Millicent a few times; raced once at Sea Lake. I've lapped round various vehicles over the years and had a lot of fun.

'Sam does the driving now and Sam's really happy with the current off-road racing plan. He drives and Dad pays. I'd be pretty happy, too, because I didn't have a dad who was into off-road racing.

'We've now got a bigger buggy – Pro Lite Class, which is up to 3.5 litre naturally aspirated. We run a 350Z motor in a buggy that would do a lighter machine than most. So this year, at Finke, Sam won his class and came eleventh outright, out of 130 buggies. It's not hard to come home with a hard-luck story but this year was good.'

Son Sam's desert driving skills came to the fore around 2011 when Kelly Theobald arrived in Birdsville. Kelly was a writer, a blogger and an accomplished photographer.

Kelly and Sam went out together for a couple of years, during which time they drove her Volkswagen across the desert. It was a remarkable feat that resulted in Kelly writing a children's book about their adventure, *Onslo*, which was the name of the car.

Sam and Kelly separated not long after. Sadly, in 2015, Kelly was driving a vehicle on the Birdsville Track south of the town and rolled. She died at the scene and her passenger was badly injured.

Sam is also one of the first people called upon to drive the ambulance when people are injured out in the desert.

In August 2012, there was a call that a motorbike rider west of Poeppel Corner had caught his foot in a tree root and broken his leg. His foot was twisted entirely around – he was in extreme pain. Birdsville's then police officer, Neale McShane, Sam and a nurse left Birdsville at 8.30 p.m. The motorbike rider was on a mattress in the back of a ute, slowly being driven over the dunes in an effort to cut down the distance and time between him and badly needed pain relief.

The rescuers got to the vicinity of Poeppels at 2 a.m. and rendezvoused with the rider soon after. As Neale said in *Outback Cop*:

> Normally, you wouldn't drive through the desert at night if you didn't have to. However, this bloke was in excruciating pain and his mates were so happy when they knew that we were coming out, that help was on the way. A lot of times that's what people want to hear; that someone cares about them and they're coming out to meet them.

A few weeks later, more motorbike riders were on the Warburton Track when one of them came off and was badly hurt. He couldn't ride so his mates left him in a swag and rode into Birdsville, where they went and saw Barnesy.

They said, 'Oh, can you go down and pick up a bike? And while you're there, pick up our mate, too.'

Barnesy said, 'Oh, what's he doin'?'

They said, 'Oh, he's hurt himself.'

Barnesy put two and two together and alerted Neale that a rescue might be required. Neale found the injured rider's mates relaxing in a room at the Birdsville Hotel. They weren't much help in detailing the nature of the rider's injuries, but it became clear he'd been left on his own for quite some time. It was decided that Barnesy, Neale and the nurse would head out that night.

Barnesy went in his car. Neale went in the police car. John White – who'd been rescued by Neale and Barnesy back in 2009, and was now a friend of both and a regular Birdsville visitor – drove the ambulance with the nurse.

It was 250 kilometres to the accident site. Along the way, the rescuers passed a number of dingoes, and they started to fear the worst. Fortunately, when they got to the rider, he hadn't been torn to pieces – but he did have broken ribs and a punctured lung. He was eventually driven back to Birdsville and flown out by the Royal Flying Doctor Service.

When I lived in Birdsville, Barnesy used to bring crashed vehicles into town on his truck and leave them there until they could be transported elsewhere for repairs or to be written off. Inevitably, the crashed vehicle was an object of interest for visitors, who then inundated the Birdsville cop and Barnesy with questions about what had happened. It was a good way to get people talking about safe driving in the outback: drive to the conditions and, if necessary, slow down. However, the questions just kept coming. Neale, the cop, cracked first.

He asked Barnesy if there was any chance of moving the truck out of sight.

Barnesy said he'd been thinking the same thing. He was answering so many questions he couldn't get any work done.

Actually, that was what he'd been doing with me for the previous hour. During that time, Sam Barnes had been busy all around us. I couldn't help thinking there might be another generation waiting to take over when Barnesy called it a day. Not that he's planning to do so soon.

His explanation of his enjoyment of desert rallying could apply just as much to why he's spent thirty-five years in the outback.

'We're always working on the buggy. There's always something. It's just in our blood. It's what we do. Some people play golf, some go fishin' and we go off-road racing. Yeah, spending more time in the outback.'

Leg Twelve

We were homeward bound once more. However, the outback wasn't finished with us just yet. The road to Windorah had reopened the day before but then Brown Creek near Betoota, which had been dropping, had risen during the night. It had torn a couple of holes in the road that crossed it – holes which had nearly swallowed a couple of vehicles that drove into them unawares.

When we got to Brown Creek, there was a council worker on one side and new Birdsville Cop Stephan Pursell on the other.

'Follow his directions,' we were told.

As we headed into the rushing water, Stephan held both hands straight up to indicate 'Go straight'. Then one hand down meant 'Go left', the other hand down meant 'Go right'. He was guiding us around two holes a metre deep that were hidden beneath the torrent. Stephan couldn't see them; he just knew where they were.

I couldn't help noting the irony of Birdsville's new police officer leaving the big smoke (Maroochydore) behind to live in the middle of nowhere, and he was still directing traffic.

There was more water than ever all the way across the outback to Quilpie, where we spent a night at the beautifully restored Heritage Inn. The next day, there were even more flowers than there were on our outward journey, and we had them almost entirely to ourselves. The rain had discouraged a lot of travellers. In some parts roads were still closed. So we poked along, enjoying the scenery for hour after hour.

We found a beautiful creek crossing where we pulled up for morning coffee among the river red gums. We'd been cracking along at such a pace, it was the first time we'd had a chance to settle down and enjoy a quiet outback experience. It was just us, a few birds, a soft breeze rustling the leaves above us and the gentle chatter of water running over the crossing.

We caught up with the rain down in New South Wales and sloshed our way over to the upper Hunter, then enjoyed the wonderful, winding road down from the Great Dividing Range into the cleft hewn by the river, gradually opening to the broad, fertile, rolling plains of the valley itself.

It was a pretty big day's driving, but when Michelle asked if I was getting tired, I replied, 'I don't think I could ever get tired of this.'

Leg Thirteen

Flew Newcastle–Brisbane–Perth. Daylight flight over southern Queensland, the Flinders Ranges, South Australia's salt lakes, the Great Australian Bight and WA's Great Southern.

Those are my notes for an entire day's travel over the great Australian vastness. They were more extensive than those of most of my fellow travellers, though, who were engrossed in the tiny screens attached to the seats in front of them.

This was my final journey in search of outback legends. This leg, though, wasn't taking me to a location in the outback. Instead, it was going to take me back in time, to an era all but forgotten and to experiences known to incredibly few.

It would also lead me to a vehicle that had soaked up that history and its passengers' adventures like a sponge. Like Tom Kruse's Leyland Badger or John Flynn's Dodge Buckboard, there was no doubt in my mind that the truck itself was the stuff of legends.

11.

The Last Ring Pounder

Bedford Truck

(c.1934–)

PART ONE

There are few places as hot, remote and empty as the north-west of Western Australia. It has always been and still is a challenging frontier. Nevertheless, from the 1860s, intrepid pioneers ventured there. They established sheep stations along the De Grey River at Port Hedland (1650 kilometres north of Perth) and by 1886 there were 63 000 sheep in the West Kimberley region (2400 kilometres north of Perth).

Initally, it was possible to shear the region's small flocks with local Indigenous and European blade shearers. By 1901, with 300 000 sheep in the West Kimberley and 1.8 million in the pastoral areas, full-time shearers were needed. Eastern states contractors such as Young and Co. and Federal Shearing Company started organising teams of shearers to travel up from Perth each year. They went by ship then donkey cart to the woolsheds, braving cyclones and flooded rivers. The era of what became known as 'expeditionary shearing' had begun.

After trucks were introduced in the 1930s, the men called it 'truck shearing'. They called the trucks 'ring pounders', referring to the beating their backsides took on long journeys over roads that often existed in name only. Many of those men (and a few women) have passed away, having shared only a few tantalising memories of what they went through. Others are still alive and can recall the adventures and hardships they experienced. Their stories are best told in their words.

The Journey

Reg Dunbar, 'expert' (responsible for machinery) and partner in contracting firm Synnot and Dunbar:
'[From the 1930s] the shearing trucks used to go to the Kimberley by boat as deck cargo. Transport costs were by cubic capacity, which is why our trucks were cut down to the windscreen and no cab. The fifteenth of November was the last date to leave for Derby before the wet season started. The men came by boat in February, although towards the end of the forties they started to fly up.'

Don Munday, shearer; handwritten description on a photo from 1931:
'It was tough going over the Liveringa Flats along the Fitzroy River to the Myroodah Crossing. It was as hot as hell and the water was damned near boiling. My feet looked like "Cooked Pigs Trotters".'

Gerry Young, presser (responsible for baling wool):
'We called Synnot's cut-down trucks "lizards". They were very low, with no top on them, and they looked like lizards crawling through the spinifex.'

Trevor Keating, shearer and museum curator:

'Sometimes they'd take the trucks up by boat from Fremantle up to Derby and they'd fly the shearers up, but in '43 the Japanese was strafin' the West Australian coast so they went inland. Marc Synnot [son of Synnot and Dunbar founder Fred Synnot] took a hundred men. There was five truckloads of shearers and rouseabouts for five different stations and a truckload of stores. That was in this wet year. It took twenty-six days, pushin' and pullin' these trucks, with no pay, to get from Perth, from the Ozone Hotel, to Derby. Crossing Anna Plains it took 'em three days to do a mile and a half [3 kilometres].

'Marc Synnot said, "There was one argument. I was drivin' the lead truck and it was open and there was two shearers sittin' in the back and I could hear 'em arguin'. What they were arguin' about was who was the best professional ballroom waltzer."

'The two men who were arguing had both been manpowered [forced to work in an occupation excluded from military service] out of Fremantle Prison to make up the numbers.

'Marc said, "They got to Marble Bar, they circled the trucks and the men, a couple of mouth organs were produced, and they made these two old shearers dance. Waltz. And they danced till they dropped. And they called it a draw.

'Marc said, "The men that done that journey of twenty-six days, they were tired, they were hot and they were sunburnt, and they were tough. Any man that done that epic journey, it was a credit to 'em. We wouldn't have got there apart from the men."'

Ron Law, shearer/son of a shearer:

'I remember Dad being away shearing and going with Mum to meet him off the *Kyabra* at Fremantle when he came home.

'I loved the yolky smell of his swag. I think that's what got me into shearing; that smell in his clothes and swag and the wonderful stories of the outback. I had to get out there myself. I hadn't even seen shearing until 1941, when I went into a team. I was manpowered during the war. I went away with [contractor] Stan Baston, one of Gosden and McGinnity's protégés around the Gascoyne. I was a shedhand the first year and started shearing the following year, when I was sixteen.

'I only went to the Kimberley once . . . 1944, with Synnot and Dunbar. We went to Broome [2240 kilometres north of Perth] on the *Koolinda*. It kept close to the coast to keep away from Jap submarines.

'In the early days the roads were just ruts. We'd make our own tracks across the river beds; put spinifex down to get across, a lot of pushing and pulling. If the river was flooded we couldn't cross at all; many a time everyone's sat on the back of the truck all night. We couldn't get out and unroll our swag because it was too wet. Synnot's trucks were all open – no top or anything – just back-to-back seating down the middle. We'd sit each side with our feet on the drop-side and all the swags tied on.

'I was on one that Marc Synnot tipped over out of Broome; the three who were hurt were in the front with no protection. We righted the truck and took the injured ones into Broome. No-one died, but Franky Rutherford, the expert, nearly died; his chest was crushed. When they got him into Broome Hospital the doctor said, "Put him in a bed, he'll die." In the morning, Franky was sitting up asking for a cigarette.

'I did miss the shearing at first when I retired. The time of the year when the mob was going north I'd feel like the ducks. Want to migrate.'

Peter Cleaver, shearer:
'Bill Young's truck had garden seats across the back; we called them the old "ring pounders". God, they were hard. When we got to the first station we'd pinch wool and make cushions. I rode up on top of the swags with my feet on the hood to miss the dust; it was only gravel roads and the dust comes up behind you. It was murder.'

Bill Young, contractor, 1933 to 1991:
'I used trucks to carry the gear for a long time, even after the men travelled in their own cars. It would take two full days to travel from Perth to Carnarvon; the roads were terrible, full of bumps. It took one day to get to Geraldton. That road was maintained but the others north of Geraldton weren't. Between Geraldton and Northampton the road was always rough: it was bad, terrible, all hills and corrugations. By gee those trucks would bounce about! Poor devils in the back. We had big single tyres – not dual wheels – because stones would jam between the duals. We tripped up and down those roads for years. Those damned roads!

'There was no service stations between Northampton and Carnarvon; traffic wasn't heavy then. I carted tins of every damned thing. I made a 50-gallon [227-litre] petrol tank for the truck, a reserve tank, and also carried a 44-gallon [200-litre] drum of petrol. A couple of times I travelled up by ship but not with the men; it was three days from Fremantle to Carnarvon by ship.'

Peter Cleaver, shearer:
'The track into Tamala, Shark Bay, was through sandhills and we put boards under the wheels for traction. It was shocking. We'd take the boards out and run to the front of the truck. We were all

racing like bloody mad to get them out and up the front. Once the truck was going we couldn't stop. Bill was just crawling along in first gear. One wet year we had to pull the truck out of a bog at Williambury. Bill had a big cotton rope on the front. I'd get up the front of the rope if I could; the ones who pushed would get covered in mud from the wheels spinning. We were a mess! The "good old days". We were lucky to get the truck across some of the dry creek beds. They were deep gullies; the motor would be on one side and the tray touching the bank we'd just left.'

Chris Fyfe, shearer. In 1949 he saw expert Arthur Dunbar fix a ring pounder's radiator after a branch punched a hole in it during a creek crossing:

'Arthur surveyed the hole through the radiator. He took the radiator off and, with a hacksaw blade, cut a square hole in it to expose the cores and then pinched the ends with pliers. He soldered up the exposed ends, heating the iron in a fire we had going. What he had was a perfectly good radiator with a square hole in it. He put it back together, drained the oil out of the engine and put in fresh oil. By this time we'd dried out the distributor leads. The truck burst into life first try and he drove it back to De Grey. On the Sunday he took off the front wheels, greased the bearings, and put them all back together. I'll always remember: "Good as gold," he said.'

Jim Pringle, shearer:

'I applied to Synnot and Dunbar and in March 1949 presented myself at the Esplanade to get on the shearers' truck. It was due to leave about ten o'clock – I got there at seven.

'We took three days to get to the first shed, Boodarie near Port

Hedland. The truck had a cover over the top and a back-to-back seat down the middle – there was no cab and no doors. Four people could sit across the front seat, one on the outside of the driver. We'd take turns opening gates and rotate seats every two hours. If the trip was long enough, we went right around the back and up to the front again. At sixteen, I considered it an adventure.'

Jack Mildwaters, shearer. Recalled what may be the only ring pounder fatality, in 1949:
'A rousie from the Noonkanbah team fell off the back of their truck and died. That was the old ring pounder, back-to-back seating, shift around two places every four hours. This kid fell off while they were shifting around.'

Bert Latham, shearer:
'I shore with Scotty Fleay at Onslow; he lived there. The team flew up and he took us out to Boolooloo on the back of his truck; it was a bloody old Fargo and we pushed it halfway there. They'd all be drinking and stop to go to the toilet. Every time we stopped we couldn't get the truck started so we had to push it. The further we went, the drunker they were getting.

'Our gear was at the back of the truck. I was sitting on one side and we were smoking and throwing our butts out and the wind blew them in on the gear. I could see smoke. The truck was making a lot of smoke anyway but it was getting thicker.

'I yelled out, "The truck's on fire!"

'There was canvas over the back and Ray Tussingham jumped over to kick everything off. He grabbed the frame – it was red hot – and he burnt his hand but he kicked all the gear off. We'd have all gone up if he hadn't.'

Ted Dreckow, shearer:
'[In '52] Yarraloola had very big rains and was flooded; no chance of dry sheep. The roads were officially closed and any damage to them had to be paid for. A few, including Jimmy Pringle, walked the 80 miles into Onslow to catch the boat to Fremantle; it took them three days.'

Colin Christensen, shearer. From 1949, after the WA government started subsidising airfares to encourage development in the north, shearers started going up by plane. Once they arrived in the north, they travelled from shed to shed in the ring pounders:
'We flew from Perth. Noonkanbah had its own airfield and we went up on the old Fokker Friendships [planes]. MacRobertson Miller Aviation [flew them].'

Harold Christensen, shearer. Colin's brother also flew:
'DC-3. All the gear used to go up on the boats. The trucks, our cases and the food supplies.'

John 'Snow' McMeikan, shearer/truck driver:
'In 1953 I was given the job of driving [contractor Eric] Kennedy's truck. I enjoyed the responsibility; it was better than riding in the back. The fumes used to pour in and Old Jim the dog would fart all the time. The blokes would get drunk and didn't seem to care. The station tracks were pretty rough and everything was covered in red dust.'

Peter Letch, wool classer/contractor:
'[In 1958] after Moogooree we went across Butcher's Track to get to Shark Bay; it was badly overgrown and the bushes would slap

us as we went along. The ones up front would yell "heads" and we'd put our hands up and cover our heads. One of the shearers got a lump of bush and every time they yelled "heads", he hit this whinger across the head. "Oh. That one got me! That one got me!" He never woke up; he got hit every time.'

Harold Christensen, shearer:
'The truck travel was an experience in itself. The back of a shearers' truck was a wonderful way to see the country; there was an uninterrupted view in every direction. The trucks went like clocks: Arthur Dunbar made sure of that. We spent a lot of time off the trucks, pushing them out of bogs and fixing punctures. Apart from that we never broke down.'

Tom Pringle, shearer:
'With Synnot we had to ride on their truck – there was a roof but no sides. If it rained we got wet and if anyone up front spewed, we got it down the back. We were young and fit and sitting on the truck day and night didn't worry us. Talk about pushing the truck? One year from Mount Anderson to Myroodah, through Liveringa, we pushed the truck for miles through 3 foot [90 centimetres] of water.'

Darryl Grey, wool classer/contractor:
'In the 1960s we had plenty of times when we were all night pushing and pulling a truck out of a bog. We had to go to a place called Callie and this bloke definitely wanted us there tomorrow to start shearing. It had been raining, raining, raining. We couldn't go on the main roads because they were all closed. So the contractor decided to go through on the station tracks. We

were bogged and so on, but we got to this station, where a guy named Murphy owned the place, at dawn. The overseer went and asked him if he could get some meat for the cook because we hadn't had a feed. Murphy asked the overseer how many men were in the team.

'He said, "Fifteen."

'So Murphy went and got fifteen chops out of his fridge and from then on he was known as One-Chop Murphy.

'We were crossing the De Grey River. Frank Marks [the contractor] was sittin' in the front of this truck going across this river and the water's pretty high and it got on the motor and cut the motor out. All the shearers and that immediately grabbed their swags and everything off the back of the truck and headed for the edge of the river. Of course, that takes the weight off the truck and it floats further away.

'I'm walkin' alongside [shearer] Geoff Hooper – a real good guy, a big guy – and as we're going along Frank Marks is still in the front of the truck and he yells out, "Geoff! Geoff! What am I gonna do?"

'Geoff turned around and he said, "Scuttle 'er, Frank. Scuttle 'er."

'The guys all got their gear over to the riverbank, came back, and got on with pulling it out.

'The thing is, you went on the back of a 1300-weight Bedford with fifteen men and all their gear and all their stores. You wouldn't be allowed on a vehicle today, like that. Never ever heard of fatal accidents, crashes or things like that. Everybody just did by common sense: yeah we'll fit another one on that, another one on there.'

Peter Piavanini, shearer:
'My expedition to the Port Hedland area was 1962. We got on the truck at the Ozone Hotel. That's where every shearin' team in Western Australia took off from.

'They called 'em "ring pounders". Aptly named. Every washout these trucks'd go through they'd hit the gully and all the swags'd jump up and all the beer in the cases, and some'd smash.

'They got bogged. They were only tracks. They were only wide enough for one truck. That now is a major highway but they called it the Madman's Track. That was the name of the road from Paynes Find to Port Hedland [1229 kilometres]. I don't know how it got its name but I assume it was because you were mad to go up it. There wasn't any civilisation for near on 800 mile [1287 kilometres]. There was Nullagine. That was a tin shed for a pub.'

John Williams, shearer:
'I caught the truck from outside the Ozone Hotel in Adelaide Terrace. From there we went to Sylvania Station but there must have been a lot of rain north of Meekatharra and we had to camp at the Meekatharra racecourse overnight. Two nights to get up to Sylvania Station. That would have been 1963. I was nineteen.

'It wasn't a bad truck, but cold at night, wind blowing in; you're sitting on bench seats and all the luggage and tucker was in the back of it, inside a cage, so it didn't fall out.

'We were coming back from shearing somewhere and a lot of the guys drank and then they had to have a leak. This particular boss was a bit deaf and they'd yell out "Piss-o, piss-o" but he never heard. So I was sitting at the back of the truck and he was having this wee out the side of the truck and I copped all of it in the face.

'The longest trip we did was out of Daly Station, out of Sandstone, to Mandora Station, that's between Broome and Port Hedland and we went almost non-stop, a thousand miles [1600 kilometres]. They would fill the truck up with juice, it would go for four hours before it'd run out of fuel and then they'd fill it up again because they had 44-gallon [200-litre] drums on the back of the truck. Then another driver would take over. We stopped at Meekatharra for something but no stopping for a sleep. Just the back of a truck for hours and hours on end till we got to Mandora Station.'

Trevor Keating, shearer and museum curator:
'When I went up, in 1969, we were goin' out to Warrawagine Station. We'd run out of spare tyres so they were fillin' the tyres up with spinifex grass. It's amazing history. It's the only place where this truck travel happened.

'Then you got charged for travellin'! We pushed and pulled the bloody trucks all the way to the north-west and then they bloody charged us.'

Arthur 'Banjo' Paterson, shearer:
'On Synnot's truck he charged five pounds to ride on it but you pushed it through miles of mud and sand. They oughta been payin' us to push it. There was no way in the world would they have got through without twenty guys. At times you were bogged anyhow. We've been bogged in the De Grey, spent a day there trying to get out.'

Trevor Keating, shearer and museum curator:
'I went in 1968 and 1969. I come from the eastern states as a sixteen-year-old boy and landed a job as a rouseabout. Even then there wasn't many cars goin' up to the north. You were isolated up there. You couldn't get to town and the contractors liked it like that.'

The Destination

Dudley Tuckey, classer:
'At the outbreak of the war with Japan we were shearing at Corunna Downs. The Americans moved in very smartly with their long-range bombers; we'd count them at dusk as we heard them fly out and again as they came back in the morning. On many occasions there would be two or three missing. I didn't let on I was in the shearing industry and joined up; I was in the 28th Battalion.'

Arthur Clarke, presser:
'The first year I went up [in the 1940s] we carried a couple of chaff bags and filled them with wool to put on the beds because the stuffing had gone from the mattresses. We had hurricane lamps and no fridges; the meat was hung in the meat house and if there were holes in the netting it would be walking with maggots the next morning. If it started to move across the plate, we knew it was trouble.'

Bill Young, contractor:
'During the war . . . the Japs were a bit troublesome up the top and we heard they might come further south. We were shearing at Minderoo and camped in the quarters not far out of Onslow. This

night one plane did come down; it circled our quarters, right round, big white quarters only 20 miles [32 kilometres] from Onslow.

'Town had rung and said, "Get out of those quarters."

'The big presser, Askevold, and I were mates. He was lying on the bed, "Let 'em come."

'When it came over, we got stuck in the door; great big fellow he was, the presser. By gee! The plane was so low I swear to God you could touch him. Moonlight it was and he came down and circled around us trying to find Pot Shot, the depot where all the troops were. We didn't get any more planes. That was a terrible thing, the noise from the plane like that, right down on top of you.'

Jack Edge, shearer/contractor:
'I hadn't heard about the Pilbara or Murchison but I soon found out. It was snowing when I left Tasmania [in 1942] and at Marble Bar it was 120 degrees Fahrenheit [48.9 degrees Celsius]. Gosden did Warrawagine, Mulyie and Braeside and then came down to the Murchison.

'At Mulyie I got dengue fever; I couldn't work. I'd go to bed and get cold and get up and start to perspire. I was sitting out on the wood heap when an Aboriginal lady came along.

'She said, "You very sick boy."

'I said, "Yes, I am."

'She gave me some black-looking stuff in a jam tin to drink. I thought I couldn't be any worse so I drank it. Three hours later I was right again. I never knew what it was but it got rid of the fever.'

Herc Weston, expert:
'At Mount Philip [in the 1950s] I took ill with appendicitis. The station owner's wife, Mrs Oakley, couldn't raise the Meekatharra

Hospital for help. I had been unconscious for some time when the cook brought in a huge poultice and placed it on my stomach; it brought me around and I was OK after an hour or so. Looking down the bed I noticed a pick and shovel by the door; in came Luigi Basseneli, the villain. "Looks like we won't need these after all."'

Arthur 'Banjo' Paterson, shearer:
'The conditions, you put up with them then but you'd never put up with them now. There was no real refrigeration. The cook – most of the places had a kero fridge but that was for twenty men. The quarters were pretty rugged. The food wasn't too bad but it wasn't too good either.

'Liveringa, the first year we went there, we had these big 4-gallon [18-litre] square tins. They were ex-army dried potatoes, dried swedes, and it was terrible that. I don't know how the army blokes fought on it. Then you had to put that lime juice in your waterbag to keep your stomach in order and that used to rot the waterbag in three weeks.'

Colin Christensen, shearer:
'Noonkanbah was the biggest shed in the state. Everyone wanted to go to that shed to say they'd been to Noonkanbah. Liveringa was about as big.'

Harold Christensen, shearer:
'May 1952 I started to shear. I did one year on the goldfields and then I followed Colin and I went north and I had three years in the north-west with Synnot and Dunbar. It was a wonderful experience and I enjoyed every day of it.'

Colin Christensen, shearer:

'Of a nighttime you didn't need anything on your bed. It was that hot. Very hot during the day and a lot of people never acclimatised to that heat and gave the game away. It sorted out the men from the boys.'

Harold Christensen, shearer:

'Noonkanbah was all a big dormitory style. There was two big rows of beds because there was thirty-four men there, and on the end of that dormitory there was seven showers. You had two sheets and a mosquito net and the mosquitoes were shocking. At midnight, seven showers would be working. You had two sheets and you put one on the bed and you laid there until you were perspiring so much that you'd take the dry sheet and put it on the bed, hang the wet one over the wire, have a shower and that would be the procedure for weeks.

'People coming out of the city never knew how to look after themselves properly. The fly problem – they'd all get dysentery, and spend half the night on the toilet. The knowledge that you accumulated, before you went to the Kimberley [the Christensens grew up in Wiluna], was a big help because you could weather the storm. As we went on and we became senior members, we used to take it upon ourselves with these young boys coming up from Perth and just away from mum and didn't know anything about washing and all that sort of thing. The first thing, when they came to breakfast, you'd say to 'em, "You had a wash this morning?"

'"Oh."

'"Go and have a wash. Don't come to the breakfast table without having a wash."

'We used to take 'em under our wings and teach 'em to wash their clothes and do all the right things . . . for survival more than anything else.'

Bruce Oldfield, classer/contractor:
'In 1956 I was shedhanding at Yanrey when an atomic bomb was exploded on the Monte Bellos, roughly 150 miles north of us. We actually saw the mushroom cloud. Another incident I remember was at Minderoo. We had heavy rain and [contractor] CJ [Deykin] set off to drive his car to the homestead. We rousies watched him leave from the quarters, saw the car become bogged and we all scampered out of sight; there were rousies running in all directions. The shearers pushed him out.'

Alf Shaw, shearer/contractor:
'The flies were the worst thing, the little bush flies. When we went for our lunch we'd grab a plate and dive under the mosquito net and try to keep the flies out of it. There was a bit of a competition when we were having tea: who had the most flies in their gravy? The little bush flies would fall in; the cook couldn't help it. We pushed them to one side. One bloke had fourteen; he won. I only got about eight. It was quite funny. We all got the Kimberley "trots" and the flying doctor came out and needled us. It was bad; we were all pretty crook. There were a couple of suspected typhoid cases and they were flown into Derby Hospital and then to Perth. They never came back in the team again.'

Darryl Grey, wool classer/contractor:
'In those days [the sixties] you used to have mostly coloured guys mustering, and that was the best time in my life, where you got

sheep brought into the sheds properly. After that, aeroplanes came in, motorbikes, and they did half the sheep, three-quarters the sheep and get you to come back in three months and shear another thousand. When they had the coloured stockmen and the horses, that was the best years as far as organisation.'

Peter Piavanini, shearer:
'When I went to the goldfields in 1961, we did a run around the goldfields and I was that absolutely homesick I would have got on the next wool truck or mail truck. I was desperate to get 'ome. I'd never been out of town and I was so homesick.

'I just happened to be matched up with a guy called Graham Tyers, who's a legend. He was my mentor. Real nice guy. Shore forty a run. Doesn't matter whether they were wethers that high or lambs that high. And, the training organisation, he was the trainers' trainer. Very level-headed nice fella. He took me under his wing and we proceeded to do all the sheds up to Wiluna and all that country.'

John Williams, shearer:
'Loved it. Never homesick. I liked the isolation of it all. I like being in the teams. I'm pretty keen on photography. I'd take photos of Sturt Desert Peas if it was the right season at the right place. Take photos of kangaroos.'

Darryl Grey, wool classer/contractor:
'Our conditions that we lived in were abominable. Shocking. Nobody did anything for shearers' conditions. Western Australia was trying to be unionised but the unions did nothing for you over here.

'We were up at Mardie, which is west of Karratha about a hundred and twenty kays, workin' on the weekend, and the union organiser who controlled Port Hedland in the iron ore days, he was the king of the north. He was the boss. He came down and he was going crook on us: why are we shearing on the weekend? It's against the law.

'I said, "Look, you guys come up three weeks from Perth, work for three and you go home for a week. That's what you do. And we're workin' three weeks and the blokes want to go home for a week, rather than sit up here, away from their families, just for nuthin'. And that's what we're doing. Working."

'A shearer, Stan Whitehurst was his name, he worked for me for about twenty years, Stan, very humorous guy, and this fella went up to him and said, "What are you doin' workin' on a Sunday?"

'Stan looked at him and said, "Because I lost ten bucks at cards last night and a box of piss on Swan Districts."

'The next guy was Gary Haines, a great big fella who's now a shearing contractor. He [the union organiser] asked Gary what he's doing shearing on a weekend. Gary just mumbled something at 'im. So he put his head closer to him and Gary grabbed him and pulled his head down, had the handpiece in his hand and he said, "I've been in the industry for twenty years. You've never done a thing for me in my life except try to fine me for doing something wrong."

'He slammed him back against the catching pen door. This guy got up, walked past me and said, "You'll be hearing from me and the police this afternoon."

'Never heard from him again. Unless they've got a mob behind them, they don't stand up.'

The Work

Gerry Young, presser:

'Every year we had to acclimatise ourselves to the Kimberley heat. I sweated so much I would take eight to ten salt tablets a day. Over the weekend I'd put on 9 pounds [4 kilograms] and by smoko Monday morning I'd lost it again. We were there six or seven weeks and when we moved to the Pilbara we had to re-acclimatise to that climate.'

Paul Morrissey, shearer:

'The worst place I ever went to was Marilla [in the 1940s]. Sheep were dying under a bough roof at five o'clock in the afternoon. I've seen them come in under an iron roof and drop dead, but they were dying under the bough roof. It was about 120 degrees Fahrenheit [48.9 degrees Celsius], three weeks before Christmas. We reckoned the Russians had a big magnifying glass up there on a satellite, beaming down and burning us out. Wakka Sheridan couldn't shear; he got heat exhaustion.

'The mill was up on the hill and the pipe to the tank – which was a fair way – was on top of the ground. We'd come back of a night for a shower and the water's boiling. The only thing we could do was get as many tubs as we could, fill them up at nighttime and leave them there for after work. What a bloody set-up that was. Talk about solar power. No need for the cook to boil any water for washing up or boiling the billy; it was already bloody boiling.'

Arthur Clarke, presser:

'One year [in the 1940s] the Calwynyardah owner came over; their sheep were all down, crippled with grass seeds and their shearers wouldn't shear them. They lost thousands of sheep that year. We were asked to come over and shear what sheep were standing up, but when we saw them, there was nothing we could do. To shear them we would have had to wear long sleeves, gloves and two pairs of trousers, the grass seeds were so bad. The stationhands were hand-shearing the legs to clear the seed and get them up and walking. Others they dragged into heaps and burnt, flies all over them. They hoped the ones they shore survived; all the prickles were still screwed into their skin. Shocking.'

Colin Christensen, shearer:
'One shearer from Victoria was going to be a gun from the start. Although we tried to explain to him about adjusting to the heat, he either couldn't or wouldn't understand. He made himself sick trying to keep up with us. One day he was vomiting down the chute, on the verge of collapse. I gave him some salt tablets to help him out. Eventually he came good.'

Arthur 'Banjo' Paterson, shearer:
'When I was a rouseabout, I went away when I was eighteen, left from the Ozone Hotel and went on the back of a truck. Synnot and Dunbar. 1950. Went to Port Hedland, Boodarie Station.

'I was a bit out of sorts when I got up there, didn't know anybody, only who you met on the back of the truck. The shearers knew all about it but the rousies didn't. The sheep were full of sand, the fleeces were terribly hard to pick up. They'd just fall to bits with the weight of sand in them.

'Being a green rouseabout and not knowing much about it, I was picking up this fleece and you had to get back quick to sweep the board, get the bits you've missed and everything. I'm doing this and this shearer says, "Look, I'm slipping all over the board. I can't keep me feet on the floor they're slipping that bad. After you finish sweepin' the board, reach out the porthole will you and grab a handful of sand and sprinkle it around. Stop me slippin'."

'There's sand everywhere and here's me scoopin' it up and puttin' it back on the board. They were just havin' a go at me. I was too silly to wake up.'

Colin Christensen, shearer:
'Dengue fever was one of the big problems up there in those days. The contractors usually carried sulphur tablets.'

Harold Christensen, shearer:
'Big jar of them and if he thought you was a bit off, gettin' the flu or somethin', you'd be shearing as fast as you could go and he'd come down and stand there and everybody had their own water-bag hanging up there and he'd give you three or four of these sulphur tablets and make you have a drink of water. Not too long because you was wastin' time.'

Colin Christensen, shearer:
'Salt tablets was another thing. You used to sweat that much you had to take salt tablets. Salt and dextrose. The waterbags were 2 gallon (9 litres). You never got cold water.'

Harold Christensen, shearer:
'If it was a real stormy bad day, you'd drink three of those water-bags full in the ten hours that you were on the job. Kimberley Cool we used to call it. Hot water.'

Marcus Synnot, contractor, from Patsy Adam-Smith's 1982 book
The Shearers:

> At Noonkanbah, one-hundred-and-one-thousand sheep were
> shorn in five weeks in 1954; forty-four men in the shed, twenty
> shearers on the board. They shore twenty-thousand one week,
> one-thousand per man per week. That was a world record. We
> shore over four-thousand-four-hundred one day and the learner
> had tears in his eyes: he had shorn over two-hundred that day
> and still dragging the chain! Of course, he was a good learner!

Peter Letch, wool classer/contractor (and rouseabout):
'Blina was the first shed [in 1958], only four shearers. It was my
first experience of a shearing team apart from the farm. It was so
hot and away to hell out in the sticks. I thought I was going to die.

'Bill Waldby, the classer, said, "I don't want you to walk.
I don't want you to run. I want you to bloody well fly!"'

Norm Cook, shearer:
'At Landor [during the 1959 drought] we had to wait for sheep.
They'd bring in a small truckload at a time and we'd shear them
in less than a run. We'd shear a sheep, push it down the chute,
then go out and stand it up. Poor things were just bone and awful
to shear; their skin was very thin.'

The Cooks

Dudley Tuckey, classer:
'The conditions when I first went up there [in the thirties] were
appalling. We're supposed to be human beings but we were
treated like bloody dogs. The crockery was old chipped enamel.

There was no refrigeration in those days and the cooks had to be very careful with the food and make sure there weren't any blowflies in the meat room or there was trouble. The poor cooks . . . no flywire doors on the cookhouse or mess room, a million bloody flies and two sheep a day to cook. The stoves were massive and generated a lot of heat. Cooks with those big teams earned every penny they got.'

John 'Snow' McMeikan, shearer/truck driver:
'Our cook was Happy Hamersley and she was a fantastic cook. Crumbed chops, sandwiches, cream puffs and lamingtons for smoko. Always a cold lunch for those who preferred it and a huge roast at night. If a fly landed on a meal, out it went! Happy could get a bit cranky – as with most cooks – but loved to tease the young rouseabouts. She'd been giving one rouseabout a hard time – he hadn't had a decent feed for a couple of days – and I gave him a plate of curry and got into real trouble. She went to throw a plate of hot curry at me and when I put my hand up to protect myself it went down the front of her dress! I was in the shit for a while but we became good friends.'

Wakka Sheridan, shearer, 1950s:
'Rex McCausland was the best cook I was ever with. He was a gambler but he was the prince of cooks. We always knew we would eat well if we had Rex. It was amazing the variety of meals he could produce under those conditions. He'd been a pastry cook so the smokos were always outstanding and different. The cook is the most important member of the team; everyone is happy if the food is good.'

John Matthews, shearer/contractor:

'One night [at Liveringa in 1954] we were woken up by this kerfuffle going on in the kitchen. The cook yelled out, "Bloody rouseabout, if you don't get out of here this minute, I'll hunt you out."

'We could hear him ranting and raving, the light from his hurricane lamp moving around. Next thing there was an almighty scream and we heard him getting out of the place. There was a 15-foot [4.5-metre] python in the kitchen and it had smashed nearly all the crockery.'

Billie Vaughan, cook:

'Towards the end of the sixties I worked with Syd Deykin in the north-west. He called to see us one time at Yuin; the kitchen was hot as there was only a wood stove. He talked to me through the window – he reckoned it was too hot to come inside; it was all right for me though.'

Doreen Bowditch, cook:

'[In 1964] we went to another shed, an outback shed, when it was raining. I said, "Gee, I'm getting wet. There's a hole in the roof." We had to shift beds around.

'In the kitchen I said to [shearer husband] Les, "I can't reach this table."

'There was a great big old-fashioned bath for washing up and a little stepladder so that I could get up to wash the dishes. They had to put two railway sleepers down so I could reach the stove.

'I said, "Look. This chair's broken. Don't sit there." I said to another chap, "Don't sit on that chair. It's broken." They both sat on them and both fell off under the table.'

Billie Vaughan, cook:
'Most places the conditions in the kitchens were shocking. There were no separate facilities for women cooks although by this time [the 1960s] it was not unusual for women to be cooking in a shearing team. I would hang a sign on the toilet door when necessary. A lot of the kitchens had dirt floors, probably the same as they were before the war. Rarely was there enough cooking equipment in the kitchen, often only a few saucepans and a dozen or so lids, none of which fitted. At one place in the Ashburton I was pitching all the lids outside into the alley between the kitchen and the men's huts when the owner came along; he decided not to come into the kitchen.

'At some places there was no water laid on to the kitchen, just a small tank of water outside and I'd have to suck on a hose to siphon water for cooking or washing up; I think that was at Mardathuna. I would start in the dark – about four o'clock – and use the Tilley light because the noise from the generator would have woken the shearers.'

Characters

Larry Foley, shearer:
'[1956] was when I met the unforgettable Albie Phillips, an extremely good Aboriginal shearer from Perenjori. Albert Pandora Phillips, he said, was his full name. One of the great characters in the game. I was shearing next to him at Wagga Wagga Station [near Paynes Find] and we were into some very good lambs. I managed to get around him for one; I shore fifty-one and he shore fifty.

'He stuck his head out the let-go chute at count-out and called to Shorty Keefe, the classer, "If this little bastard's gone around me, I'm pulling out."

'Kidding, of course, but Shorty got the point.

'"Dead heat," he called when he counted my pen.

'One run a gun doesn't make.'

John 'Snow' McMeikan, shearer/truck driver:

'I only ever voted wet [that the sheep were too wet to shear] once and that time the frogs were jumping out of them. [Shearer] Paddy Tuppin would say, "It's the dry bastards that'll kill you, Snow!" . . . Paddy would say, "Your heart has to be in the right place for this caper, Snowy. There's good money in shearing, but by hell, it's a long way in!"'

Don Mercer, classer:

'[In 1960] I had Arthur Dunbar with me as an expert for a short period. Marvellous man. I found he was a thorough gentleman, helpful and level-headed and an absolute joy to be with. A couple of incidents show the calibre of the man. At Wooleen the steam engine used to run the shearing plant. To clean his false teeth, Arthur had a habit of placing them on a ledge near the steam outlet. One day he was called away and when he returned his teeth had started to melt. Realising he couldn't manage without them, he immediately clamped them in his mouth to retain the shape.

'"They were a bit hot," he said.

'On another occasion his fingers got caught in the belt which drives the overhead shaft so – without looking – he doused them in kerosene, wrapped them firmly and continued his work.

'When he unwrapped them, he commented, "I put my fingers on crooked."'

Harold Christensen, shearer:
'I thought Marc Synnot was a really, really good boss. You knew exactly where you stood with him every day. Sometimes we'd be going back to the shed after lunch and he'd be coming over because he'd done the count-out. And depending on how we were working, if we were shearing a lot of sheep, he'd say, "It's good to see you boys busy."'

Colin Christensen, shearer:
'Marc Synnot, we all thought he done a splendid job because as well as taking thirty-six men to the Kimberley he had to organise all that food and everything in Perth.

'He didn't know what was in front of him. One year at Noonkanbah we had 6 inches (150 millimetres) of rain overnight. Every vehicle on the station, with that country up there, there was that much water they just sank to the ground. We were a fortnight there. They couldn't bring the sheep into the shed because it was all too boggy, and somebody took up a couple of tennis balls, we fashioned a bat out of a bit of wood and played French cricket in the water. We just had to wait for the country to dry out.

'One day a chap who'd had a few drinks picked on [Marc], saying he was going to knock his block off. Marc tried to talk him out of it. After this fellow took a couple of swings at him, Marc stepped in – bang, bang, and he was flat on his back.

'Marc just said, "Tut, tut. Silly boy."'

The Pubs

Peter Jorgensen, classer/contractor:
'[In 1959] I had a shedhand, Bert, a complete alcoholic. He'd be

drunk twenty miles before we'd get into town, psychologically. I'd go into town and the first thing I did was to hand Bert over at the police station. They knew him and would lock him up; that way he would never have a drink. We'd do our jobs around town, pick him up and away we'd go. If we didn't do that he'd destroy himself. He understood and thought it was all right. Drugs are probably a bigger factor now than alcohol; they seem to affect a lot of the younger ones.'

John 'Snow' McMeikan, shearer/truck driver:

'If we stopped at a pub getting them back on the truck was quite a job. I'd get a couple out of the bar, turn back for the others and those outside promptly went back in again. Frustrating, but funny at times.'

Darryl Grey, wool classer/contractor:

'Synott and Dunbar. They were coming down from Port Hedland and they had to go past Whim Creek. Karratha wasn't going at that time [the fifties]. Coming from Hedland it was the only pub until you got down to Roebourne. The contractor didn't like stopping at hotels because you couldn't get people out of them.

'So as they're going past the hotel someone yelled out to Marc, "A swag's just gone off the back. We've gotta stop and get it."

'And Marc Synnot said, "It's too late. You'll have to get a new swag."

'And they said, "It's yours, Marc."

'The truck had to stop. They went straight into the pub. It took him four days to get the shearers out of the hotel.

'They didn't like stopping and if they camped overnight they'd always stop on a rocky hill, somewhere it was uncomfortable to sleep, so everyone is up and off early in the morning. It was a traditional thing to find a terrible place to camp.'

Tom Pringle, shearer:
'Everyone knew I was a non-drinker. Others would take my ration of a bottle of beer a night and – if I was lucky – they'd pay me. In our team of six shearers, five didn't drink; that was unusual. Of the five, four ended up with farms and the other bloke became a shearing contractor. The sixth was a hospital orderly at the Southern Cross Hospital; I met up with him when I had a plaster cut off my arm.'

The Runs

Gerry Young, presser:
'The first couple of years I was away, I didn't get back to Perth until 21 December, and on one occasion I left again on 25 December. I was home four days. I wasn't married, but it didn't make much difference after I was married. Once I was away, that was it.'

Arthur 'Banjo' Paterson, shearer:
'It would be '53 I went up as a shearer. Liveringa, then we came down to Port Hedland, Mallina, Warambie, Mardie, Wooleen (on the Murchison). I only went to the Kimberleys twice as a shearer.

'That run went from April, probably, to middle of November. We left Port Hedland, we were shearing just out of Port Hedland. I don't think we saw another town till we got back to Perth.'

Reg Dunbar, expert:
'Some of the best shearing sheep were at Dirk Hartog Island [in Shark Bay]. The best tally, in 1950, was 1684 for six shearers. In 1951 Elwyn Platt from New South Wales shore 306. I spent nineteen consecutive years going to Dirk Hartog Island. After being out in the bush for months, living on mutton, Shark Bay was the place I looked forward to.'

Darryl Grey, wool classer/contractor:
'For me the trucks finished about 1965. From then on blokes could get in their own cars.

'There was a favourite place, Dirk Hartog Island, where Synnot ended up at Christmas time. He used to get all these places on the coast that were brilliant for fishing, so they were the best places to go away on.

'When I was a young kid going away rouseabouting, I was told about this run of Synnot's. It was the best one to go on. I go along to get a job in St Georges Terrace, in the office, and the lady in front wouldn't let me have an interview because I didn't have a white shirt and tie on – to get a job as a rouseabout!'

Trevor Keating, shearer and museum curator:
'You'd get the job and you'd go to the Ozone Hotel. It was in Adelaide Terrace and they'd do the rollcall and they'd load you on. The whole shearin' team on the back of one truck and away you'd go. In 1969 I went on as a seventeen-year-old rouseabout and we went to Marble Bar; that's right up the top in WA. From there we went east out to a station called Warrawagine. You'd stay out there. You might be a month at one station. Then they'd load you back on and go to the next station. You were away for

months and months and months. Sometimes when you'd leave a station, the contractor would go a hundred mile [160 kilometres] out of his way to get to the next shed to avoid a pub.'

Syd Deykin, contractor:
'We had one run which started the first week in January out of Geraldton, went right through the Gascoyne, Ashburton, back to the Murchison and finished up at Thundelarra, out of Paynes Find, a few days before Christmas; that was the longest year I ever did. Because we could offer a long run we were able to attract good shearers.'

The Mateship

Darryl Grey, wool classer/contractor:
'It was amazing the camaraderie when I used to go on trucks. There were no women in those years but men were living together for months on end and there hardly ever seemed to be any fights. The thing that seemed to keep them like that was that they were very strict on manners at tables. I reckon a lot of humour, being forced to have good manners and work like hell, it all melded together real well.'

Harold Christensen, shearer:
'I can sit here and say, I spent longer shearing than [brother] Colin did – my career went over about ten or twelve years, or fourteen years – but I enjoyed every single day I was there. It was a very, very clean, healthy lifestyle, a lot of good comradeship, you made good friends. We're still good mates. And it'll never be lost. If we had a fella in the team and he was a bit of a snag, he

very soon found out that he could either join in or join out. When you're looking people in the face every single hour of the day for weeks and weeks on end, you had to get used to it. The quicker the better. I think we were most fortunate to live in that era. To be young guys in that era and all this work was going.'

Peter Piavanini, shearer:
'Got married when I was twenty-one; I done a lot of truck work before that, in those five years. You meet all these blokes, it's a funny feeling to meet all these guys. There's something there. I don't know what it is. Just a camaraderie, that you done "in the north", because the north was a pretty remote place in those days. There was no such thing as a doctor or a nurse anywhere. No flying doctor. There was in Port Hedland but most of the places, like De Grey, probably had a strip, but most of 'em, some were startin' to get a little bit modern but it was pretty basic stuff.'

Valerie Hobson, OAM, contractors' wife and truck shearing historian:
'Shearing was the most nomadic of all outback jobs. The environment of the shearing teams developed and accentuated solidarity and loyalty. The team was a self-contained mobile processing factory. All worked, lived and travelled under difficult, uncomfortable, isolated and often climatically harsh conditions with little or no intrusion from outside influences. Truck travel was a great leveller; in wet weather much time was spent pushing and pulling the vehicle out of bogs. This was accepted as part of the overall experience and a sense of humour carried the team through. From this was born an amazing camaraderie and mateship not experienced by their eastern states counterparts.

All these factors contributed to the unique bonding, which exists still, more than fifty years on. They were strong, independent and competitive individuals, yet they tolerated and accepted each other's idiosyncracies.'

PART TWO

The days of the ring pounders didn't so much come to an end as gradually fade away. As mining started to take off in the north-west in the late 1960s, road infrastructure improved sufficiently for shearers to take their own vehicles. The 1968 decision to include Indigenous workers in the pastoral award, which ended what was effectively slavery on some stations, meant many properties ceased to be financially viable. Increasing dingo numbers didn't help matters. And then came drought.

As shearer and contractor Digger Redman told Valerie Hobson in her 2002 book *Across the Board*:

> During the five-year drought – 1969 to 1974 – Edjudina Station went from twenty-eight-thousand to seven-thousand sheep. At one stage I had twenty-six stations on the books and they'd ring and tell me when they had a thousand sheep in. They couldn't get them all in at once. Before this they'd never had more than two dry seasons in a row. The situation was desperate; some stations didn't have a shearing team at all. They'd just get a shearer when they could get a few sheep together.

Wool classer and contractor Darryl Grey told me the influx of New Zealand shearers also had an impact.

'All the New Zealanders started coming over and there were some brilliant shearers but there's no control over New Zealand shearers. We had rules that at nine o'clock lights out and into bed, no noise. The New Zealanders would party on until two o'clock in the morning, get up the next day and all shear 200, and the Australians couldn't get out of bed 'cos they're that crook. This used to go on all the time, so you lost control of the shearing teams and it got harder to make money as a contractor because you lost control. The wool industry never died a sudden death. It just sort of broke apart.'

While the sheep industry in the nor-west of Western Australia is now virtually non-existent, it's not forgotten. Many of those who were involved in it still gather to remember those times and swap their stories. It was them, and the oldest of the very few remaining ring pounders, that I'd come to see.

Before the truck shearers' annual reunion at the Ravenswood Hotel, on the Murray River south of Perth, I'd been warned that they'd probably be unwilling to talk to me. The opposite was the case. When they learned I cared enough about their history to travel all the way from eastern Australia, they went out of their way to help me.

Valerie Hobson, OAM, an eighty-something outback legend in her own right, was first among them. I'd met Valerie the year before at the writers' event at the Shear Outback museum in Hay, New South Wales, organised by the late Ian Auldist. I'd referenced her book, *Across the Board,* in *The Shearers* and was inspired by the many stories she'd gathered about the truck shearing days from the people who went on the trucks.

The day before, she'd organised for me to see the last ring pounder. It was in the Revolutions Transport Museum at Whiteman Park, north of Perth. However, it wasn't on display. It was in the storage facility at the rear of the museum.

Valerie and one of the ring pounder's passengers, former shearer Barry Mainwaring, pointed out the features of the truck. It was a rough, hard vehicle, battered and worn after many, many dusty outback miles. There was a bench seat down the centre of the tray. There was no roof and the front cab had been removed. There were storage lockers built along the side, hooks for hanging waterbags, wooden footrests attached on the front wheel arches so that the outside passengers on the front seat had something to brace against. There were spare springs for the leaf-suspension and an axle stowed under the tray.

Incredibly, the 1934 Bedford still runs! It even has its original manual, only missing the cover. Incredible, after travelling so far.

Valerie explained how one old shearer told her he was sure he'd been a passenger on this particular ring pounder. He pointed out a groove on a side-board. He'd made it so he could rest his feet more comfortably.

The ring pounder used to be displayed at the Perth Royal Show, with old shearers telling visitors the stories of the truck shearing days. They'd gradually been pushed to the back of the pavilion until they felt they were no longer welcome.

Despite the setback, the shearers were still active in preserving their history. Barry said: 'After the launch of Valerie's book, in August 2002, the Shearers and Pastoral Workers Social Club was formed and has held get-togethers in November. We started a museum in Carnarvon. The shearers set up the museum. A heritage group now runs it.'

After leaving Whiteman Park, we travelled down to Trevor Keating's truck shearing museum, south of Perth. The exhibits were first rate, but housed in a rented, rat-infested pig shed. Entry was by invitation only. Efforts to find the museum, and the last ring pounder, a permanent home had so far proven fruitless.

The already-excellent exhibits really came alive when ex-shearer Trevor told the stories that were attached to them. He's still shearing and opens his museum by appointment. Yet he faces an uncertain future.

'It was Val that started it. Her book *Across the Board*. She's the one that got my passion goin'. The bottom line is, I'm the only one doin' the history of the truck travellers. And if it goes, well, we've lost it.'

Down at the Ravenswood Hotel, the truck shearers' reunion was preceded by the annual general meeting of the Shearers and Pastoral Workers Social Club. Some of the members wanted to know why the last ring pounder was no longer on display at the Perth Royal Show. Marc Synnot Jnr, whose family owns the ring pounder, explained the logistical and financial obstacles.

The committee then detailed plans for a film about the truck shearing days, and the logistical and financial obstacles they were trying to overcome to self-produce that.

The reunion comprised sixty men ranging in age from their sixties to nineties. They told their stories long into the afternoon, while I dragged as many as I could to a quiet place to ask questions (the answers included in Part One, above). To me they were the stuff of legends, yet in the pub they were surrounded by young people who had no idea, and would scarcely believe the things the nor-west truck shearers had seen and done.

At the end of the day, those who'd booked accommodation gathered in Valerie's room and talked into the night until tiredness overtook us. The next morning, we returned to Valerie's room, where she and Barry Mainwaring had catered breakfast. I ended up cooking sausages, bacon and eggs for nine. When it was all ready and still hot, I hunted the shearers, historians and my wife to the table. They all said I'd make a good shearers' cook. They didn't know I'd pretty well exhausted my culinary repertoire.

After breakfast, I asked Valerie how many of the contributors to her 2002 book were still alive. She sat down with my copy and checked off all the people who were gone or she was not sure of. It was about half.

It was then that I realised where the real challenge in saving the last ring pounder lay. Without the stories of the truck shearers – the pressers, contractors, cooks, classers and rouseabouts who rode on the ring pounders – it was just a truck. It was the memories associated with it that gave it resonance. And those memories were disappearing, one by one.

No wonder so many people overcame their reticence to talk to me. Anyone who recognised and valued their history was always going to get their attention. They fully understood what I was trying do with this chapter – and with this book, when it comes to it. If you've read this far, the last ring pounder won't have been forgotten. Meanwhile, our living legends don't live forever. Make the most of them while you can.

Quotes from the following have been reproduced from Across the Board *(2002) by kind permission of Valerie Hobson: Reg Dunbar (deceased), Gerry Young, Ron Law, Peter Cleaver (dec.), Bill Young (dec.), Chris Fyfe, Jim Pringle, Jack Mildwaters (dec.), Bert Latham, Ted Dreckow, John 'Snow' McMeikan (dec.), Tom Pringle, Dudley Tuckey (dec.), Arthur Clarke, Jack Edge (dec.), Herc Weston (dec.), Bruce Oldfield, Alf Shaw (dec.), Paul*

Morrissey (dec.), Wakka Sheridan (dec.), John Matthews (dec.), Billie Vaughan (dec.), Doreen Bowditch (dec.), Larry Foley, Don Mercer, Peter Jorgensen, Syd Deykin and Digger Redman (dec.). Some quotes from Peter Letch, Harold Christensen and Valerie Hobson are reproduced from Across the Board and others from author interviews.

Quotes from Trevor Keating, Colin Christensen, Darryl Grey, Peter Piavanini, John Williams and Arthur 'Banjo' Paterson are from author interviews.

The quote from Marc Synnot from The Shearers is reproduced by Arrangement with the Licensor, The Patsy Adam-Smith Estate, c/- Curtis Brown (Aust) Pty Ltd.

The Last Leg

After the truck shearers had gone their separate ways, some to the farms they'd bought, others to jobs they still have in the shearing industry, Michelle and I headed up the Kwinana Freeway to Perth in our rented two-wheel drive.

We encountered no floods, storms or hail along the way, which meant we had a free afternoon before flying home. We went to Perth's botanical gardens, paying particular attention to the section on the nor-west plants and landscapes. It was the nearest I'd get to it, but I already felt closer in other ways.

Could we fly up? There was nothing to see. The nor-west sheep are all gone. The wool industry that once contributed fifty per cent of Western Australia's export income and two per cent of Australia's is a shadow of its former self. The sheep stations in the pastoral areas have all gone over to cattle and the shearing sheds have decayed or been flattened by cyclones.

The next morning, we flew the first leg of Perth–Brisbane–Newcastle in a commercial jet. After journeys that had presented a variety of challenges, it was a bit of an anticlimax. I sat in the middle of the plane – patch of blue to the left, patch of blue to the right, inflight movies in front. I couldn't get so much as a glimpse of the outback rolling past beneath. All I had were the memories of the last ring pounder, getting further away behind me, and filling a notebook on my tray table.

After a pretty adventurous year searching for 'outback legends', I was closer to understanding what defines them.

I'd once watched tourists flock around the former Birdsville mailman, Tom Kruse, during one of his last visits to Birdsville, while the locals flocked around then Birdsville 'mailman' Tom McKay, on his regular visit to deliver their groceries. I don't think anyone else noticed but I'd seen the two Toms exchange a look of recognition that said, 'We're no different, you and I.'

Neither of them have sought fame and recognition. It happened to find one of them; even then, it was pure chance. Had the producers of the film *Back of Beyond* (1954) chosen someone else as its central character, they'd almost certainly be famous, instead of Tom Kruse.

As June Andrew put it, everyone in the outback is inspiring in their way. Of course, she doesn't regard herself as being special, but if you follow the logic, if she lives in the outback . . .

Sally Brown grew up wanting to be inspired and Danielle Doyle recognised that her predecessors were inspiring. Yet both have that quality that impresses them: they just get on with things.

Shannon Warnest didn't just find something he was good at it, he pushed himself to be the best at what he was good at. When he'd achieved all it was possible to achieve, he devoted himself to helping others do the same: not just to be better shearers but better human beings. Murray Hartin has also done a great deal to make life better for his fellow man, and it doesn't bother him that people know his poems *Turbulence* and *Rain from Nowhere* better than they know him.

The drovers of Camooweal are quiet men and women who've lived lives that embody the bedrock of the Australian character, while Fred Brophy's dream has kept a rich part of another aspect of our history alive. He's both inspired and challenged generations of Australians, both in the boxing ring and when he's replied to 'You can't' with 'I will'.

Don Rowlands has endured all that life has thrown at him and refused to bow to anyone. He and his community have much to teach the rest of Australia about how non-Indigenous and Indigenous people can build a better future.

And when you're stuck in the Simpson Desert, there's one person you'll definitely be glad to see: Barnesy. He embodies that outback quality of 'going the extra mile', except in his case it's usually hundreds of kilometres.

All of these people are very different, but they also have much in common. They're the salt of the outback. They're not legendary figures from long ago and far away. You can rub shoulders with them here and now. They're as close as the internet, where you can read the blogs and Facebook updates of some of them. They don't belong to another era. They're our outback legends.

In Brisbane, we had a couple of hours before our flight to Newcastle, during which a line of storms rolled over the east coast of New South Wales. The final leg of our flight was in a Dash 8 prop job more in keeping with outback workhorses like Fokkers and DC-3s. Like them, it couldn't fly above the storms, which meant that during our flight we hit some turbulence. Then, lots of turbulence.

As the experience grew increasingly unpleasant, a word popped into my head.

'Outside!'

I was chuckling by the time the pilot announced that one of the vibrations in the aircraft was due to ice on the propellers but that he'd turned on heaters that would soon melt it. Having travelled sideways down the Birdsville Track, sweated on the windscreen shattering on the Hay Plain and navigated submerged holes in the road crossing Brown Creek, icy propellers were par for the course.

Had it all been worth it? Of all the obstacles involved in reaching the outback people I found inspiring, the biggest was the reluctance of most of them to be recognised as 'legends'.

You might not agree with the choices I've made, and I know there are other people who are worthy of inclusion. Does it matter that they weren't? Probably not to them. It probably matters more to the people who are looking for them.

They're there, of course, often in plain view.

Right back at the beginning, when I asked Terry Picone to be one of my outback legends, he said, 'I'm not that person.'

I finally knew how to answer him.

'You are to me.'

REFERENCES

CHAPTER 1: 'ARTHRITIS'

Burling, Jill. 'Moree's Picone Story'. *Moree and District Historical Society*, no. 30, December 2008, p7.

Hitchins, Max. *More Fact, Fiction and Fables of the Melbourne Cup*. Hitchins Marketing, Sydney, 1997.

Hurley, Donna. *Northern Daily Leader*, 22 June 2002, p18.

'1925–1962'. *North-West Champion*, 6 December 1962.

Poulos, Bill. *Picone Bookmaking Family Steeped in History*. Deluxe Café, Moree, 2014.

Poulos, Bill. 'SPECIAL FEATURE: Picone family the giants'. *Northern Daily Leader*, 4 February 2014.

Weate, Bill. 'Picone'. *The Bookmaker*, March 1992, p15.

CHAPTER 2: FINGER ON THE PULSE

Cadden, Rosemary. 'A Day In The Life Of June'. *Along Those Lines*, 10 October 2015. www.alongthoselines15.wordpress.com/ 2015/10/10/a-day-in-the-life-of-june.

CHAPTER 3: THE REAL DEAL

Author interview only.

CHAPTER 4: SHANNON'S WAY

Adams, Prue. 'Raising The Baa'. *Landline*, ABC, 3 August 2008.

Schwartz, Dominique. 'Golden Shears'. *Landline*, ABC, 20 May 2012.

REFERENCES

CHAPTER 5: POEM FROM NOWHERE

Hartin, Murray. *Rain From Nowhere*. 2007.
Hartin, Murray. *Big Jack*. 1990.

CHAPTER 6: LARGER THAN LIFE

McHugh, Evan. *The Drovers*. Penguin, Melbourne, 2010.

CHAPTER 7: THE LEAGUE OF EXTRAORDINARY WOMEN

Doyle, Danielle. *Miss Chardy: Laughter In The Outback*.
    www.misschardy.com.

CHAPTER 8: LAST MAN STANDING

Brophy, Fred. *The Last Showman*. Penguin, Melbourne, 2014.

CHAPTER 9: A VOICE IN THE WILDERNESS

Author interview only.

CHAPTER 10: BARNESY

McHugh, Evan. *Birdsville*. Penguin, Melbourne, 2009.
McShane, Neale, and Evan McHugh. *Outback Cop*. Penguin,
    Melbourne, 2016.

CHAPTER 11: THE LAST RING POUNDER

Adam-Smith, Patsy. *The Shearers*. Nelson, Melbourne, 1982.
Hobson, Valerie. *Across The Board*. BackTrack Books, Gidgegannup,
    2002.

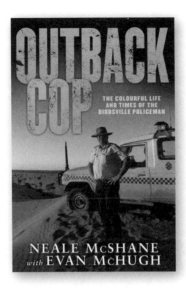

Birdsville is one of the most remote police postings in Australia. It can be lonely and uneventful for weeks, then the dramas come thick and fast: from desert rescues to rising floods, venomous vipers to visiting VIPs.

Throw in heat, dust and flies and it's not a job for the faint-hearted, unless you're Senior Constable Neale McShane, who has single-handedly taken care of a beat the size of Victoria for the past ten years. How do you feed 4000 unexpected dinner guests? Where do you find a Chinook helicopter when you need one? Who's your backup when the population explodes for the famous Birdsville Races? And what do you do when you're the person the Flying Doctor is flying out?

Among these inspiring tales of danger and death, dreamers and 'dumb tourists', you'll encounter a little community with a big heart that stands shoulder-to-shoulder with a larger-than-life policeman who's become part of Australia's outback legend.